Through the Eyes of a Dancer

Through the Eyes of a Dancer

SELECTED WRITINGS   WENDY PERRON

WESLEYAN UNIVERSITY PRESS

Middletown, Connecticut

Wesleyan University Press

Middletown CT 06459

www.wesleyan.edu/wespress

2013 © Wendy Perron

Manufactured in the United States of America

Designed by Rich Hendel

Typeset in Arnhem and Aller by

Tseng Information Systems, Inc.

Wesleyan University Press is a member of the
Green Press Initiative. The paper used in this book
meets their minimum requirement for recycled paper.

Library of Congress Cataloging-in-Publication Data

Perron, Wendy.

Through the eyes of a dancer : selected writings / Wendy
    Perron.

pages   cm.

Includes bibliographical references and index.

ISBN 978-0-8195-7407-7 (cloth : alk. paper)

ISBN 978-0-8195-7409-1 (ebook)

1. Dance. 2. Dance criticism. 3. Dance—History. I. Title.

GV1600.P47 2013

792.8—dc23   2013017390

5 4 3 2

This book is dedicated

to the memory of my mother,

Dorothy Perron (1918–2009),

and the future of my son,

Nick Perron-Siegel.

Contents

Illustrations

Acknowledgments

First, thanks to Deborah Jowitt and Marcia B. Siegel, whose course in dance writing I fairly devoured many years ago.

I appreciate all of my editors, starting with Richard Philp at *Dance Magazine*, who gave me my first opportunity to publish in 1973. Robb Baker pulled me in to the *SoHo Weekly News* and let me have free run of the downtown scene. On his (later my) "Concepts in Performance" page, I could define performance however I saw fit. A big thanks to John Rockwell, who opened the door to the *New York Times* when he was editor of the Arts & Leisure section there. Annette Grant at Arts & Leisure actively sought freelancers and was a dream to work with. Elizabeth Zimmer at the *Village Voice* taught me the value of using lively verbs in reviews. Other editors at the *Voice*, like M. Mark, Burt Supree, and Ross Wetzsteon, helped me with the organization of feature stories.

I'm grateful to my fellow dance addicts at *Dance Magazine*: Kina Poon, Hanna Rubin, and Khara Hanlon (and past editors Siobhan Burke, Kate Lydon, and Emily Macel Theys). They look at my writing as much as I look at theirs. And of course *Dance Magazine* in general, for giving me the opportunity to travel down many roads, and for letting me repurpose some of the evidence here.

I also have to thank two friends who were over-the-top generous in reading my entire manuscript: the aforementioned John Rockwell, and Robert Walsh, who had already brought his editorial expertise to my Salinger memoir at *VanityFair.com*. My former dancing partner Risa Jaroslow gave me helpful comments on my opening chapters.

Good friends who have indulged in dance making and/or dance discussing over the years include, but are not limited to, Ninotchka Bennahum, Irene Borger, Holly Cavrell, Blondell Cummings, Barbara Forbes, Theresa Ruth Howard, Risa Jaroslow again, Liz Lerman, Denise Luccioni, Kathryn Posin, Susan Rethorst, Tamar Rogoff, Vicky Shick, Stephanie Skura, Louise Steinman, Cathy Weis, and Bill Whitener. The sense of camaraderie I have with each of them goes deep. I've also had lively conversations with many of the devoted freelance writers of *Dance Magazine*.

For a mind that mingles aesthetics with social conscience, and for hours of stimulating discussion, I bow to Sally Banes. I've been inspired by her writing and her thinking over the years. It was she who assigned two of the longer pieces herein and worked closely with me on them.

I have to mention Deborah Jowitt again for setting a magnificent example of a dancer/choreographer who writes. She integrates literary brilliance, generosity of spirit, and a bone-deep understanding of dance.

Sally Sommer sent me an angel, Jaime Kight, who gave me lots of techno help as well as valuable comments and challenges in the early stages. Thanks to my son, Nick, for further help with preparing photos.

I thank the photographers for allowing me to use their images. Some of them have dancers' eyes too.

One of the nice things about having taught so much is that former students crop up all over the place. One of them, Victoria Bijur, has become a literary agent; when the time came, she gave me the lay of the land in book publishing.

Liz Lerman, my old friend from our first year at Bennington College, told me what a good experience she'd had with Wesleyan University Press. Suzanna Tamminen, director of WUP, guided me through the pre-production process; she also gave me a crucial framework when she suggested that I provide each piece with more context—through my current eyes.

I am grateful to the New York City subway for not only connecting me with the hubbub of humanity every day, but also for providing a place where I could work on this project in short stints.

The steady stream of intern applicants to DanceMedia (the parent company of *Dance Magazine*) has shown me that there's more interest in becoming a dancer/writer than before, allowing me to envision a core readership for this book.

Last, and really first too, I thank my husband, Jim Siegel. I'm fortunate that he loves dance and welcomes my enthusiasms as well as my gripes. He sees everything I write before it leaves the premises; for this book he's gone over each page several times. He catches the tiniest mistakes and helps with the biggest organizational decisions. His curiosity, support, and love have buoyed me during this whole process.

Introduction

I was not the writer in the family.

My older brother Reed wrote poetry and would sometimes let me in on the questions he was pondering: What is a poem supposed to do? How is my poetry different from anyone else's? His letters to me from college and medical school were funny, wise, full of wonder, and alive to paradox.

My brother Tommy, only eighteen months older than I, wrote incessantly. He was colossally unstable and I have hundreds of pages of his brilliant, deranged stories, somewhat like Gogol's *Diary of a Madman*. I didn't read them until well after he died, a suicide at thirty. Among his delusional ramblings was a casual mention that he would die soon and that he would leave his typewriter—his only possession—to me.

Even while using Tommy's typewriter, though, I was not really a writer.

I was, from early on, the dancer in the family. My mother had studied with Martha Graham and danced with Jane Dudley. The year I started kindergarten, she opened a school of "creative dance" in our basement in New Milford, New Jersey. One of my earliest memories was helping my mother brush sticky black stuff over the cement floor before laying down the linoleum tiles. Looking back on that moment, I've often thought that I was also laying down the foundation of my life.

In my mother's classes we would clap out rhythms with gusto, leap above that linoleum floor until we felt like we were flying, orbit a pillar until we fell down drunk with dizziness. We also worked in pairs, improvising slow-motion fights. When I was in our living room, if I heard my favorite record being played in the basement below—I especially liked "My Playful Scarf"—I would run downstairs to join in, no matter what age group was having its lesson (thus igniting the first arguments between my mother and me).

When I was seven, in 1954, my mother augmented my training by taking me to weekly ballet lessons in nearby Englewood with Tatiana Dokoudovska, a former dancer with one of the Ballet Russe companies, who later founded Kansas City Ballet. She pounded a stick on the floor to keep time, which didn't exactly foment joy in executing the steps. But I got my first dance crush there—a thirteen-year-old pony-tailed girl named Jennifer, who, to my young eyes, was an ideal dancer.

The next year we moved to another nearby town, Ridgewood, where Irine Fokine ran a ballet school and my mother's basement was no more. I lived for Christmas vacations, when I'd spend all my waking hours rehearsing or performing *Nutcracker*. (Miss Fokine's mother, Alexandra Fedorova, was the first to bring the *Nutcracker* to the United States in one-act form). I was lousy at pointe work and had no turnout, but I felt beautiful while moving through port de bras, and the piano music got into my blood.

Always seeking the best for me, my mother took me to audition for the summer program at the School of American Ballet in New York City when I was twelve, so I studied there for that summer, and again three years later. For the two summers in between, I joined Miss Fokine and her band of ballet-aspiring teenagers to spend happily dance-obsessed summers on Cape Cod, which is the point where I begin "One Route from Ballet to Postmodern," the memoir that constitutes my first section, "The Sixties."

During my last two years of high school, I was coming into Manhattan twice a week for classes at the Joffrey school and once a week at the Martha Graham school, where I was in the advanced teenage class. (I did my homework on the bus.) Ballet and modern seemed like they were two different planets, and I was always trying to figure out which one I belonged on.

I loved my ballet classes, but the Graham technique helped ground me. I remember once when Martha herself taught class. We were doing the "pleadings"—that's where you lie on your back and you curve up in a contraction. Martha threaded through the group to watch our contractions. When she came to me, she squatted down, slipped her hand under the small of my back and commanded, "*Crrushh* my hand!" The way she enunciated the word was so guttural, so absolute, that I then did my first authentically urgent, naval-to-spine, Graham contraction. The woman really knew how to use verbs!

During the more dramatic combinations across the floor, our regular teacher, David Wood, would call out in his sonorous voice, "Wendy, be angry. I want to see your *anger*!" I was a melancholy, wistful kid and didn't exactly tap into my reserve of anger on cue.

But there was a moment of revelation with David that helped me to forever connect mentality to muscle. We were doing a combination of taking two steps backward, turning to the other side and reeling over into a halting high contraction. To get us to really dig into it, David said it was like suddenly discovering you were on the edge of a cliff and were caught by the terror of it—like your heart leaping to your mouth. (Fear I could do much better than anger.) An epiphany, as in "Ohhhhhh, there is a *reason* I am doing this high contraction!" helped me make the heart-brain-body connection. Actors call it motivation.

I worked hard in all these classes but, at the same time, I also watched my fellow dancers and tried to analyze why one's dancing appealed to me and another's didn't. Applying my yen for observing, I started teaching early. At sixteen I gathered my two little sisters and their neighborhood pals into our playroom for weekly lessons.

––––––––

Although I kept a diary in high school, I never imagined I would make use of my writing. I was a slow reader and a slow writer, and my whole expression went into dancing.

At Bennington College, my freshman "Lang & Lit" teacher was literary critic Stanley Edgar Hyman. He liked my writing and my critical thinking. But cranking out a paper was an ordeal, causing me to spend many hours in the all-night study room. I majored in dance, which is why I had chosen Bennington, famous for its modern dance department. My minor was psychology, not literature.

In those days Bennington sponsored a student tour for upper-class dance majors every other year, which for me fell in my junior year. It was a heady trip for college kids to perform one-night stands with their own choreography in about twenty cities. After that, I was chomping at the bit to go dance in New York, senior year be damned. I remember a long phone call—at that time there was just one pay phone for a dorm of thirty girls—in which my mother convinced me to stick it out one more year. During that last year, I choreographed a lot, including a solo that I later performed at Dance Theater Workshop. Deborah Jowitt, one of the founders of DTW, reviewed my solo in the *Village Voice*, saying that my dancing had a "blazing purity." I was off and running as a downtown dancer/choreographer.

I worked with many of the choreographers at DTW and was also seeing plenty of dance. I noticed that I was more involved than my peers in talking about what I had seen, and that I kept these discussions (or possibly monologues) going long after the others played out their interest. It fascinated me how one performance, or even a single movement, had a huge impact while another just didn't. Only by talking about it could I get closer to understanding it.

So when Deborah Jowitt and Marcia Siegel offered a course in dance criticism at Dance Theater Workshop (now New York Live Arts), I was interested. I think the attraction was less that I would learn how to write and more that I wanted and needed to talk about dance.

We would write reviews, read them aloud to develop an ear for rhythm and word choice, and then get written comments. I remember that Marcia circled the word "doing" on my paper and suggested I use a more specific verb. What an eye opener! I've been struggling with verbs ever since. Dance is naturally a rich source of verbs. You don't have to stretch to find them. You not only walk, run, or leap. You glide, spring, curve, stagger, float, entwine. But still, the right verb can be elusive.

In that course we discussed questions like, What is a critic's job—to evaluate and judge, or to elucidate? Deborah and Marcia were (and are) very different kinds of writers. Though they agreed that description was essential, they used it differently. Description, for Deborah, led to deep insights, whereas for Marcia it led to sharp evaluations. I respected them both so much that I never decided which kind of critic I was. I still don't really know.

I only know that what you see on the stage comes in at the eyes and then spreads to your muscles, bones, brain, and heart. I try to allow my whole self to respond to a performance, just as my whole self was involved in dance and choreography. (Of course, that means the ears too. To this day, whenever I hear music that I've danced to, I have a visceral reaction.)

After three cycles of the course, I wanted to write some real reviews—for *Dance Magazine*. When I told Deborah of my ambition, she encouraged me to call Richard Philp, then managing editor, and send him some sample reviews from the class. The word I got back was, "You'll be okay to review modern dance, but Doris Hering says you don't know enough about ballet." That made me happy and mad. But of course Doris, who had practically run the magazine single-handedly at times, was right. I knew nothing about the ballet world, either then or historically. I didn't even know that Miss Fokine was the niece of Michel Fokine.

My first assignment from Richard, in 1973, was to cover a new group of college boys called Pilobolus. When I went to see them, Arthur Miller was in the audience. Wow. My favorite playwright. I shamefully confess that my first thought was a competitive one: Why was Arthur Miller attending this dance performance and not mine? Which, of course, is a good example of the pitfalls of dancers reviewing other dancers. I don't think my review was particularly insightful or well written. In fact, when I reread the handful of reviews I wrote for *Dance Magazine* that year, I didn't see much that was worth preserving (which is why they are not collected here).

It was later, at the *SoHo News*, that I found my groove. I didn't have to worry about whether I was balletically informed enough, and something about writing for a downtown audience gave me my voice. I felt I could bring readers into the world I had just seen. But when I started getting more offers to write than to choreograph, I backed off. Anyway, sitting at the typewriter was bad for my back, and I was already, in my twenties, getting killer spasms that took days to recover from.

One of my heroes at the time was Susan Sontag, both for her feminism and for forging a new way to talk about art. In her revolutionary essay "Against Interpretation," she advocated for a criticism that didn't interpret or "excavate" so much as represent the "sensuous surface" of art. Her approach fit the new kinds of dance that were exploding into view. You couldn't excavate a work by Merce Cunningham, Yvonne Rainer, or Trisha Brown. You had to sense it, pick up clues from it, not analyze it.

A new friend appeared at my doorstep. Someone must have steered Sally Banes, a young writer from Chicago, to me because she wanted to talk about all the choreographers I was most interested in: Trisha Brown (with whom I was dancing), Yvonne Rainer, Steve Paxton, David Gordon, Simone Forti, Kenneth King (with whom I also danced), Meredith Monk, and others. (This interest of hers fueled her landmark book, *Terpsichore in Sneakers*.) She matched my craving to talk about the artists I loved—artists who were deeply connected to our times. The way we were both thinking and looking, dance wasn't in a separate silo from life. As a writer, Sally put performances in the context of what was happening in the world, ushering in a fresh breeze of social consciousness.

The eighties was my most active period as a choreographer and teacher, and the least active as a writer. On faculty at Bennington from 1978–1984, I felt a two-way giving between myself and the students. The situation lent itself to a kind of choreographic lab, to which they brought their own individuality. Their openness allowed my choreography to flourish. And, I have to admit, teaching gave me more confidence in my choreography. The little bit of writing I did was tied to my dance making and teaching. I didn't think or feel like a critic; I still identified as a dancer and choreographer. In fact I felt very opposed to criticism as it was practiced, which is why I came forth in 1991 with a tirade against critics, "Beware the Egos of Critics" in "The Nineties." (Some of those ideas are echoed in my last blog post, "A Debate on Snark," in the last section.)

The nineties was a crossover decade for me. I was choreographing less but getting involved in dance in other ways. For three years I served as associate director at Jacob's Pillow Dance Festival, during which time I thought of myself more as a gatherer than a dance maker. Even when I made a piece for the Lincoln Center Festival, for which I assembled four groups of performers, I felt like a gatherer—a precursor to my current job as editor of *Dance Magazine*, where I bring disparate entities together in each issue.

By 1999 I had made about fifty dances over a thirty-year span, while writing was a side gig. My company had performed annually in New York, and sometimes toured as well. I was one of eight dance artists, including Bill T. Jones and Stephen Petronio, profiled in Michael Blackwood's documentary *Retracing Steps: American Dance Since Postmodernism*. During all those years, I was always working on a new piece—in my mind if not in the studio. Only gradually did choreography get pushed to the side and writing to the center. I started pitching features for the *New York Times* Arts & Leisure section. The following year I accepted a part-time position as New York editor at *Dance Magazine*, and was named editor in chief in 2004.

Even before coming to *Dance Magazine*, I was given the opportunity to review ballet, by both Elizabeth Zimmer at the *Village Voice* and Paul Ben-Itzak at *DanceInsider.com*. This effort paralleled my dance life: I had tried to incorporate ballet into my choreography at different times. In the eighties I gave a beautiful ballet dancer named Barbara Forbes a solo in a piece of mine. I felt sure that there was a way to infuse ballet with my eccentric kind of body logic—or vice versa. I eventually made two solos for the supremely classical Peter Boal of New York City Ballet, and one for former American Ballet Theatre star Martine van Hamel. Through these projects and through *Dance Magazine*—and through watching Wendy Whelan onstage—I found my way back to ballet, which I had spurned as a downtown choreographer and feminist.

———

Although writing and choreographing are very different physically, they both hold you in their grip mentally. The stream of decision making won't let you go; it haunts you; it keeps you up at night. Away from your desk or your studio, you are still going over things in your mind. You have to make a mess of it before you can clean it up, meaning you have to follow certain threads that will pull apart previously well-knit sections. In the "cleaning up" phase, you reread what you've written or you re-watch what you've made, over and over again. You want to be sure it has the rhythm you want, the continuity, the emotional tone, the infusion of life. Every tiny change sends you making other changes. You work at the details, polishing the parts until the thing shines as a whole.

———

I think I actually defined my writing style more quickly than my choreographic style, maybe because words are so much a part of our communicative equipment. I just had things to say—through the eyes of a dancer. Somehow my dancer's eyes gave me more freedom in print than in the choreographic process. Maybe I felt safer watching other people's work than in exposing my own. At any rate, it took about seven years of choreographing before I felt I found a voice, before I made a solo that felt totally me—or totally the adult me. Whereas in writing, I felt I had a voice as soon as the *SoHo News* opportunity came up.

My voice changed when I joined the editorial staff of *Dance Magazine*. I was no longer writing for the general public as I had been with *SWN* or the *New York Times*. This publication was for dancers and about dancers, and it felt like I was speaking to my own tribe. My previous job had been the administrator for the New York chapter of Physicians for Social Responsibility. I was editing a newsletter about the medical hazards of nuclear weapons production, climate change, and gun violence. While I believed passionately in those causes, I didn't feel I brought anything special to the table. The physicians I worked with had made a lifelong commitment and were far more knowledgeable than I.

When I got the part-time job at *Dance Magazine*, I felt I knew the people I was working for; I was one of them. I knew what a hard life dancers and choreographers have. I feel lucky to have a post-performance life in the field I love. I see many performances a week, and every time the curtain goes up, I still get a tingling of anticipation.

At the magazine, I launched into writing reviews, features, interviews, and reports. When the Internet seeped into our everyday lives, blogging gave me a different way of writing—less formal, more subjective, more spontaneous. As you can see in the last section, I felt I was tapping into a large, roving conversation behind the scenes.

———

Since I've chosen the title *Through the Eyes of a Dancer*, I feel I should say how a dancer sees—or at least how this dancer sees. First of all, we see movement *everywhere*, whether it's a child skipping down the street, a train pulling out of a station, or grass flattened by the wind. We pick up on what changes as well as the stillness of what remains the same. We see energy: where it starts from, how it surges or wilts. We see style—how one person walking is different from another person walking and what part of their body they are protecting.

All of this contributes to rhythm. The rhythm of a single action can be as fascinating as the rhythm of a whole ballet. And rhythm is what guides me as a writer and editor. One could call it flow. When I'm having trouble with a review or story, I try to pay attention to the flow. A few of the pieces I've chosen here have less to do with dance than with rhythm, and I would count my excited little meditation on radio personality James Irsay in "The Seventies" in this category.

But mostly I chose this title to say that, though I no longer have the legs, the back, the arms of a dancer, there is some part of me that is still a dancer. My eyes were trained in thousands of classes to pick up movement quickly, just as my legs were trained to open in a plié or my back to elongate when arching or curving. You learn to use your eyes to see where the movement starts from and where it reverberates in the body. And because I have spent many hours looking at empty space and imagining how to fill it with human energy, I also have the eyes of a choreographer.

There is one more reason for this title. I want to emphasize that everyone's eyes are different, that all critics write from how they see things. We tend to give "the critic" great authority. We think that person has seen so much and knows so much that she or he must be right. But when looking at a work of art, there is no one correct way to view it or to judge it. So I am saying, This is how I see things through *this* pair of eyes, with *this* particular life in dance behind me.

———

How has the dance world changed in the last four decades? Admittedly, it will be hard to tell from this collection. My own direction in writing started from downtown dance and performance and wound up at more mainstream dance, much of it ballet. But over the long haul, a few things come to mind, all of them overlapping. Here are five of them.

First, ballet and modern (or postmodern) dance have drawn closer together. Choreographers in Europe who blend articulate legs with deep torso movement, like Jiří Kylián, Mats Ek, and William Forsythe, have had a huge international influence. Here in the States, Twyla Tharp has done a lot to meld the two, as I point out in my feature on her in my fifth section, "From 2000 to 2004." More recently, ballet choreographers Christopher Wheeldon and Wayne McGregor have opened themselves up to modern dance influences, while modern dance bastions like the Alvin Ailey American Dance Theater have come to rely heavily on ballet for training.

Second, like everything else, the dance world has gone global. I've been fortunate to catch glimpses of the dance boom in Israel, Russia, Cuba, France, and England. Not only ballet, but also modern dance, jazz, postmodern, tap, hip-hop, flamenco, butoh, gaga, and Indian classical dance have spread beyond their birth countries and evolved. Too, there's more traffic between companies and countries than ever before. Because of social media, a dancer in Sydney, Australia, can feel connected to a dancer in Houston—and maybe get a job there.

Third, since videos of other dance cultures and eras are accessible on the Internet, each choreographer has the potential to be a deejay and remix any combination of dance forms. Hip-hop, Bollywood, salsa, the Ballets Russes,

Mary Wigman, and Fred Astaire are all at our fingertips. While the question of authenticity was relevant a decade ago—in my feature on butoh in "The Nineties," the question came up, Do you have to be Japanese to do butoh?—that's less of an issue now. And with the growing diversity in all segments of our society (that's not to say racism isn't still a problem, especially in ballet), dance artists are crossing cultures to make new physical languages. Examples of people who have created stimulating hybrids are Trey McIntyre, with his mashup of ballet, postmodern, and social dance, and Jared Grimes, who mixes tap, hip-hop, and vaudeville (both appear in the last section). As Harry Shum says in "The Times They Are A-Changin'," my update on diversity, "I make my own salad."

Fourth, attitudes toward gender have opened up. With influences like Contact Improvisation and Mark Morris, there are less marked differences between men and women in action and affect. All-male ballet companies like Les Ballets Trockaderos de Monte Carlo and Les Ballets Grandivas are popular internationally—everyone likes to joke about gender. Even with some ballet choreographers, occasionally the woman bears weight. (In most of the ballet repertoire, however, men and women are still polarized in what they do and wear, which to my mind is part of the reason it often looks old-fashioned.) And with more young people choosing to become transgender, it's not highly unusual to see a transgender person in modern or postmodern dance concerts.

Lastly, dance on all sizes of screens has proliferated. As I write this, we're in the midst of an epidemic of dance programs on reality TV. Although these shows can be irritating—repellant, even—they pull in new viewers to our humble (economically speaking) art. Dance in film has become popular too. And with the accessibility of editing programs in personal computers, a new generation of video dance has sprung up.

———

The selection in this book is far from comprehensive. The dance world has grown exponentially, and I don't claim to have a handle on all its myriad facets. Even from my own experience, this collection offers just a slice—well, a few slices—of what I've seen and done. (One omission, for example, is Ailey's *Revelations*. It thrills me every time I see it, but I just never happened to write anything substantial about it.) The reviews, features, musings, and tirades gathered here have been chosen because I believe they contribute to the ongoing conversation on dance. I am reprinting them pretty much as they originally appeared, but have cleaned up the language wherever I spotted something redundant or confusing or inaccurate.

One of the things that interests me in looking back over time is that my own reactions to certain artists have changed. For instance, when I first saw Pina Bausch in 1983, I never would have guessed how much I would grow to love her work—or how her work would open up in its emotional tone as it kept the wildness of its compulsions. Likewise, when I first wrote about a Wayne McGregor piece in 2009, the adolescent brutality rubbed me the wrong way, and only later did I see the beauty in his work. That ability to change, both for the artist and the watcher, is one of the great rewards of hanging in there.

I've divided the book into seven chronological sections. Each starts with a brief introduction to say something about my life at the time and/or what was happening in the dance world. I conclude with an afterword about my mother, because that's how my own dance story began.

The Sixties

A few years ago, when I came upon an old program from my days as a teenage ballet student, I noticed that the date of our summer recital in Cape Cod was the exact same date as the first Judson Dance Theater concert. So when Sally Banes asked me to contribute a memoir-type story to her anthology *Reinventing Dance in the 1960s* I couldn't resist making the connection. The aesthetics and lore of Judson, that crucible of dance reinvention, have been such a big influence on me that it was a crystallizing moment to realize how far I'd been from those aesthetics in 1962.

From Sally's point of view, the sixties stretched into the seventies, so it was fair game for me to include something about that later decade as well. This account of my early dancing life lays out some of the preoccupations that recur throughout this collection: the intersection between ballet and modern dance, the magnetic pull of Russian ballet, the terrors and triumphs of improvisation, Trisha Brown (with whom I started dancing by the end of this memoir), and Judson Dance Theater, the collective that cracked open modern dance on the way to postmodern dance.

Just a note to say that this first section is the only one in the book where the title ("The Sixties") describes the period written *about* rather than the time of the actual writing, which in this case was around 2002.

One Route from Ballet to Postmodern

from *Reinventing Dance in the 1960s: Everything Was Possible*, edited by Sally Banes
with the assistance of Andrea Harris, University of Wisconsin Press, 2003

On July 6, 1962, the day of the first performance of the members of Robert Dunn's workshop at Judson Memorial Church, I performed with my ballet teacher on Cape Cod. Miss Fokine (Michel's niece, Irine) took a group of students to Nauset Light Beach, where we had class for two hours every morning and late afternoon on an outdoor platform and swam at the beach down the block in between. At the end of this idyllic summer, we gave a recital for local residents. I was fourteen.

After every performance, summer or winter, Miss Fokine would pick on one poor kid who had done something transgressive, like letting dirty toe shoe ribbons drag on the floor. On this occasion, after our performance of the "Grand Pas" from *Paquita*, she entered our dressing room and came right at me, pointing and yelling, "Look at your hair! You look like an African Fujiyama!" We had been on the Cape for six weeks, and whenever my mother wasn't around to cut my hair it grew like a bush. From that moment on through the rest of high school, I grew it long so I could tie it back in a bun like the other girls. When not in class, I ironed my hair or applied a god-awful-smelling chemical to straighten it. I didn't know Fujiyama was a mountain, but I thought whatever it was, it probably wasn't African.

That fall the Bolshoi was coming to the Metropolitan Opera House, and

Me, at seventeen. I still love to stretch. (Jerry Bauer)

they were looking for American teenagers to fill the crowd scenes of Leonid Yakobson's new *Spartacus*. Miss Fokine's mother, Alexandra Fedorova, still had connections to the Bolshoi, and arranged for a bunch of us to audition. I was among the lucky group chosen to perform. We were onstage when Vladimir Vasiliev leapt like a panther and turned like a gyroscope. When Maya Plisetskaya dragged the cart like a beggar woman, we all had to point at her and laugh. Backstage, Galina Ulanova walked a few steps behind the meltingly lovely Ekaterina Maximova. My fantasy was to become the next Anastasia Stevens, the American-English girl who danced with the Bolshoi and also translated for us. Plus, she had beautiful reddish frizzy hair (frizzy—like mine!).

In the summer of 1963, I went to the Delacorte Theater in Central Park to see the new Joffrey Ballet. Because the performance was free, crowds of people would come, so you had to get your ticket in the morning and camp out in the park all afternoon. I remember seeing Gerald Arpino's *Sea Shadow*, with Lisa Bradley, hair long and free, undulating on top of a man. She was both pristine and sensual, and utterly gorgeous. The possibility of this kind of dancerly sexuality appealed to my budding sense of myself. That night I decided to study at the Joffrey school (officially the American Ballet Center) starting in the fall, even though it meant commuting from New Jersey.

I loved the Joffrey school, especially Françoise Martinet, who wore white tennis shoes even for pointe work. The classes seemed less strict than at the School of American Ballet, where I had studied during the summers of 1960 and 1963, and the atmosphere was not quite so hallowed.[1] Lisa Bradley, Noël Mason, Ivy Clear, Trinette Singleton, Charthel Arthur and Marjorie Mussman were all taking the advanced class, which I watched whenever I could. I usually took the intermediate class with Miss Martinet, Lillian Moore, or occasionally Mr. Joffrey. I tried hard to be a worthy ballet student, and when Mr. Joffrey asked me to stand front and center as an example to the others, I was thrilled almost to the point of delirium.

A few modern dancers took class too. I didn't want to be a modern dancer—that's what my mother had been. I had studied "interpretive dance" with my mother and other teachers since I was five. I had taken the June course at the Martha Graham School of Contemporary Dance that summer of 1963, and I continued to go every Friday, but it remained a sideline for me.[2]

One day as I was walking to Washington Square Park between classes, I saw one of the modern dancers from the Joffrey class—Sandra Neels—on the steps of a church on Washington Square South. She called out to me, saying, "You should come to some performances here. They're really interesting." I just said, "Uh huh." I don't think I was even curious. I didn't go see modern dance unless my mother dragged me. (Sandra danced with Merce Cunningham from 1963 to 1973.)

I've gone back to that moment many times, wondering if anything would have mobilized me to check out the performances at Judson. My two magnetic poles at that time were *Swan Lake* and *West Side Story*. I would listen to the radio, roving up and down the dial in hopes of hearing one or the other. I had seen *West Side Story* on Broadway and memorized all the songs. The same year, I danced in my ballet teacher's *Swan Lake* and adored it. I could have rippled my arms to Tchaikovsky's music for days.

As my high school graduation approached, I developed three possible plans. The first was to attend New York University and continue studying at the Joffrey school, with the hope of getting into the company. The second was to go to Juilliard, where I could study both modern dance and ballet. The third was Bennington, which was my mother's first choice, and for that reason it was my last.

I forced myself to assess my prospects in ballet realistically. Although I was a lyrical, musical classical dancer, my turn-out and pointe work were less than sparkling. In the Graham technique, you had to dig deeper into yourself, and that intensity had a gritty psychological appeal. So, after being accepted at Juilliard, I watched a class there—I believe Antony Tudor was teaching. I realized that if I chose that route, the next four years would be entirely familiar to me, as I had taken ballet and modern classes virtually all my life. On the other hand, the day I visited the Bennington campus in Vermont happened to be a beautiful fall afternoon, suddenly illuminating the world of art and literature and learning. I chose to follow the unknown rather than the known.

It took me my whole freshman year to change over from being a ballet dancer to being a modern dancer. I had to be broken like a horse is broken before you can ride it. Bill Bales lit into me for my habits—the swan-like neck, the prissy footsteps, the jutting chin, the delicate fingers. I had to purge myself of these mannerisms and find the ground underneath me.

During my college years—1965 to 1969—I often came to New York City and saw early Dance Theater Workshop performances. Jack Moore, who had cofounded DTW with Jeff Duncan and Art Bauman, was teaching dance at Bennington. On one of these trips I saw Rudy Perez perform his solo *Countdown*. He sat on a chair and took a drag of a cigarette in surreal slowed-down time while the *Songs of the Auvergne* played on tape. When he stood up, you could see stripes of blue paint on his face. Was it war paint? Was it the tears of a clown? The markings of a quarterback? The dance was ineffably sad, yet rooted and powerful.

And I went back to the Delacorte in 1966 and saw Carmen de Lavallade in a solo by Geoffrey Holder. She was the most beautiful woman dancing I could imagine. The vision of her spiraling in a white dress lingered in my mind for days. It was the first "modern dance" I fell in love with, but it wasn't weighty and angular like "modern dance" or insistent in any way. It was like dreaming of an island far away.

I was feeling more comfortable as a modern dancer and wanted to choreograph, simply because it was so hard to do well. I remember a time in Jack Moore's composition class, probably in my junior or senior year, when the assignment was to make a beginning and an ending. We would each then choose someone else's beginning and someone else's ending and make our own middle to sandwich in between. I remember being in the studio alone, trying to begin my beginning. I started with a big reach up with my head and arm—an ecstatic reach to the heavens. I was playing with it, trying out different ways of doing it. I started breaking it up into parts. Through endless trials, I found a way of reaching the head up, then bringing the arm up sharply, and then as the head came down, leaving the arm up. Within two seconds, the arm movement intercut the head movement. I worked on it until I could do it without thinking. It was an unusual coordination, but a certain energy came from breaking it up. It was no longer a breathy or ecstatic thing, but broken, like shards. When I showed it in class, the other students responded immediately, and more than half of them chose it for their beginning. I felt something had happened. I had undermined a unit of assumed movement and made something new. Looking back, I see that I was deconstructing a standard modern-dance reach—my first encounter with postmodernism. I feel that much of my choreography can be traced to that moment.

College changed me, but the sixties did too. I remember sunny days when we would take our dormitory furniture out on the lawn. Someone's stereo would be blasting Aretha Franklin's voice from a dorm window, and everything was fine in the world. To me that was the sixties: wearing a light-as-air Indian shirt and beads and hearing Aretha wail over Commons Lawn. Some of us were dancing and some were reading. Ooooh it felt good. Singing "R-e-s-p-e-c-t" along with Aretha was a glorious way to grow up.

One night during our college dance tour in the winter of 1968, I stayed at a friend's pad in Boston. She sat me down and said, "You have to hear the new Beatles album." It was *Sgt. Pepper's Lonely Hearts Club Band*, and I was overwhelmed. The ingenuity, the drive, the lilting but somehow rebellious melodies, the camaraderie, the lightheartedness, the trippiness (yes, we got

Taking technique class at Bennington, with my beloved friend Harry Sheppard standing behind me, sometime between 1965 and 1969. (© Josef Wittman)

stoned first), the sense that Anything can follow Anything, were astounding. (Did the Beatles know about John Cage?)

So my new poles were Aretha Franklin and the Beatles. The go-for-broke, sing-from-your-guts celebration of womanhood on the one hand, and this zany collaboration, the revelation that you could be brainy and also have fun, on the other.

College taught me that while it's worthwhile to be a good girl, it's also worthwhile to break the rules. The Bennington campus had 350 acres of rolling hills and picturesque landscape. Viola Farber, the former Cunningham dancer who taught at Bennington briefly, asked us to choreograph for an out-of-doors spot on campus. I was feeling pretty dismal, nursing a broken heart that I pretended was "sophomore slump." I wasn't in the mood to celebrate the joy of life on the grassy knolls or under a lushly spreading oak tree, so I found a small alley between a garage and a chicken coop that was littered with hangers, old tires and beer cans. Mostly I got entangled in some wires and stared at the ground. Decades later, Viola, recalling that assignment, blurted out gleefully, "And you picked the ugliest place on campus!"

In the fall of 1968, Judith Dunn came up to Vermont to teach, with musician Bill Dixon in tow. Also a former dancer with Cunningham, Judy had assisted her husband, Robert Dunn, in giving the composition workshops that led to Judson Dance Theater. (She had since separated from him.) I loved her yoga class and learned the sun worship from her. To demonstrate the lion posture, she would get preternaturally calm and then, with a ridiculously fierce thrust of her head, stick her tongue out and down and pop her eyes wide open. She would hold that posture for two full minutes. I was impressed by her commitment.

But I hated Judy's technique class. Her idea of the new relation of music to dance was that Bill would play any loungey jazz thing on the piano while we repeated her combination. She emphatically did not want the piano to set the tempo and did not want us to do the steps "to" the music. But she scolded us when, inevitably, we each performed it with different timing. This seemed illogical and irresponsible, and I quit the class.

But Judy's presence opened things up. She challenged the tradition of a single, end-of-semester concert in Commons Theater so that we could do performances in other spaces and at other times. But one such performance, masterminded by Cathy Weis, one year behind me (now a video/dance/performance artist), and an MFA student named Mary Fussell, was already in the works. Cathy and Mary turned Jennings Mansion, where music classes were held, into a complex, dreamlike environment. On the ground floor was a genteel ballroom where Ulysses Dove[3] and I danced with guests and graciously escorted them to the level below. The basement practice rooms had been transformed to represent organs of the body: one room was the heart, another the lungs, another the liver. Audience members entered rooms that had billowing fabrics and throbbing sounds. They were given costumes to don, so the separation between performers and audience was blurred, and people went from room to room in a pleasantly confused state. Tuli Kupferberg of the Fugs came to campus to heighten the confusion. [I would say this event was a precursor to the "immersive theater" that we've recently seen emerge from England.]

I knew that Judy was conducting a serious improvisation session on Friday mornings, but I never signed up for it. Out of that class came her strong improvisation performance group of the next few years. I knew that something very interior, very intuitive was going on that I wasn't privy to, or didn't have access to in myself. Just the fact that it was a three-hour session was daunting.

Also, I had had an experience that crystallized my fear of improvisation. One Thursday afternoon during the weekly dance division workshop, Jack Moore decided, for a change of pace, that we should improvise. He named a few people to go up onstage and "improvise." (This was Commons Theater, where Martha Graham and other modern dance "pioneers" had premiered major works in the thirties.) Someone put a box full of hats onstage. As Jack was calling out names of people to go up and experiment in front of everyone, his eyes alighted on me and he added my name. I froze. Like a stone, my body suddenly got heavy and inert. Even if my future had depended on it, I couldn't have budged from my seat. I shook my head vehemently. "Oh come on, Wendy, it'll be fun," said Jack in his most inviting voice. "No," I said. This went back and forth a few more times as I totally humiliated myself. I had had good solid training in both ballet and modern dance, and I knew myself as a dancer when I had access to those techniques. Improvisation meant losing control and looking stupid.

Jack finally dropped his case, and I got to sit back and watch the adventurous ones onstage. They played with the hats. They covered their eyes with the hats, stomped on them, tossed them around. At best, what they did was either cute or clever. I was glad I hadn't acquiesced. But amid the sea of silliness, one phenomenon surfaced: Lisa Nelson, a student one year behind me. Her concentration was a thing to behold. Her quickness and connectedness between her dance self and the hat self were astonishing. She did things with the hats that I was sure no one else on earth had ever done. I couldn't take my eyes off her. She seemed to be getting signals from outer space, or I guess inner space. (Many years later, she teamed up with Steve Paxton, and they created PA RT [1978], a collaborative duet which they performed for years.) To this day, she is my favorite improviser.

During my freshman nonresident term (now called field work term) I studied at Paul Sanasardo at Twenty-first Street and Sixth Avenue. His class was known as the hardest modern technique class in the city. I was up for it. In that class were Sara Rudner, Cliff Keuter, Elina Mooney, Kenneth King, Diane Germaine, Manuel Alum, Sally Bowden, Bill Dunas, Mark Franko, Judith Blackstone, and Laura Dean. I loved watching these dancers just as I had loved watching the dancers at the School of American Ballet, the Joffrey and the Graham school.

But studying with Paul Sanasardo was a mixed experience. As galvanizing as his rigorous barre and combinations were, his narcissism was out of control. After giving orders in his richly booming voice, he'd watch himself in the mirror, his eyes glued to his own image. He treated his dancers brutally. Manuel Alum and Diane Germaine, his two star dancers, were routinely scorned and humiliated in class. It was disturbing. I did not aspire to work with a man like that.

One person who seemed not to belong in an advanced technique class was Bill Dunas. He would do triplets across the floor with his head wagging back and forth, which I interpreted as an excuse-me-for-living attitude. I was then blown away by his performances at the Cubiculo in which he appeared between blackouts in intensely characterized roles. Every move he made, every look on his face, was drastic. No complex movement or virtuosic technique emanated from him—just an existential hunger and rawness. Later, in 1972, I learned *Gap*, the basic three-minute dance that he put into each piece in a different way. I remember open arms with fists, feet planted apart. The head tucks and the arms loop around each other, then you come up strong, as defiant as before. I fell in love with him—and this love, for a change, was requited.

During the summers of 1967 and 1968, I attended the American Dance Festival at Connecticut College. I took Sarah Stackhouse's ecstatic classes in Limón technique, Graham classes with David Wood (who had been my main teacher at the Graham school), Doris Rudko's course in Louis Horst's choreographic method, and Lucas Hoving's own hybrid class. For those of us already having back trouble, Betty Jones offered extracurricular sessions in the "constructive rest position," based on the work of Lulu Sweigard. The second summer I danced in a reconstruction of Doris Humphrey's *New Dance* (1935), directed by Jennifer Muller and supervised by José Limón. But more important was that Martha Wittman, of the Bennington faculty, had asked me to assist her in teaching composition, and I got to observe her serious but unorthodox approach. She experimented with group process and improvisation as routes to choreography.

So when I graduated from Bennington and came to New York in 1969, I was no longer satisfied by modern dance as I had known it—the austere beauty of Limón's *Moor's Pavane*, the chiseled angst of Martha Graham in *Lamentation*. I was drawn to performances of the legendary improvisation group, the Grand Union—their family-like reunions where you wondered who was going to misbehave. The group included David Gordon, Trisha Brown, Douglas Dunn, Barbara Dilley, Steve Paxton, and Nancy Lewis. We'd watch them get on each other's nerves—brilliantly. They were our Beatles. We all had our favorites. "Were you there the time Trisha stayed under a blanket for about an *hour*?" "Did you see how David insulted Nancy? Do you think he really meant it this time?" "Did Douglas wear that preacher outfit 'cause he felt alienated?" "The women's dance was really sweet this time." "I don't know what David and Barbara were doing with those pillows, but I loved watching them."

I remember the Grand Union performance at New York University's Loeb

Student Center when they played the popular song "Lola" by The Kinks about a hundred times. One of the group would just walk over to the phonograph and turn it on. This was against all the rules we had learned in college warning us about using popular music. But this alluring yet insolent song about ambiguous sexuality captured the moment perfectly. Everyone was trying out everything. Choosing that song exemplified the conflation of high art and popular art that was heralded by Susan Sontag. This was like bringing your furniture out on the grass and listening to Aretha. The defiance, the sensuality, the do-your-own-thingness of it!

My first year after graduating, I was on scholarship at the Martha Graham School and dancing with Rudy Perez. I learned a lot from him about applying collage techniques to dance, but after a year I realized that he wasn't going to allow me to take time off for my own choreography.

I often took class with Maggie Black, a popular ballet teacher whom modern dancers trusted because of her emphasis on alignment. At the end of one class, Sara Rudner and Rose Marie Wright, scouting new dancers for Twyla Tharp, approached me and invited me to come to Twyla's studio. In a one-candidate audition, I was told brusquely, "You'll do." But I felt uncomfortable in the movement and told her later on the phone that I wouldn't join them. I had not yet seen *The One Hundreds* (1970), the piece that blew my mind with its inventiveness and sent me scurrying to audition for the "farm club," the temporary group of seventeen young dancers she assembled to learn repertoire. Working with her was a juicy challenge for me as both a dancer and an observer. Out of Twyla's body flowed a stream of ingenious, intricate, infinitely varied and open-ended movement. A clear love of the body in motion—as opposed to positions and as opposed to motion in the service of narrative—was the motivating force. "You must feel personally about every move," she told us while showing the steps, thus confirming what I had always felt about dance.

In 1971, at the Whitney Museum, I saw Trisha Brown's *Walking on the Wall*, in which her performers, aided by specially made harnesses, walked on the wall. The illusion was so strong that you could swear you were looking out a window and down to the sidewalk. It was very trippy, as though everyone in the room was having the same hallucination. She also performed *Skymap* (1969), for which she asked the audience to lie on our backs, look up and listen. We heard Trisha's earthy yet mischievous voice inviting us to use our imaginations to cross a fantasy terrain. It was an amazing feeling to know that everyone was making similar thought pictures while packed like sardines on the floor. (Is this a descendant of Anna Halprin's community pieces?) I wanted to remember every word and write it down. [Note: The text for *Skymap* is now collected in the MIT Press book *Trisha Brown: Dance and Art in Dialogue, 1961–2001.*]

In 1973 I saw Yvonne Rainer's *Inner Appearances*, her prelude to *This is the story of a woman who. . . .* It was on a program organized by James Waring called "Dancing Ladies." Her sole action was vacuuming—a decision that was both logical (considering so many women spent so much time at it) and daring (in that vacuuming was not traditionally considered the stuff of art). I was completely engrossed in her written text, projected sentence by sentence onto the back wall. One of the lines, which I wrote down on a scrap of program, was, "Social interaction seems to be mostly about seduction." I felt that Yvonne was like Susan Sontag, her high level of intelligence joining together with her high intensity of emotions. There was a force to this piece (which was before the term "performance art" was commonly used) but also a restraint that was moving. I was also knocked out by the protest she embedded in her bio in the program notes. Although James Waring had been her mentor, she railed against the title "Dancing Ladies": "Five years ago I might have appreciated the humor and quaintness of 'Dancing Ladies,' but in a time when more and more women are struggling for a sense of individual identity in ways that are new and unsettling, such a title is—at best—anachronistic in its ignoring of that struggle and—far worse—condescending. . . ." I loved that she just couldn't leave it alone. Yvonne was one of the few people who had the guts to live the slogan of the times—"the personal is the political."

Through Bill Dunas I met Kenneth King, and I danced in his *Praxiomatics* and *The Telaxic Synapsulator* (both 1974). The cast of *Praxiomatics* included David Woodberry and three people who had performed with Robert Wilson: Charles Dennis, Robyn Brentano, and Liz Pasquale. I loved dancing with Kenneth. Somehow he created an environment that dissipated my fear of improvisation. By now I had done some improvisation with Art Bauman and while auditioning for Daniel Nagrin when he started his Workgroup (I ultimately was not accepted). But I really felt free with Kenneth. He was a very technical dancer and appreciated technique in other dancers. I was fascinated by his character work, for which he would go way out on a limb dramatically. Kenneth is the philosopher/artist, wizardly in his thinking. His *High Noon*, based on Nietzsche's writings, was dark and mysterious, studded equally with moments of Nietzsche's truth and Nietzsche's craziness. [Update: Kenneth is author of *Writing in Motion: Body—Language—Technology* (Wesleyan University Press, 2003)].

Talking about truth and craziness: around this time I was reading Jill

Performing my solo, *The Daily Mirror*, in Trisha Brown's loft, 1976. I added a
new string of movement every day for 100 days. (© Babette Mangolte)

Johnston's collection of *Village Voice* reviews entitled *Marmalade Me*. It
sizzled with her highly personal take on dance and art. Her writing bypassed
the usual organization of paragraphs and cut to the heart of her searing and
poetic vision. Hers was a real sixties voice. It got me curious about Judson—
and interested in writing too. I took three cycles of a course in dance writing sponsored by Dance Theater Workshop that was co-taught by Deborah
Jowitt and Marcia B. Siegel. (I may have this backward: it could be that the
course is what led me to read Johnston.)

When I started dancing with Trisha Brown in 1975, I felt I had come home.

In addition to seeing her walk on walls, I had seen some of her dances in a gallery. The year before, I had written a survey of what I called "loft dances" for *New York Magazine* (which never made it into print), and in it I declared Trisha my favorite choreographer. I described her dancers as having "collapsible bodies." I was trying to identify not only the special quality of looseness but also the possibility that they could drop to the floor at any moment. It was like collapsing your assumptions, like emptying your mind. Whatever you were thinking, it could just end. Trisha's quicksilver mind matched her collapsible body. No need to hold on to the uplifted body, the virtuosic, the heroic. Just a need to keep dancing. It was radical almost like Jerry Rubin and Abbie Hoffman were radical.

In Trisha's studio in SoHo we were making a piece called *Pyramid*; the score was a diabolical progression of accumulating and de-accumulating. The first day, Trisha explained the structure and had us make our own series of movements. When we asked what kind of movement, she said something like, "It should be simple and complex, steady and erratic, strong and delicate, logical and irrational, grand and humble." This series of paradoxes threw me just the kind of choreographic bone I love to chew on. About Trisha, I wrote in my journal, "Her movements are more natural than natural. . . . You can see her thoughts in the dancing, how she questions everything." And Trisha didn't mind my bushy hair. By that time Angela Davis had emerged as a cultural icon, so I started thinking that my natural hair state was a Judaic version of the Afro.

During this period, I was also writing reviews for the *Soho Weekly News*, right around the corner from Trisha's studio. Since I wasn't crazy about reviewing my friends, I mostly kept away from dance. Instead, I covered the new, anything-goes performances—stemming from experimentation in theater, music and visual art—that were later dubbed "performance art." Robb Baker edited a section called the "Concepts in Performance" page, and it was the only place where this type of thing was covered. When Robb left, I became the editor of that page. And after I left, Sally Banes, who had started writing for it, took over.

Tragically, in the late seventies Judith Dunn developed a brain tumor and could no longer teach. While she was on medical leave, the Bennington College dance division looked for a replacement—and found me. Soon after I arrived in 1978, we were discussing ideas for the next repertory class at a division meeting. Martha Wittman, who was still on the faculty (an eloquent dancer, she later joined the Liz Lerman Dance Exchange in her sixties), suggested teaching Judy's *Dew Horse* (1963/1966). I wanted to expand the idea to doing a whole semester's worth of works from Judson Dance Theater. Another faculty member, designer/videographer/performer Tony Carruthers, loved the idea. Between Tony and me, the project grew to include residencies with Trisha, Yvonne, Steve Paxton, and Lisa Nelson; a lecture by Sally Banes (who was writing her dissertation on Judson at the time;[4] reconstructions of Steve's *Flat* (1964), Yvonne's *We Shall Run* (1963), and Trisha's *Homemade* (1965); a series of videotaped interviews; and an exhibit of photographs that toured internationally. Later we reconstructed many more pieces at the Danspace Project of St. Mark's Church in New York. This was all part of the Bennington College Judson Project, which took up much of my time from 1979 to 1982. (I continue to give a slide lecture on Judson Dance Theater.)

Much of the work I saw in the seventies led me to look for its roots in Judson: the mind trip of Rudy Perez, the intensity of Kenneth King, the paradoxical nature of Trisha Brown, the mythmaking improvisation of the Grand Union, the hard-won intellectual feminism of Yvonne Rainer, the brazen writing of Jill Johnston, and the emergence of performance art. Judson was a time to clear the slate and start over. The allure for me was returning to a heady beginning that I hadn't witnessed, when sparks of possibility flew across the skyscape of the American mind.

NOTES

1. But I thoroughly enjoyed the training at the School of American Ballet. In my diary of 1963, I paired the name of each of my teachers with her or his most repeated utterance: Antonia Tumkovsky ("Cheek to me"), Maria Tallchief ("Stomach in, chest out"), André Eglevsky ("Arms simple"), Lew Christensen ("Learn to listen"), and Muriel Stuart ("Now rest, darling").

2. Nevertheless, I was very involved in the Graham classes. The Friday class was the advanced teenage class, and many kids from the High School of the Performing Arts took it, including Christian Holder, who later became a star of the Joffrey Ballet. On Friday, November 22, 1963, while in my high school history class, I learned that President Kennedy had been shot and killed. After general chaos and crying in the girls' room, I decided to take the bus in to New York City for my Graham class anyway. Only about six kids showed up for class, but David Wood taught as usual. He said, "We're dancers, and dancing is what we do, no matter what tragedy has occurred. We will work through it."

3. Dove later danced with Merce Cunningham and Alvin Ailey and became an internationally acclaimed choreographer who mounted works on many companies until his death in 1996.

4. This dissertation was later published as *Democracy's Body: Judson Dance Theater, 1962–1964* (Ann Arbor: University of Michigan Research Press, 1983).

The Seventies

The three years I wrote for the *SoHo Weekly News* roughly coincided with the years I danced with Trisha Brown's company—1975 to 1978. My deadlines were on Fridays, so I would stay up late Thursday night, stalling till around midnight, and then devour a pint of Häagen-Dazs coffee ice cream. After that there was nothing else to do but sit down and write the damn thing. I'd stay up till four or five, cutting and pasting, which in those days meant scissors and scotch tape—many times, many versions. By the time I got to rehearsal, a short walk through SoHo from my apartment on Sixth Avenue, I was a wreck. Afterward I would go around the corner to the *SoHo News* office on Spring Street and submit my review.

Getting the "job" at the *SWN* followed a twelve-hour, winter-solstice, dance-and-music event that was a collaboration between choreographer Stephanie Woodard, composer Peter Zummo, and myself. Audience members arrived at a loft in SoHo throughout the night with their sleeping bags. Robb Baker, who wrote on experimental dance in the *SoHo News* and *Dance Magazine*, was one of them. He was so appalled by the lack of press coverage of this interdisciplinary marathon that he invited all three of us to write for his section of the *SWN*, which was called the "Concepts in Performance" page. He wanted the kind of work we did to be more visible.

The seventies was a time when performance art—though it wasn't yet named—seemed to explode out of nowhere but actually emerged from alternative work in theater, music, and visual art more than from dance. That suited me just fine because I didn't want to write about my friends, who were mostly dancers. Nevertheless my "reviews" covered David Gordon, Lucinda Childs, and the legendary Grand Union improvisation group.

At the *SoHo Weekly News* I had the freedom to write on whatever I pleased—at ten dollars a throw. I could define any event as a performance. My choices included a juggler who didn't want to do tricks, a radio announcer who improvised, and a daredevil high-wire walker named Philippe Petit. The longer pieces include a comparison of Fred Astaire and Mikhail Baryshnikov, and a feature called "Exporting SoHo" on European audiences gushing over New York's downtown artists. I have a juicy interview with Susan Sontag that touches on art, feminism, life, and death. The essay on "Dumb Art" for the *Village Voice* is really a shameless attempt at taste making, calling attention to a certain strain of instinctual, or preverbal, art.

Barbara Lloyd (Dilley)

61 Crosby Street, New York City

written for Dance Writing class, June 1971

Decades after I wrote this for Deborah Jowitt and Marcia Siegel's writing course, Deborah asked me about the review I'd written on Barbara Lloyd (who was later known as Barbara Dilley) dancing nude. I had no memory of it and said, "I never saw Barbara Dilley naked." But when I looked in my old files, there it was — a carbon copy, typed on two pages. I include it here because it's a link to the communal, trippy sixties — which came before the feminist, equal-time-for-female-pronouns seventies, as you can see in the second sentence below.

There is a trend in avant-garde dance toward the more casual. By this, I mean that it is no longer necessary to watch every moment of the performer's actions, and the performer himself has more leeway regarding the movements he does. This requires more personal investment from the dancer, and the audience too must bring more of itself to the performance.

A good example of this new kind of piece was Barbara Lloyd's solo, *Dervish*. The audience was seated in a large circle, and before it started, candles were given to about every fifth person. It was dark, except for one lighted candle, which was passed along to ignite the next person's candle, and so on. It was during this long process (about forty candles) that we began to see Miss Lloyd, nude except for garlands of flowers on her waist, ankles, wrists, and head, moving in the center of the loft. She stayed in that spot, pivoting steadily on one foot and using the other to push off from, while her upper body moved fluidly. Some of us thought that she would do this until all the candles were lit. She did, and after she continued in this vein still longer, we realized that the entire dance would consist of this turning. The dance lasted fifty or sixty minutes.

A whole range of thoughts occupied me: I admired her endurance; I hated her endurance. Would she keep going until all the candles burned out? I blew my candle out. I imagined her completing the dance and vomiting right there. I imagined myself vomiting. What must she be thinking of? How is her pivot leg behaving? How many times had she rehearsed the dance full out?

There was an atmosphere of unity, and it seemed that Miss Lloyd, and everyone there, accepted whatever I might be thinking. The dance existed for meditative purposes. Just like a red and white checked tablecloth. Or like the tiles on your bathroom floor.

Toward the end, Miss Lloyd was making simple sounds—humming and clicking and such. The audience, partly from a togetherness feeling and partly from restlessness, joined in by improvising vocally on her leads. It became ritual.

Usually at a downtown dance concert, I see a few people walk out before the end. No one walked out that night.

Followable Dancing: Mary Overlie and David Gordon

Whitney Museum of American Art, New York City

SoHo Weekly News, March 4, 1976

The unison between David Gordon and Valda Setterfield that I describe in the second half of this review floors me anew. In a way, it was the foundation for the next thirty-six years of their work together, though they haven't actually danced with each other all that time. Their onstage partnership is very different now—his dancing ability has faded as his playwriting talents have risen; her dancing and speaking onstage have gotten even more burnished over time. But the two are still profoundly in tune with each other. In David's new work, The Beginning of the End of the . . . *(2012), he sits on a platform reading from his brilliant, fractured, maddeningly self-questioning script (drawn partly from Pirandello) while she anchors the show with her dependably charismatic aura. Her British composure complements his scruffy New York self, just as her still-lithe dancer elegance complements his sedentary, writing-plays-in-his-mind stubbornness. That synergy has been the backbone of his work since they were married in 1960.*

In a time when everyone is trying to do/be everything, a dance that is concise and quiet and eloquently constructed is something to be savored. I saw two such gems on the Whitney series: a delicate, entrancing solo by Mary Overlie and a brilliant duet by David Gordon.

On entering the space, Mary Overlie had an intentness that immediately brought a rowdy audience to a stunned silence. The poignant blend of authority and vulnerability in her face and the look of her beige-covered body will stay with me for some time.

The twenty-minute dance was called *Small Dance* and she danced small, directing our attention to the quavering of her hand, or the sudden sinking of her chest. Shimmers gently shot through her body. Stillness was drawn out until it finally burst into motion. The flurry of motion was not really a contrast to the stillness because, like the yin-yang symbol, her motion had stillness within it and her stillness had motion. Overlie was hovering on the edge of something. I kept thinking of a hummingbird and I kept my eyes glued.

In the program notes, Overlie calls the piece "a three-way conversation between the body of the dancer, the mind of the dancer, and the audience." Because she has this idea, and because she has an excellent sense of composition (i.e., where she's coming from and where she's going), the dancing was followable in a way that I found enormously satisfying. The kind of

David Gordon and Valda Setterfield in *Times Four*: breathtaking unison.
(Courtesy *Dance Magazine* Archives)

followable that good fiction has, or beautiful music, or a stimulating conversation—it makes me want to know, makes me *care* what the next word,
the next note will be.

In dance I rarely see this quality, but I am hungry for it, so when it happens twice in one week, it is positively exhilarating. The second time was
watching David Gordon and Valda Setterfield. I have recently been loving
watching unison (Trisha Brown's *Locus* hooked me)* and there's no more
visually striking, in-sync pair than Gordon and Setterfield. Even when a
teeter and fall is built into the steps, they land at precisely the same moment
and with precisely the same sense of weight. It's breathtaking.

In *Times Four* (work in progress) the two perform a brief traveling phrase
in unison in all four primary directions before they begin a different phrase.
So each time they return to front, you know that a new step is coming. But
they slip into it so slyly that it's there before you know it and then you're
grateful for the chance to see it three more times. Sitting on the side, I saw

* Trisha Brown's *Locus* (1975) is the pure-movement quartet that Trisha and the
other three company members practiced every day as I was warming up before we
all worked on a new piece. The first part was in unison, and I grew dependent on getting my daily dose of watching the fluid, measured, idiosyncratic phrases in the quiet
sanctity of her studio.

them do each phrase next to each other; then with their backs to me, Setter-field behind Gordon; then adjacent again; then facing me. What a luxury! There was great generosity in this progression—and patience too. A patience bordering on serenity, a serenity with inscrutable faces. (I'm sure they look just like that while waiting on the cashier's line at the supermarket.)

The phrases consist of functional shifts of weight and are so well ordered that each time new ground is covered (the first time they face a diagonal, or the first time they slow down the tempo) a whole world of possibilities opens up. As with Overlie, the changes are not for the sake of contrast (contrast upsets my stomach anyway), but for continuity.

Their continuity is created with intelligence and tenderness. It is what I meant when I used the word followable earlier. It happens when a dancer resists showing all that she or he can do, but instead chooses to concentrate on the selecting, finding, making of the moves and how they proceed from one to another. And then . . . and then the dancer is the embodiment of a continuous train of thought.

People Improvisation: Grand Union

La Mama Annex, New York City

SoHo Weekly News, May 6, 1976

This viewing of the Grand Union took place in the last year of that legendary improvisation group's six-year life. Trisha Brown and Steve Paxton had already left to do their own work. I don't think it lasted much beyond this date, but oh, what a group it was. Seeing the Grand Union at a gallery, loft, or student center was part of our lives in the downtown dance world. We discussed each sighting with each other endlessly. Any Grand Union performance could be both funny and full of tingling, interpersonal tension. Even now, young dancers in downtown New York recognize the name Grand Union as the improv group that embodied the daring and unpredictability of the seventies.

Ancient Japanese swordsmen would customarily train for many, many years to attain one simple goal: to be ready to accept, and counter, a blow from any direction at any time. The swordsman's decision was not permitted to rely on any previously successful strategy. Rather, he was to take into account all the forces of the present moment, and choose the one action perfect for that moment.

The differences between this theory and the theory that the Grand Union goes by is that for the latter, there is more than one appropriate action in a given situation. It is the choice, among the range of possible alternatives, that they, and we, are interested in. When X does this, what will Y do? Or, when Z does this, what will Z then do? Each initiated action opens up a new realm of possible reactions. Each reaction opens up . . . etc. Endings are beginnings. The performers create a constantly shifting matrix of joinings and separations, rises and falls, quickenings and trailings off, revelations and suppressions.

The way the Grand Union accomplishes all this is by having near-legendary rapport as a group, and by each member having a strong identity of his/her own. Like the loyal audiences of traditional Eastern opera, we have come to know each character well; they are varying degrees of real/unreal for us; and we each have our favorites. A brief run-down is in order:

Barbara Dilley is small and soft, wears comfortable clothes that let her comfortable body extend and curl and twine. She is patient and well grounded in manner and motion. She usually avoids verbal content and when pressed, responds somewhat too earnestly. ("A leader is someone who has wisdom," she informs David Gordon.)

Douglas Dunn is lean and angular, with a determined look on his face. The black clothes and hat he wore on Sunday night made him look preacher-like, and he played into that by striking stark poses. The intention in his dancing is very evident, and he likes to channel this clarity into weight studies—lifting, catching, yielding to, testing another's weight.

David Gordon has an uncommon gift for monologue. He tops his own brilliant witticisms with more brilliant ones. He banters, puns, weaves tales, plays the prophet, plays the victim.

Nancy Lewis is tall and goofy and, although she has been compared to Carol Burnett, I see more of Holly Woodlawn in her. It is fun to watch her mercurial changes between chic, sulky, and disarmingly sensual. She is a parody of herself, letting us know by a darting glance, by a droop of the shoulders, that she doesn't believe in this stuff 100 percent. This creates a contrast to her dancing, which is full and swoopy and emanates from an inner center.

Valda Setterfield, who danced with Merce Cunningham for a long time, is long and sleek, and looks the height of elegance in whatever eccentric outfit she drums up. Her dancing is distinctive for its effortlessly clean lines and the matter-of-fact way she drops into and out of movements.

These dancers are such colorful and memorable characters that we are drawn to their performances again and again, as though to a new install-ment of a soap opera. We follow their triumphs, disappointments, dares, and frustrations almost too keenly to be bearable. We feel the challenge of spontaneity, the chaotic assortment of possibilities as we do in our own lives. *We know that there is no plan.* We witness the trust that allows them to bring their personal doubts into play. On one occasion, Lewis stood at the back of the room with a blanket over her head for a long time and finally, during a pause, asked anyone who would listen, "Am I doing anything im-portant??"

However, the group sometimes relies too heavily on bits, or types of bits, that have gone over well in the past. Each member is, at different times, lim-ited by the very illustriousness that makes him or her magnetic.

But the Grand Union is still the best improvisation group around and there are still those moments that stun you by being so utterly in the present. On Sunday, Gordon had got himself standing on a chair, slowly revolving as he told a story of (himself as) a bed-wetting adolescent who joined the cir-cus. The narrative seemed unconnected to anything else going on until he eventually directed it to the moment at hand: "I love having hundreds of people watch me turn around on top of this chair. . . . This is the best mo-ment of my life." But moment gives way to moment, and exhilaration gives way to misery: "How long will you let me go on like this. . . . You're making me turn around on the chair. . . . *This is the worst moment of my life!*"

Yvonne Rainer, who was a founder and strong influence on the group, has written that "one must take a chance on the fitness of one's instincts." (*She'd* make a good Japanese swordsman.) Part of this means an instinct for play, which might loosely be defined as non-goal-oriented exploration. Most of the Grand Union members have children, and I see evidence of that influence in their ability to play. They even use the word "pretend." Gordon: "We were pretending to be chickens mating and I resent your calling it dancing." ("Let's pretend"—that magical gateway to endless delights for children, but a term that has been dropped from the adult vocabulary.) This time they even looked like children—children playing dress-up in the morning with their pajamas still on. They all wore combinations of plain and fancy.

"Instincts" can also mean learned abilities. The instinct that improvising requires includes knowing when to let go of an action and when to forge ahead, when to claim the focus and when to give it up, and what proportion of personal wishes and fears to lay bare.

Needless to say, these are the same issues we face in everyday living. Perhaps that's why I leave a Grand Union performance not with a declaration of good or bad, but with an emotional fullness, similar to the effect of a highly charged event in my own life.

After one of the performances, a woman told Barbara Dilley, "I've seen dance improvisation before, and I've seen theater improvisation before, but this is the first time I've seen people improvisation."

Consuming Determination: Lucinda Childs

Danspace Project, St. Mark's Church, New York City

SoHo Weekly News, June 17, 1976

I am going to press shortly after seeing Lucinda perform Pastime, *a solo she made at Judson Church in 1964, at Danspace as part of its Judson Now series. She climbed inside a little boat-like container, wrapping herself in a length of jersey à la Martha Graham, and slowly extended a leg out. Simple and stunning. Her intensity as a performer had not waned a bit.*

Lucinda Childs is a riveting performer. This is not opinion: it is fact. I studied the audience and every pair of eyes was fixed, focused on Childs's face. There one could read a determination bordering on anger mixed with the alertness of a frightened animal. *Her* eyes were on the floor in front of her.

The determination is about holding a system together. She sets up a game and plays it in the most serious way possible. The rules are absolute and inviolable. We can't hope to understand the reasons why or what, exactly, the rules are. But we can see that following the rules is terribly important—urgent—like for the guy whose job it is to press the right buttons in a nuclear missile base . . . like for a child who has to *not* step on the cracks in the sidewalk.

Minimalism—and I mean only narrowing down the material in order to get a better look at what happens in a small range—can be a very satisfying kind of art and not at all elitist. *Cross Worlds*, a new solo, had the excitement of a tennis or ping-pong match. Childs traveled back and forth along a diagonal with a pattern of gallops and walks that established a driving rhythm whose irregularities eluded every counting system I applied. Usually one thinks fullness is required to be "satisfying" but here it was the sparseness that did it. Whether because she constructed a good system or because of her power as a performer, I do not know.

Childs's undaunted concentration is accompanied by a tension that locks her upper back and neck. This gives her slow, simple motions—walking, arm circling—a needed formality, but it keeps the action limited to the extremities in the quicker motions. Watching a single performer can be an intense (identifying) experience, and when it is, the discomforts of that performer seem almost contagious. I came away feeling a little tense myself, wondering what *my* neck and back were doing.

Curiously enough, Childs seems more at home in Robert Wilson's work than in her own. In an open rehearsal of *Einstein on the Beach* (March 1976), the forty-five-minute solo for Childs was a remarkable and moving performance. This too was on a diagonal track and this too was a tight system. But this system was a plan of (r)evolving images that seemed both continuous and disjointed. The dance unfolded gradually, the spare, [ritual-like gestures] of the beginning eventually becoming manic and restless. She skittered and limped and bounced while making complicated darting hand signals. Her facial expression maintained that consuming determination but the character changed with the speed of hallucinations intercepting one another. If I blinked, she may have turned from clown to baseball coach, or from didactic professor to drunkard. It was uncanny and it was beautiful.

Older Is Better

SoHo Weekly News, December 16, 1976

It's hard to believe that I wrote this when I was only twenty-nine.

So many young dancers have breezed into town in the last few years that it seems like an invasion of the small, we're-all-friends dance community in New York. For my own mental clearinghouse, I would love to be able to discount them all by deciding they're talentless or pushy or tasteless. They're not. Most of them are well trained, disciplined, inventive, and unpretentious.

A bunch of dancers who fit the above description were dancing in Mel Wong's *Glass* this weekend. They were fine. Energetic, bright-eyed, and brave. But, with the exception of Susan Emery, who has a simplicity and rootedness rare for someone her age, they seemed like they were trying to keep their heads above water. (Not helped by the inordinate amount of head and chest arches they had to do.) Of course, their well-meaningness could be called hopefulness or even exuberance. But even put in positive terms, that kind of dancing simply does not appeal to me.

In contrast, Karen Levy's and Renee Wadleigh's presence accented the quiet assurance that comes with no longer being young. Perhaps because Wong himself is in their age range—middle to late thirties—he seems to sympathize with their physicality more than with that of the younger dancers. His choreography for them is less frantic and more personal than the colder-than-Cunningham stuff he gives to the others.

Levy and Wadleigh look alike, look good together. Both have spare, tough, womanly bodies. The intensity of their dancing comes not from trying to be good dancers, but from the long cultivated habit of bringing all you have to what you do and having the intelligence to do that without narcissism. Watching their dancing, I can read the knowledge of living in them. I prefer that to all the rosy pliancy of youth. It's like outgrowing books with large print and going on to read books with smaller print.

A solo for Wadleigh had her hands gesturing near her face. It was a dance of horror, whether intentionally or not. Her deep-set, glass-blue eyes looked straight out at us with the challenging pain of a witch-hunt victim. I was reminded of Lenore Latimer's powerful rendition of "A time to be silent" in José Limón's *There Is a Time*, which I saw in '67. Again it was the hands

Merce Cunningham in Avignon, 1976: so much himself. At right are Meg Harper and Chris Komar. (© Babette Mangolte)

and the eyes—her eyes were black and screaming as her hands covered her mouth. No college kid could have looked like that.

I've been thinking about how age affects dancers since I caught a glimpse of Merce Cunningham rehearsing with his company this summer. He was at the outdoor theater of the papal palace in Avignon. His grand gray curls and darting glances were perfectly at home in the elegant old (God knows how many centuries) palace. His body was settled (by settled I don't mean slow, mind you) into the space. His face was the face of a fifty-eight-or-so-year-old man doing what he does.

Hanging halfway out a window to spy on the closed rehearsal, I suddenly had the thought that this man being so much himself and so much not anyone else is important for the world to see. In our society, it's assumed that we'll all be useless for many years before we die. In primitive societies people continued what they'd always done right up to the end. Merce Cunningham, man of the future, is a throwback.

In last week's *Village Voice*, Lally Weymouth quoted George Balanchine as saying that dancers are through "When you don't want to look at them anymore." I, for one, won't get tired of looking if the dancer is not tired of dancing.

Exporting SoHo

SoHo Weekly News, December 30, 1976

Looking back on this moment of European presenters' fascination with the American avant-garde, I realize that it's gone the opposite direction recently: American presenters are now rushing to import the latest European artists. And I think that's partly because of the seeds sown in Europe by American artists during this very period I talk about below.

An interesting aside: After I brought this story to the SWN, *the publisher, or maybe the designer, lifted the distinctive logo of the word "SoHo" from the Akademie der Künste poster and used it for their new banner. It stuck until the paper folded in 1982.*

This fall SoHo performers were being exported by the dozens to European hotbeds of new culture. Or maybe I should say hotbeds of Americana. The various European festivals, which sponsor a staggering number of events every year, this time decided to go heavy on American arts, particularly New York, and particularly SoHo. And conveniently so, because it coincided with our Bicentennial year, which has been an excuse for some European governments to ingratiate themselves with us by offering Bicentennial "gifts."

We who live or work in SoHo may not think of SoHo performances as particularly American. They don't seem particularly anything to us, since they draw from a broad spectrum of forms and standards. Some of the performing we see around here is serious, some is light-headed, some is dizzying. Some is powerful, some is pale. Some is intentionally absurd and some is unwittingly absurd. Perhaps the one common denominator is a certain irreverence, a relish for the unexpected. I see it as the wish (or the will) to challenge existing definitions of performance. It is this rebelliousness, whether you think of it as naive defiance or as the pioneer spirit, that makes SoHo distinctly American.

As a member of the Trisha Brown Dance Company, I traveled and performed in several of the festivals. Two of the more extensive operations were the Berliner Festwochen, featuring a six-week exhibit called "Downtown Manhattan: SoHo," and the Steirischer Herbst in Graz, Austria, which sported a New Dance series. A third was smaller than these two: Geneva's West Broadway Festival. I observed audience response not only to Trisha Brown's work, but also to other groups. Audience reaction was definitely, well, definitely ambivalent.

Roof Piece (1971) by Trisha Brown. This photograph, taken in 1973, was used by several European festivals to represent SoHo in their posters. (© Babette Mangolte)

Indifference has been the usual response in cities unfamiliar with American contemporary performers. A writer named Linda Zamponi told me that when Merce Cunningham first performed in Vienna, "People didn't say it was beautiful. They didn't even say it was interesting. They said, "It's nothing." And in France they said their teenagers could dance better than Twyla Tharp's company.

Now, however, there is a conscientious effort to surmount that indifference. At an afternoon lecture-demonstration of Kei Takei's Moving Earth company, a Viennese balletomane stubbornly insisted it wasn't dance. That same evening, she attended a concert of Trisha Brown's, was puzzled at first, but by intermission, beamed to her neighbors, "It's fascinating, enchanting."

Tina Girouard, who was invited to show work and perform at the West Broadway Festival, called the Geneva audience "enthusiastic but reserved." At her performance, people were packed like sardines at the back of a small room. She heard them making a commotion over not being able to see. They wanted to see.

The German and French are not so polite. Some beer drinkers in a late night crowd in Berlin hooted and giggled at Joan Jonas, a performance and video artist. And in a concert I was in, a few students started clapping midway through one dance like they wanted it to be over. Others loudly defended the artistry, and at intermission the two contingents nearly came to blows.

———

Each performer or group builds up his/her/its audience over the years, city by city. The composer Philip Glass has made fifteen trips to Europe in the last five years, far more than the number of times he's toured the United States. His work has been called everything from genius to utter bore by European critics, but now he attracts a hearty, with-it audience for every performance. In this aspect, Glass is part of a long line of innovative American performers who have been more warmly received in Europe than at home.

I asked Jane Yokel of Performing Artservices, an agency that books some of these U.S./Europe exchanges, how she would explain this phenomenon. She cited the history of aesthetic awareness in the everyday life of Europeans. She calls them "more art-oriented, more aware of their surroundings." And they're more willing to go out to see a concert because television hasn't gotten hold of them as thoroughly as it has us. These are the makings of an eager and discriminating audience.

It's a perfect match: New York provides the performers, and Europe provides the theaters, money, and spectators.

The European artists, of course, aren't too happy about this situation. They receive neither the funding nor the public support that we Americans get when we're over there. The small Geneva art-going public that was enthusiastic and curious about American artists was called "blasé" by a Swiss dancer who formed a new company. A Geneva performance artist named John Armleder explained that the Swiss viewer distrusts the local product, is quick to call it humbug: "New York art seems genuine to him. But when it's happening at home, he can't believe it could be interesting to him." This bias is corroborated by Richard Landry, a musician who performs solo and with Glass. He admits that "being from New York is our selling point."

During the run of all these festivals in Europe, the indigenous artists had ways of making their discontent known. The West Berlin visual artists didn't attend any of the multitude of SoHo showings, having a basic mistrust of the "performance art" being featured. In Geneva a small group of leftist musicians boycotted the new music series, protesting that the "real" American music is black jazz. The French, being French, were perhaps the most outraged. Their government had poured more money into the Wilson/Glass *Einstein on the Beach* than into any homegrown production. A group of French actors and crew held a two-week strike prior to the *Einstein* arrival. (At the end of the Einstein stint, they bade a tearful farewell to their newly made friends.)

From the point of view of the European artist or performer, we Americans have every freedom and opportunity imaginable. Freedom from tradition is our greatest advantage. Having much envy and respect for the way the past is kept alive in Europe, I never realized how stifling tradition can be, until I discussed it with some people at the Presseburo in Graz. Of course the hold that tradition has over a working artist varies with each country and with each set of circumstances. In Austria, it's a stranglehold. "Tradition is a huge burden here," says Zamponi. "It sits on top of you and prevents you from finding new directions." I asked her if she thought that Austrian choreographers/performers would be visibly influenced by the spate of New Dance performances in Graz. The answer was a firm No.

If the artists in Europe are not adventuresome, the audiences are. They showed up in large numbers, with curiosity, and not having any idea what to expect. All ages and classes were among them. They came to see the real America—not coca-cola, not denim, but SoHo.

As I traveled I wondered about this infatuation with SoHo. When I asked, I got answers like "new" and "now." I learned that the interest is actually not new. Some of the festivals, particularly Spoleto and Festival d'Automne had been sponsoring American avant-gardists for years. What was different about this year was the scale: they brought more of us over and spent more money.

In trying to answer the question of why this sudden popularity, I found a clue in a striking coincidence concerning the publicity of the festivals. It just happened that a photograph of Trisha Brown's *Roof Piece* (1971) was used by three of the festivals mentioned above, becoming virtually the logo for both the Berlin and Geneva festivals. The photograph shows the rooftops of SoHo loft buildings hazing off into the distance. There is a dancer in a simple position standing on every third (or so) rooftop. It's an image that reveals a unique conception of the relationship of person to environment. Rooftops are like basements, or closets: they aren't meant to be seen. When they are deliberately shown to you, you get the feeling you are seeing the inner workings of something. And then to see the dancers fit in as nicely as though they were laundry hanging on a line is irresistible.

I think that this whimsical vision of man-in-his environment appeals to Europeans. But more than this, the photograph represents Downtown's answer to the usual smooth and shiny American export. Europeans have been both attracted to and skeptical of the razor-edged professionalism of our television and movies. It must appear to them (and not only to them) that our products are made by institutions and not by people. The new

American art offers them what their films once offered us: a relief from the relentless Technicolor know-how of American production, a chance to see the inner mind at work, a probing into the corners rather than the mainstream of modern thought. It makes both art and Americans seem real to them.

One of the realistic aspects of Downtown art is its shoestring budget (with notable exceptions, like *Einstein*). Lutze, a German artist who assisted René Block in organizing the Berlin SoHo Festival, told me, "We *love* to see what you Americans do on no money!"

Block, who owns galleries in both Berlin and New York, speaks tenderly of the "communal, cooperative spirit" that he believes SoHo has and that Berlin had in the Dada and Bauhaus days. He points out that SoHo was formed in large part by European immigrants. To this day, the galleries in SoHo remain friendly to European artists. This is the other side of the welcome that Europe is now extending to experimental Americans. Block sees the possibility of establishing a dialogue, a link between Europe and the United States, between the past and the present: "Now is the time to connect again."

Improvisation: The Man Who Gets Away with It

SoHo Weekly News, January 6, 1977

I was thinking about improvisation so much that I decided to write a series on it. I led off with a quote from Frances Alenikoff, a dancer/choreographer/writer who had made a solo for me a few years before. I decided to extend my definition of improvisation to James Irsay, my favorite wayward radio host.

> In improvisation the moment is the crucible. A risky business. No time for second thoughts or rearrangements. You do it or it dies. Tools are an agile imagination, finely-tuned senses geared to synthesize inspiration, and the skills of your craft, plus the capacity to be totally absorbed in the instant — alert to its possibilities — while maintaining a honed awareness of the shape of the whole. —Frances Alenikoff, Craft Horizons, *April 19, 1972*

I have someone in mind who fits the bill sublimely, ridiculously, irresistibly. A veritable unknown, his performances are a rare treat that have suddenly become even rarer. I will say the name, and the obnoxious loveable voice will either pop into memory or not. You're either a fan or you're not.

James Irsay gave his last live radio show on Monday of last week. After doing two shows a week on WBAI (listener-supported Pacifica station at 99.5 FM) for five years, he's decided to study and teach piano in a more organized fashion, at Indiana University. If you're interested in classical music, if you're interested in improvisation (not at the piano, but at the microphone), try to catch WBAI's Program Announcements (at 9 AM, 6 PM, and 11:55 PM) on the chance that they'll air some made-in-Indiana Irsay tapes.

The format of the show has been a monologue that introduces, comments on, and interrupts classical music selections, with room for brazen flights of fancy. He is a passionate, irreverent critic of classical music. He improvises with his record selections the way an inspired, slightly mad music-appreciation teacher might: "This part should roar out at you," or "He's not nervous enough here." To point out an imperfection he'll play a tiny passage of a record over and over again till you want to scream. And then he'll scream. Or he'll say to the record, "You never learn, do ya."

With the record as his partner, he can be hilarious — or merely educational. But going solo is when he really gets into the risks of improvisation. Risk is the chance you take to let go of yourself and seize the moment. The self you let go of is the stale self of impacted layers of ideas or rules. The moment, by definition, is that which has never existed before. Full recognition of that exact time and set of circumstances requires redefining yourself. The chance is that you may reveal something new about yourself before you have the time to approve it privately first.

Improvisation is a stream of (un)consciousness organized by a sense of form. Not everyone can find the paths that lead to that stream, and not everyone, once the stream is found, is interesting. (And that I have no explanation for.)

Children are more likely to have clear pathways to their fantasies of the moment than adults. Children and James Irsay. Irsay is like a precocious child, unhampered by any sense of propriety, who makes surprising intellectual leaps and connections. Like a child too, he is compulsive about saying things that no one else will. (I suspect a major influence was Lenny Bruce's "Lecture on Snot.")

Being alert to the instant means knowing when to prolong, develop, refract, or drop what you're doing. One day during the recent WBAI fundraising marathon, exasperated at the poor results, Irsay reeled into "Maybe maybe maybe if if if I I I say say say everything everything everything three three three times times times you you you will will will get get get the the the point point point." He kept it up for an alarming amount of time, then escalated to five repetitions of each word. When he stops a riff like this, he stops suddenly. The pleading ends and the sneering begins: "Okay let's listen to how much money is left so I can stop this *ridiculous filth*."

Improvising is composing as you go. Irsay balances chaos with his awareness of the whole. A more or less theme-and-variations structure ran through each program and, on the long-term scale, through his five years on the air. He'd return to a theme the way a good composer does: seemingly accidentally, but with all the added information of what followed since it was last introduced. I was continually astounded by the range and freshness of his riffs. When he discussed a favorite composer, Chopin for instance, he always offered a new insight—and usually a new way to pronounce the name too.

I'll miss what WBAI calls "Music and insults from the man who gets away with it." I'll miss that voice of the moment-to-moment manic-to-depressive monologue, that voice of wit, perversity, and the insistently risky business of guessing as you go.

Update: I am happy to say that, as of April 2013, Irsay has returned to WBAI with his own program on Friday mornings. He is as brilliant, funny, and educational as ever— music appreciation teacher extraordinaire.

Only an Illusion: On Street Performers

SoHo Weekly News, July 14, 1977

A woman I met in Paris in 1972 had told me to keep an eye out for her ex-boyfriend,
a street performer and tight-rope artist named Philippe Petit. I started seeing him in
Greenwich Village soon after, and later learned of his death-defying hike between the
Twin Towers. At the same time, New York was—and still is—rich with street performers.
Here I chose three to focus on. (I was so enamored of buskers that twenty years later I
choreographed a piece for the Lincoln Center Festival using real subway musicians.)

A street performer is tough in the same way that a streetwise kid is. He's got
to know his stuff, be a fast talker, and be ready for anything. He's got to feel
out good or bad vibes almost before they happen. He's got to know when to
jump out of a tight spot and into a good one.

Any performer is an adventurer of sorts, daring himself/herself to overcome all obstacles and emerge triumphant. But the usual indoor performance situation looks tame by comparison to the added obstacles a street
performer pits himself against. For one thing, he's got to keep an eye out for
the cops. Although the police are more an annoyance than a danger, they
can slap him with a fine that ranges from two to thirty dollars for obstruct-
ing the sidewalk. For another thing—and this affects every minute of his
work—he must accumulate and maintain an audience if he is to survive. A
delicate seduction is necessary: one wrong move and the audience dribbles
away, little by little.

Some New Yorkers, myself included, like to stroll aimlessly on a warm
still evening, ready for the familiar surprise of running into a really good performer. It's one of the things I love about New York in the summer. Scattered
around Sheridan Square and Sixth Avenue there's always a bunch of performers, varying widely in genre and quality. There are mimes, magicians,
all kinds of musicians (I notice more chamber music than ever before), and
stray orators. Some attract a small crowd immediately, while others play directly to two or three stragglers. I even saw one drummer playing to no one
but a pile of bagged garbage.

The more consistent performers can be counted on to occupy a particular
spot at a particular time. They seem to share a camaraderie with each other,
and along with that goes a courtesy about where to play/perform. I spoke
with William McQueen, a magician, at the side entrance to Chemical Bank,
just off Sheridan Square, and he calls those few square feet "Otto's spot." It

was Otto's beat first and Otto can have it any time but sometimes offers to share it with McQueen.

McQueen is a rangy black man who's been a magician for twenty-two years. He says he'll have his own show called "The Incredible Black Magic Show" in the fall, but he says he prefers working on the street to working in a theater. (He works along Sixth Avenue between Fourth and Eighth Streets when he's not at "Otto's spot.") He says the money is better and he seems to enjoy the flexibility and challenge of his current setup. "The streets will bring out the best in you. Sometimes you can't build an audience, but when you do build an audience, you can't get rid of them."

McQueen's specialty is coins. He also does stuff with a disappearing red scarf and a rope that gets cut up and miraculously unites itself. But he is most amazing with the coins. His hands, with long supple fingers, are like a waterfall that conceals and reveals and washes away unlikely traces of objects. It is mysterious from a respectful distance of three yards, but it is astounding when he shows you close up and slowly. Sometimes he does his tricks so small and offhandedly that people walk by without noticing that anything special is happening. That talent comes in handy when the police walk by. But McQueen can also turn on his showmanship at will, thereby controlling the thickness of his crowd.

He sustains a running commentary on his tricks, fooling us with deception, deceiving us with honesty. "It's only an ee-lusion," he chants slyly. He talks about retention of vision—you continue to see an object for one-thirtieth of a second after it leaves your field of vision—and about the invisible law principle, which I figure has something to do with the way an audience appears and disappears.

———————

Otto is a ventriloquist and has trained himself for nine years by watching and experimenting. When Otto speaks for Phil, his puppet, you can see his lips and throat move, but the illusion remains intact. Mostly because the two characters are clear-cut, convincing, and work together as a team. Phil takes on the traditional dummy's role of the innocent and grotesque/adorable troublemaker. Otto is the straight man, feeding Phil his lines and putting up with his naughtiness, which is sometimes genuinely funny. Phil gets laughs by being fresh to the audience, like when he says to one guy, "You're ugly, did anyone ever tell you that?" He also takes a swipe at some political figures, like saying he wants to visit the White House because that's where all the other dummies are. (That line worked better last year.) One of the best parts of the act is the end, when Otto tucks Phil away in a small duffle bag. Phil protests and carries on even though his body is hidden and all we see are his legs being folded up and zipped away. He is clearly no longer activated gesturally, but the voice alone sustains the illusion of life — a variation on the concept of retention of vision.

————

One of the most extraordinary performers I've seen anywhere is Philippe Petit. He is the man who tightrope-walked across the Twin Towers three years ago. You can see that spirit of daring in everything he does. In the tradition of French circus folk, he spent years training in all aspects of the circus, and worked on the streets of Paris before coming to this country. He continues to train himself by trying out new tricks and new combinations of tricks on his corner of Bleecker Street and Seventh Avenue.

Petit is an extremely stylized performer. When he takes a particular stance, his small body (always dressed in black) is firmly rooted but ready to bounce into something new in a flash. His impish face radiates alertness. His body always assumes a definite shape; his face always reflects a character. Not a word is spoken. His act includes a smoothie top hat routine, some fine inventive juggling, a spin on his unicycle, and for the new *pièce de resistance* he juggles flaming torches while walking on a rope that he rigs up between the traffic lamp and a NO PARKING sign.

He is clowning every minute. He'll feign a yawn in the middle of his most elaborate juggling stunt. He plays pranks on members of the audience, like coaxing a woman to try juggling and then showing us that he has slipped off her wristwatch in the process. As with the ventriloquist and the magician, his audience loves to be fooled, if it is fooled artfully.

Petit has an uncanny sense for knowing what's going on near him and what to do with that information. A juggler must keep his eyes on the balls, and he does, but if someone in the audience lights a match. Petit, without interrupting his routine, will parody a blowing out motion.

His entire act is about twenty minutes long and I advise seeing it more than once, not only because he is a master, but also because he goes for untested stuff each time. He is not at all bothered when he fumbles; in fact, fumbling well is part of the act. I sometimes think he uses his little corner as a practice spot for larger projects.

Petit will perform this Friday, Saturday, and Sunday, all shows, with the Big Apple Circus in Battery Park. After that, he will probably be back on his beat at Bleecker and Seventh on Friday and Saturday evenings. Do not miss him.

Starting from Nothing: Michael Moschen

SoHo Weekly News, September 22, 1977

I went to the Big Apple Circus looking for Philippe Petit and found Michael Moschen. I didn't know anything about circus arts, so this piece became a hybrid that's part review, part interview (in italics), and part profile. Today Moschen, who received a MacArthur "genius grant" in 1990, is widely considered a visionary artist who transformed juggling into a concert form.

When juggler Michael Moschen walks into the center of the ring, you forget that circuses are supposed to be dazzling spectacles. Instead, you are immediately drawn in by an unassuming figure with curly hair and a boy-next-door smile. He makes you feel not like part of a motley obstreperous crowd, but like a specially invited friend. He starts juggling three small balls as cordially as if he were mixing cocktails. Then he does a very *sincere* fake cough and you wonder what this guy is up to.

> *I didn't know how to open my act. I didn't want to start with a big trick. I like to start with nothing and build from there. I want people to see me, and me see them, and have the juggling between us. I cough, and then I look up and start making eye-contact all around the ring, to find out who's there and why and what they're thinking, to get myself comfortable.*

The Big Apple Circus is the perfect place for Michael Moschen. The tent is comparatively small, and the audience is sitting close enough to get to know each character and catch the details of each act. It's a European-style circus that allows the performers to develop an identity as well as a rapport with the audience. It avoids the commercialism of the mammoth three-ring American circuses.

> *I don't like the American circuses. They're not personal. The performers do the routines they've been taught and there's no love for what they do. I don't want to work for huge audiences where they don't know who you are. This is one of the best performing situations I've ever had. It's intimate here. Everybody's involved in all the work. With nine shows a week, we have to spend a lot of time down here [Battery Park City]. It's tiring and wearing on your mind, but I like it because everybody's hearts are in it.*

Although the Big Apple Circus delights both children and adults, there is a marked difference between the responses of those two groups. Michael feels his solo act is geared more toward adults than toward kids.

My most comfortable audiences are at night. Kids just want to see somebody fall down, or do acrobatics, or throw the balls up as high as he can. They don't see the subtleties. I'm not interested in tricks. I don't use a trick unless it fits into the act. I can juggle five balls, but I won't do it in my act because it's still just a trick. I want my act to be a whole unit, a story.

———————

Michael began juggling when he was twelve. His brother and best friend bought a book on it "one boring summer" in Greenfield, Massachusetts. He was, he admits, a jock before that—football, basketball, baseball—but also always did things with his hands, including pottery. In one year, he and his brother and friend taught themselves everything about juggling, or so they thought. When they attended an international juggling convention in Hartford, they were amazed by the range of possibilities. At subsequent conventions, Michael became fascinated with what could be done with just three balls. Being enamored of simplicity, he told me, "I even saw a guy juggle with *one* ball and it flipped me out!"

He and his friend came to New York and shared a tiny apartment in which they practiced a partner act six to eight hours a day. ("Now I'm lucky if I practice one hour a day.") After three months, they got a gig at Great Adventure, an amusement park outside of Trenton, doing thirty-six shows a week. When he returned to one of the conventions, Michael entered a contest and won a prize, which gave him the confidence to develop a solo act.

Now twenty-two, he has attracted the attention of some of the finest jugglers in the country. But you don't have to know the discipline to enjoy his performing. He is easy-going, moves beautifully, and, although his is not a comedy act, his reserve of clownishness highlights certain movements— one by one, several balls, each looking like an egg in the nest of his hair, roll off his head; Michael staggers forward to catch each one. It is not a trick. It *contains* a trick. It is an integration of movement, rhythm, character, and virtuosity.

Still, he wants me to know that he is a juggler first and a performer second. In truth, he thinks very much like a performer.

I know what I'm doing each second. What I do for myself is different from doing it for an audience. If I have an unreceptive audience, it's real hard to keep my energy up. There has to be some give and take. My approach is through movement and space. I like to watch movement and find the logical progression in it. In my act there has to be a reason to go from one movement to the next. Also, it's important that my movements be full and clean and solid. I take a lot of my strength from the ground. I have strong legs—I'm a lower body person. It feels comfortable, real at home, to be low to the ground. Also I'm afraid of heights.

It was hot and humid the day I saw the circus, and Michael flubbed his last bit, the one where he blows on a ball and it rolls along the "V" made by two fingers and hangs just underneath, gently defying gravity. He told me later it was because there was too much moisture on the ball. I thought he would feel awful about dropping the ball, but he claims mistakes aren't important to him. He doesn't want to be, or feel he *has* to be, a "superman juggler."

He likes that little blowing bit not as a gimmick, but because when it works—and he says it usually does—it is a quiet finish to his act. "It's an illusion, something a little strange. A nice little nothing."

Masters of Surprise: Baryshnikov and Astaire

SoHo Weekly News, September 8, 1977

There is no way I could have guessed that Mikhail Baryshnikov would become more than a superstar ballet dancer. As artistic director of American Ballet Theatre, he led that magnificent company for a decade; he started his own adventurous modern dance company (White Oak Dance Project); and he created his own presenting space, Baryshnikov Arts Center, in midtown. At this writing, he still performs internationally, either as a modern dancer or as an actor in plays he produces (oh, and there was a whole season of Sex and the City*). His two studios and a theater in* BAC *are buzzing with activity, including generous residencies to promising dance artists and other groups. Nor would I have guessed that our worlds would overlap at all. I attend performances at* BAC *often; I've done a photo shoot with Misha; and he has graciously presented an award at a* Dance Magazine *event. So it's a bit embarrassing to see how narrowly I viewed this artist who is now such a mover and shaker.*

However, I stick to my thesis that there was something about his dancing that called to mind Fred Astaire. While working on this story, I enjoyed mentally jumping across barriers between Hollywood and the Metropolitan Opera House.

As I have said, I was my own editor at the SoHo News*. There was no one to tell me to include a "nut graph" that explains what you will do in the story, or to tell me not to refer to two different books in the opening paragraph. I was on my own, so it sometimes reads as free association.*

When Fred Astaire was starting out in vaudeville, his sister Adele was the better half of their act. According to Arlene Croce's *The Fred Astaire & Ginger Rogers Book*, he opted for aloofness over insecurity. Some observers (Marshall and Jean Stearns in their book *Jazz Dance*) thought his manner projected the sentiment, "Okay, Adele's the star, so I'll help her out, but I'm bored to death."

This "boredom" developed into a look of supreme confidence, of never trying for something he couldn't have. Which is also the feeling I get from watching Mikhail Baryshnikov. Although Baryshnikov could never be described as bored looking, he is certainly not over-eager onstage. These two performers have a miraculous self containment that I find irresistible. At the same time that we are convinced that the dancer is doing exactly the right thing at the right time (technically and philosophically) we also see that he is not doing it in order to please us. It can be pleasantly maddening.

Fred Astaire and Rita Hayworth in *You'll Never Get Rich*, 1941.
(Courtesy *Dance Magazine* Archives)

A MATTER OF WEIGHT

Although Baryshnikov and Astaire don't look alike, two qualities distin-
guish them from other dancers and put them in a class of their own: They
are a physical quality of liquidness and a mastery of surprise. The liquidness
comes from a release of all tensions (very modern) and the weight dropped
low. Their most notable colleagues, respectively Rudolf Nureyev and Gene
Kelly, carry their weight higher—up around the shoulders and chest—giving
the whole body a "meaningful" look. With my two favorites, no one part

of the body takes on exaggerated tension, so the energy flows unstopped and the dancer is just as ready to drop into the floor as to bound into the air.

The feeling of center is not particularly visible. You know Baryshnikov must be strongly centered because he can do all those exhilarating leaps, but he doesn't let you see how he holds himself together. He simply doesn't subscribe to the excessive verticality that marks (or mars) other ballet dancers. No other classical dancer would or could dare effect the looseness that he experiments with. In the production of *Giselle* on television a few months ago, as Albrecht wild-with-grief-over-Giselle, he finished off a rash of pirouettes by letting his head drop back while he was still turning with his leg extended to the side. (It looked as if he were on the verge of swooning, not unlike the melting feeling Fred has when he's about to join Ginger. Both these men know how to look hopelessly, deliriously in love while dancing.

PARTNERSHIP AND NARCISSISM

And yet I am not at all convinced that Baryshnikov is crazy about Makarova, or Fred about Ginger either. But that's OK with me because I am transported by the dancing, not the acting (though of course they are really inseparable). And better than being believably in love, they transcend the conventional male partnership. They are both smaller and suppler than most men, which makes for a more equal match with the women. Neither is/ can be the strong gallant guy who's just letting the girl show off. And never will you see either one approach the girl with insidious seductiveness, as the average male performer does, with inflated assurance of his own attractiveness. Baryshnikov, like Astaire, is just *there* for her. He may lean into her but he never seems to reach from where he is to where she is, just as he never reaches out to the audience.

This reaches the point of outrageous narcissism in Fokine's *Spectre de la rose*, where Baryshnikov, as the fantasy of a young girl, is so exquisitely limp and gaudy (an exhausted rock star) that he's practically *dripping* all over her. But he never extends a hand or, I think, even looks in her direction. This goes beyond Astaire, whose characters, however fanciful, are civilized and sensible by comparison.

Both men have partnered dazzling women. Ginger Rogers can more than hold her own as a comic, a dancer, and a romantic figure. And Gelsey Kirkland is, of course, heartbreakingly lovely. (Baryshnikov has danced with plenty of other women too—I don't know who his current steady lady is.) But, as wonderful as these two women are, they can be something with their respective partners that they cannot be alone: surprising—camouflaged vir-

Mikhail Baryshnikov in *Daphnis and Chloe*, 1974, choreography by Mai Murdmaa for Baryshnikov's "Creative Evening" at the Kirov (Mariinsky) Ballet, in Leningrad. (© Nina Alovert)

tuosity sneaking up on you. It's impossible to keep up with them, so slippery is their timing. Croce says about Fred and Ginger in *Follow the Fleet*, "These two are like brilliant comedians who crack superb jokes without waiting for the laughs." And Marcia Siegel said of Baryshnikov and Kirkland, "You hardly realize they're doing something phenomenal till they've done it."

With a really magical dancer, you cannot tell what he will do next. Astaire, pouncing up onto a desktop with no more preparation than a cat needs. Baryshnikov, his arms suddenly going as limp as a scarecrow's in *Petrouchka*. They make us aware that anything can happen at any moment. Will he break into a leap, a slide, a spin? Will he just stand there and smirk? Will he waltz? Whatever he does it always seems the perfect choice.

Astaire and Baryshnikov use their faces differently. Baryshnikov still has a slightly martyred look from his days in the Soviet Union, though less than some traditional ballet danseurs. But his face changes appropriately with each role, from the Vaudevillian deadpan of Tharp's *Push Comes to Shove* to the gullibility of Franz in *Coppélia*, to the pathetically thwarted Petrouchka. Astaire, however, radiates an ever present, ever-so-slight edge of mischievousness no matter what role he plays. He's delighted by the game of life, every twist and turn of it.

Then too, Baryshnikov is sexier. He's sexy just standing in first position, and that is no minor feat. Maybe it has to do with his narrow hips and big legs held tight and loose like that, and his torso modestly caved in above. Or maybe it's that ever-changing center, the slightly asymmetrical look. His stance seems very American to me. The dewy-eyed cowboy. Not quite James Dean, but maybe a mixture of Montgomery Clift, Joe Dallessandro, and Sylvester Stallone. Knowing he's Russian makes him even more of a curious phenomenon.

Astaire, on the other hand, strikes me as European. His passionate courtesy, his glowing elegance and charm, seem a residue from an old world. And his patience in allowing his body to speak—to speak of love—can teach something to us of the contemporary world. Who needs bedroom scenes when Fred and Ginger are dancing their intoxicating best?

We always need a few people around to confuse us. In Baryshnikov and Astaire we have two performers who are amorous but not possessive, sexy but not macho. They create suspense without a build-up, and let virtuosity slip past a veil of neutrality.

Interview with Susan Sontag:
On Writing, Art, Feminism, Life, and Death

SoHo Weekly News, December 1, 1977

After reading Susan Sontag's Against Interpretation *(both the essay and the book containing the essay), I couldn't get enough of her. She became a role model as an artist, a critic, and a feminist. The occasion of this interview was the release of her book* On Photography. *I met with her in her apartment near Columbia University, camouflaging my awe by acting casual and even, at times, almost rude. But she took it in stride and gave me a remarkably candid interview. It was startling how willing she was to treat me as an equal. At one point she cites my Fred Astaire and Baryshnikov article—not that she had read it but she remembered my talking about it earlier. And yet there are places in this interview where I cringe when rereading it.*

I completed this piece while on tour with Trisha Brown. I remember hastily spreading my rough draft out on the hotel bed and cutting and pasting it together to meet my deadline.

Even though very little of the interview focuses on dance, I include it here (in a shortened version) because Sontag, who died in 2004, had a huge effect on my—to use her word—sensibility.

Before Susan Sontag came along, everybody knew the difference between high art and popular art, form and content, artistic and social. Sontag confounds those stale dichotomies by writing what she sees—*all* she sees in what she sees—and how she sees. She has crystallized a sensibility that defines our era, while keeping philosophical uncertainties intact. She has shown us that, in any good art and art viewing, intelligence and sensuality are inseparable. Her essays of the sixties are required reading for anyone who wants to look at contemporary art (or life) seriously.

Reading her is not easy. She leads us through the convolutions of her thoughts as a genuine attempt to keep edging toward truth. She can condense three centuries of art into a sentence, and she can spread one image of a film over twenty pages. She can be detached while making expert aesthetic assessments, and she can be unabashedly subjective. Introducing "Notes on 'Camp,'" she writes, "I am strongly drawn to Camp, and almost as strongly offended by it. That is why I want to talk about it, and why I can." She points out a paradox, examines it from all sides, and then leaves it in a state of glorious non-resolution.

No, reading her isn't easy. Only thrilling.

Sontag has had cancer surgery, and cannot be certain that the malignancy won't spread. Never one to separate her life and her work, she recently gave a lecture at New York University that was about, and entitled, "Illness as Metaphor." In it, she defended the "kingdom of the ill" against the (Reichian) idea of a patient being, however subconsciously, responsible for his or her disease. But, she told me later, when it comes to recovery, she believes that the individual will plays a part.

The will to live has kept Sontag alive. When she speaks, life-affirming energy radiates throughout her body and the space around her. She has a beautiful face, a thicket of black and silver hair, and gently moving hands. She is a warm, caring, and focused person.

Listening to her, just as in reading her, I was exhilarated by the blend of intelligence and passion. Her voice is low and authoritative and completely unaffected. She would sometimes hedge for the right word, even stammer. When she got over the hitch, other words followed, rushing on like a river.

We talked of many things before, after, and in between the actual tapings, including the choreographer Kenneth King, the somatic healer Charlotte Selver, *Vogue* magazine, WBAI Community Radio, and Merce Cunningham. Neither of us could tell when the "interview" began. I turned the tape recorder on in the middle of a discussion on writing:

———

SS: One of my notions is that one should be able to do everything. I used to worry a lot about the relationship between fiction and nonfiction. Now I worry less about it because I want to write essays that are like fiction and to write fiction that's like essays. In the story I had in the *New Yorker* ["Unguided Tour," Oct. 31, 1977], there are things that could be in an essay.

WP: I noticed about that story that the rhythm is very different from the rhythm of the essays.

SS: I find it easier to write fiction. And much more pleasurable. The essays are a terrible trial.

I usually feel that after I write something, it's harder to write the next thing because that has to be different. It's mysterious, going from one thing to the next. In the end, the new thing always resembles what I've already done, but I have to think it's different in order to do it.

I wish that I could write more. My main problem is that I write very slowly. There's an immense process of gestation, and I'm always in arrears. What I'm interested in is always *now*, but I'm still working on things that I was interested in a year ago. I was very interested in the metaphors and myths of illness when I got sick. I had already known about these ideas but didn't have the passion to go with them until I got sick two years ago, and then my interest became an active one. And I'm only just now working on it: revising the material I gave in lecture form to be a publishable essay.

The essays are part of long-range thinking, which changes because I write something. There is not one of my essays that I'm not in some kind of argument with. There's always something more to say.

I've learned something about the essays from the reactions to them. The essay on Camp, which was written in the mid-sixties, had a fantastic career of its own, which does not have much to do with what I intended. And yet, I can't disavow it. I saw a review of a book of essays on art the other day. The review attacked this book and said that it "illustrates Susan Sontag's Camp." How strange. I'm just the observer, the explicator. Anybody who thinks that I *invented* camp taste didn't really read my essay.

I wrote that essay in a very innocent frame of mind. I thought that you could write like that and people would understand what you meant. I left a lot of things out which I thought I could take for granted, even the way it was written—in the form of notes.

WP: What I like about that essay is the personal thing: you're not afraid to say if you love something or hate something.

SS: Well, I much prefer talking about work that I like. It's more pleasurable to be a fan than to put things down. I don't want to be a critic, in the sense of giving ratings. I'd rather discuss things in ways that haven't been thought of, or to connect different things, as you were saying about Baryshnikov and Fred Astaire. [She is referring to an article I wrote two months before that I must have mentioned before I turned the tape recorder on.]

———

WP: Where did you live before you came to New York?

SS: I'm from Arizona and California. I was like Masha of *The Three Sisters*. As a child I dreamed of living in New York as Masha would dream of living in Moscow. And New York was every bit as wonderful as I imagined it would be. It was a place where you could be in touch with everything. And I had a tremendous appetite to *see* things.

WP: Do you still feel that way?

SS: No, I don't. Within the last week there have been seven things I wanted to do—for instance I wanted to hear the Ramones at CBGB's; I wanted to go to the Rembrandt exhibit at the Morgan Library. New

York is a feast of things to see all the time. So I try to restrain that a little, because I think one must place some limits on the amount of consumption. But ultimately one *is* a consumer, though I try to live in a non-consumerist way.

WP: Why? I know a lot of reasons, but I want to hear yours.

SS: I must stay home and be with the work; and being with the work means being in that place where it happens. And there's a lot of *vigil* near the work. You have to create this solace and space for yourself. As Kafka says, "You can never be too alone to write." But there's a part of me that doesn't want to be alone and write, that wants to go out and see these things that New York offers. Not to be in the critical role, but out of curiosity, out of the desire for pleasure. Of the many things I wanted to do this past week, I did only one: I went to the opera and saw *Pelléas and Mélisande*.

WP: Hmmm. You're right. I should reconsider my life strategy, because I'm seeing so much and doing so much.

SS: I think you shouldn't reconsider. You just have to be aware that all these things are, in some way, contradictory forms, and that's what an urban life is about—balancing all these contradictory things. But I think the best way is to go through binges. Let's say you could be alone for a couple of weeks and work on your own. That would be terrific, and then you'd decide to go to galleries and museums or see dance things and do that for a while. When I'm not working I find it almost impossible to *get* to work, and when I am working I find it almost impossible to stop.

———

WP: Where did you go to school?

SS: I went first to Berkeley, then to the University of Chicago, and then to graduate school at Harvard. Before that, I went to a dreadful high school where I didn't learn anything. In eleventh-grade English class we were given the *Reader's Digest* and told to read it and be quiet. The teacher sat in front of the class and knitted. And I was reading European fiction and philosophy and hiding it behind my *Reader's Digest*. I remember that once I was reading Kant's *Critique of Pure Reason*—I don't know how I could have understood it at that age, but I was trying to understand it—and I got caught. So the teacher made me put the book away and go back to the *Reader's Digest*.

I wasn't encouraged to do those things. It's just that I was enterprising enough to find people who had my interests and to put myself in contact with things that would be stimulating. That's very different from having a mentor, or someone who encouraged you. On the other hand, I wasn't discouraged either. But I *do* remember a little bit of "Don't be too smart: You'll never get married" and that kind of stuff, but not much. I think I was impervious; I was on the moon.

WP: That attitude, "Don't be too smart etc.," was that from your family or outside the family?

SS: Oh, my stepfather said it to me once when I was thirteen, and I burst out laughing and said, "I don't want to marry anybody who wouldn't like somebody like me."

———

WP: How do you feel about *On Photography*, now that it's out?

SS: The thing I find hardest to talk about is the photography essays because I feel that I've said what I had to say. They're part of the past for me. And even if I *could* recover the thoughts, I wouldn't be able to say them as accurately and subtly as they were expressed in the book. Each of those sentences was worked on . . . many times.

WP: What are you working on now?

SS: I can't really talk about work that isn't done. I guess I'm hopeless for a certain kind of interview. I don't like to talk about work in the past because it doesn't interest me anymore; and I can't talk about what I'm working on because it's still fluid and I don't want to make it concrete. If I talk about it, I'm afraid I'll use it up. Writing is a magical process.

WP: Can you say what kinds of things you'll be writing?

SS: I plan to do an essay next year called "The Aesthetic Way of Looking at the World."

WP: That's what you've been writing all along.

SS: Right! Now I'll really do it! I want to really talk about the relationship between the aesthetic and the ethical. I've been taking notes on it for a couple of years. But I know that when I write that essay, I will open a can of worms, and all sorts of problems I don't anticipate will arise.

But I don't want to do any more than one or two essays a year. Fiction is what I'm mainly doing. There will be a book of stories in March called *I, etcetera*. And I've been working on a novel on and off for about five years.

WP: What about anything political? Are you planning any projects like your film [*Promised Lands*] on Palestine and Israel?

SS: That film isn't really political. If I wanted to say what I thought about the Middle East problem, as it's called, I would write an essay. It's a nonfictional film, but it's constructed like a fiction film. As for political things, I do what I'm asked to do. Just today somebody asked me to serve on a committee that's part of PEN for the defense of writers in jail. If I could be useful, I would want to do it.

I don't like to do things that don't in some way connect with my personal experience. The first political things I ever did were some activities in connection with the support of Cuba. It grew out of the fact that I spent the summer of 1960 in Cuba, and I had a sense of what was going on there and I felt that the Cuban revolution should be defended. In 1964 I got involved in activities protesting the American war in Vietnam. Then I went to Vietnam twice. I do what I feel I have to do.

WP: You've said that you don't like party lines, but I want to know if you think feminism has had a large influence, where you think it's going.

SS: Yes, it has had a large influence, and I think its influence is entirely positive. I have no idea where it's going, I just hope that the pressure is kept up and intensified. This is a huge struggle; this is the most radical demand of all. The abolition of slavery is . . . easy compared to changing the situation with women. And it took a thousand years to abolish slavery.

Of course I get restless when somebody says that I'm not following the right line. I've always thought of myself as a feminist, long before there was a feminist movement. The point is not a "line," the point is activities that put pressure on people to change situations—all the ways women are treated and treat themselves as second-class human beings. The overall struggle is one of breaking down stereotypes. Every woman alive now will not see the end of it in her own lifetime.

WP: What's an example of how women play into stereotypes?

SS: Women are always putting their hands to their faces, much more than men do. Women smile more, to placate, to say, while they're talking, "I'm nice. While I'm asserting myself, I'm still a nice person."

WP: You're doing it now.

SS: Sure, everybody does. You said, "You're doing it now," and then you smiled. We don't just do it to each other. I can be reading in bed alone, and put my hand in front of my face. It's built into our bodies, into our way of moving. Fear, low self-esteem, insecurity, inability to localize our full energies for achievement. Every woman, no matter how enlightened she is, faces these problems.

WP: But you must feel that you've made some headway with those issues in your own life.

SS: Well, I try to keep vigilant. It's an endless struggle with myself that goes on at every moment of my life. I think I have less of it than most women do, but I still have some. I didn't have the problem that a lot of women have of being afraid to compete in a world which is professionally largely men.

———

WP: In "The Aesthetics of Silence" you wrote that "art is a form of thinking." So I want to ask you, what is art thinking now?

SS: There doesn't seem to be any leading movement in the arts (and I include literature). There is a lot of disparate, you could almost say contradictory, stuff now. I don't mind that, but people don't seem comfortable with that situation. They seem to prefer a situation in which the people that are recognized as good could be identified as working in a certain movement or school. But it isn't like that; it's very pluralistic.

The reason that I said that art is a form of thinking is that I'm very opposed to the standard dichotomies of the intellectual versus the artist, or feeling versus thinking, or the sensuous versus the cerebral. All of those polarities are phony. I like to say that art is a form of thinking because I am also attached to everything that is sensual in art.

I'm also attached to the notion of apprenticeship and craft. It's not only a question of technique, but a question of commitment and passion. There has to be a place where things can be done in a more intense way. What I'm afraid of in all these notions of closing the gap between art and life is that, well, it's not as serious.

———

At some point in our conversation, I mentioned that I had seen the preface she wrote to Peter Hujar's book of photographs called *Portraits in Life and Death* (Da Capo Press). She wanted to show me the book, so I turned off the tape recorder when she got up to get it. She sat and smoked as I leafed through the book. The first half of it contained beautiful photographs of interesting people, some of whom I knew or had seen or heard of. In the second half, all the portraits were of dead people: semi-preserved, ancient skeletons that he photographed in catacombs in Sicily. After seeing only two of these, I closed the book and said I could not look at more. Sontag told me I must. I said I'd always been squeamish about death, but that I knew I had to get used to the possibility of my own death. She looked at me with her dark bright eyes and said, "It's not a possibility; it's a fact. You will die. We're all going to die. It's a good thing to know."

I just listened to her. She had faced something I hadn't. I asked her what she envisioned happening to her after death. She said nothing happens. She said that you weren't alive before you were born and you didn't mind that, so why should you mind not being alive after you die? I turned the tape recorder back on.

WP: When you found out that you had cancer, did you think about things you wanted to do before your life ended?

SS: Sure. Well, when I thought I had perhaps a year or so to live, I had a lot of fantasies about what I wanted to do. Actually, no. I had fantasies about *having* such fantasies because I thought, "Now I should do that thing that people do when they just have a few months to live." I thought of it in terms of trips. I thought I wanted to see the Amazon Jungle, or go to Egypt. But then I quickly realized that what I mainly wanted to do was go on living my life.

WP: In the beginning of your *New Yorker* story you say that when you travel it's always to say good-bye.

SS: I have a highly developed sense of the mortality of things. And that's been sharpened by living with this disease for the last two years. But I think anyone who travels a lot—and I do—has a sense of how rapidly things are being destroyed, particularly in the last ten years, so there is a pathos in that experience of traveling. It's not only that if I go to Venice, I think maybe I'll never see Venice again, but also that I think maybe Venice won't be there to see.

Dumb Art: Beautiful but Not Too Bright

Village Voice, January 2, 1978

As a Trisha Brown dancer and a writer/editor of the "Concepts in Performance" page, I was steeped in conceptual art. Possibly as a reaction, I began to take special pleasure in art that was somehow non-brainy, preverbal. I probably was also influenced by Sontag's plea, in Against Interpretation, *to look at the sensuous surface of a work rather than "excavating" or analyzing it. For a headline, I had suggested using the phrase "dumb but beautiful," and was appalled when it got turned around by a headline editor. In any case, I enjoyed coming up with an observation that I could apply across several disciplines.*

It's abstract art. It's pop art. It's conceptual art. It's minimal art. It's performance art. It's blank art. It's dumb art.

Yes, the new trend—the new vital trend—in art these days is dumbness. It's not to be confused with numbness, or silence, or primitivism, but it shares elements with all three. Dumbness is an insistence on not knowing, a good-natured rebellion against the overwhelming number of facts and experiences that assail us each day. It's akin to the political and aesthetic rebellion of the sixties but not so earnest, not so bitter. It acknowledges the decorativeness, not to say shallowness, of the sensibility behind much of today's art. And it takes the irony in this art a step further.

Maybe it all started with the concept of the antihero. Art has traditionally centered around exalted human beings; in the past hundred years or so, ordinariness has become more interesting. Andy Warhol, the ordinary-is-good guru, directed films like *Trash*, in which characters were stubborn, frustrated and lethargic, with just enough existential self-consciousness to keep us from feeling superior to them. Through his pop art and films Warhol became a champion of the ridiculous, the simplistic. Today's dumbness descends from the *Trash* sensibility, but without the undercurrent of futility.

When Arleen Schloss performed recently at the Kitchen in SoHo, she wore a black Peter Pan tunic, a silver-spangled belt, and tap shoes. With her long bangs and conscientious enunciation, she looked like an assured twelve-year-old giving her first recital. That innocence is genuine, but she has an impressive body of work behind her—mainly experimentations with textures and patterns.

Since 1975 Schloss has been working with the alphabet as a written, spoken, or chanted set of changeable parts. *Rhythm*, at the Kitchen, was a series of abbreviations in nearly alphabetical order. She recited it quickly and, like an auctioneer, let the pitch rise on the last syllable of each breath. Mostly it was too fast for the audience to catch the letters, but when we could recognize a particular abbreviation, its placement and rhythm made it inexplicably funny. I asked for a copy of the "script"; here's an excerpt:

```
ITS A.D.
ITS B.C.
ITS C.B.
ITS A.C.D.C.
ITS C.B.S.
ITS B.S.
ITS C.B.O.B.
ITS C.P.A.
ITS B.F.A
ITS B.M.T.
ITS B.L.T.D.
ITS B.Y.O.

ITS B.T.U.
ITS B.Q.E.
ITS C.I.A.
```

(You can tell it's dumb because there's no apostrophe in IT'S.)

For eight years Schloss taught four- and five-year-olds in Lower East Side public schools. She told me that she was influenced by the kids and their way of playing, that she felt more like a student than a teacher. Teaching taught her to present ideas in the clearest, simplest way.

Robert Wilson, playwright/director/architect/performer, has worked with deaf, brain-damaged, and handicapped kids. He's been influenced by eighteen-year-old Christopher Knowles, whose mind works in an uninterrupted flow of observation and discovery. Knowles has an unerring instinct for form—his poetry is dumb, beautiful, and uplifting. My favorite is part of Wilson's *Letter for Queen Victoria*. Here's how it starts:

```
THE SUNDANCE KID IS BEAUTIFUL
AND THE STORY IS ABOUT THE SUNDANCE KID
AND THE MOVIE IS ABOUT THE SUNDANCE KID
AND THE SUNDANCE KID IS BEAUTIFUL
BEAUTIFUL
YEAH THE SUNDANCE KID WAS BEAUTIFUL
YEAH THE SUNDANCE KID IS VERY BEAUTIFUL
YEAH THE SUNDANCE KID CAN
```

DO THE DANCE
DO THE DANCE A LITTLE BIT
THE SUNDANCE KID COULD DANCE AROUND THE ROOM
THE SUNDANCE KID COULD WALK AROUND THE ROOM
THE SUNDANCE KID COULD WALK AROUND THE ROOM
THE SUNDANCE COULD RUN AROUND THE ROOM
ABOUT THE HOUSES
ABOUT THE TREES

Dumb art isn't a school; it's a sensibility that plays around the edges of an artist's work. I've used it in directing dancers—to impart the feeling of a certain step. I'll say, "Think dumb here." I was once flattered—perversely—by a review that said my collaborators and I used one-tenth of our brain power. In our process we had decided to dispense with extraneous intricacies.

Sometimes dumbness is the only valid stance.

The idea of not knowing what you know—or what you could know—has been used by dancer/choreographer Sara Rudner. She sometimes arranges for one dancer never to learn a sequence: the result is a disoriented look in performance. Trisha Brown used not knowing as the fabric of *Line Up*, which was built on improvisations by five dancers (of which I'm one). We would improvise for about ten seconds at a time, then try to recreate what we did, then set it. It took great discipline to recapture the delicate timing of uncertainty and the ability to be surprised by each other and by ourselves.

William Wegman, a visual/video/performance artist, shapes his intelligence to illustrate an elementary level of consciousness. *Shrubs with Windows and Door*, one of Wegman's many photographs with incisions, has a cute door and two cute windows cut out of a photograph of a sprawling shrub, which makes it look a bit like a jack-o'-lantern in black and white. Wegman seems to have attained a certain level of primitiveness that made him want to see windows in bushes. And he managed to tap a whole set of secret fantasies about being able to look into and out of the shrub.

Wegman is also one of the best known and loved video artists in New York. His videotapes are hilarious—even the one in which he sits on a chair and tells the dumb joke about "the female patient who goes to her doctor and says 'Doc, I'm not having any fun in life,' and the doctor says, 'Life can be a ball—go out and have a ball.'" Wegman, whose deadpan rivals Chevy Chase's, repeats this over and over, stubbornly interspersing "Get it? Get it?" Meanwhile, nestled between Wegman's legs is a tennis ball, which he occasionally tosses to his smart dog, Man Ray.

"Dumb art" and "smart art" have different connotations among painters. Smart art is when the artist knows too much, is too chic for his own good. So smart painters aim for dumb art, which means art that is not too slavish to the ideas of the day (or the year), art that instead shows a truly individual method or look.

Daddy's Old, Nicholas Africano's recent show at Holly Solomon Gallery, uses a primitive, back-to-basics approach. Each of the four paintings contains two bas-relief figures, which look tiny against a spacious background of institutional aqua. The figures are colorful, awkward, and impassive. White-haired "Daddy" appears in all of them, in different stages of knowing that he's ill. In the last of the series, father and (I assume) son stand a bit apart, father with back turned, son with hand lifted to his head. The gesture doesn't look like exasperation, but "The argument" scrawled in crayon on the wall fills in the picture. What was silent and distant becomes excruciatingly familiar.

Dumbness, or muteness, in theatre generally allows the body to speak. In the theatre of Stuart Sherman, however, the body is as mute as the voice. In his *Tenth Spectacle* (*Portraits of Places*) the drama that's erased from the human figure is infused into dozens of props: roller skates, boxes, balloons, scarves, two tables, a small globe. The objects speak for themselves; and surprising relationships crop up. Things are found inside other things: Rose petals fall from a dismantled telephone receiver; a shirt on a hanger is attached to a pair of pants and stuffed with more hangers. Sherman himself is simply the catalyst who allows us to see the magic of the objects. Brisk and matter-of-fact, he sets up one object and scoops another away. The "spectacle" is a grammar-school classroom where one bright boy dashes around to get his project done; you can picture the rest of the class tittering at his earnestness.

The new dumbness also turns up on the screen. In *Rocky*, Sylvester Stallone doesn't talk much. Neither does Shelly Duvall in *Thieves Like Us* (she talks a lot in *Three Women*, but she doesn't *say* much). Both actors are ravishing in their resolve not to cross into the realm of worldliness. They seem to be ingenuous—not devious, not even acting. Or are they even more devious than other actors? What do they know? What do they want us to know they know?

Peter Gordon is a composer who concentrates on the simplistic. His first album, *Star Jaws*, will soon be out on Lovely Music, Ltd., a new record company for new music. There's something stubborn and naughty in Gordon's music; he does things he knows he shouldn't—like writing a song called

"Machomusic." Gordon's voice is a bit Lou Reedish; he says the words more than sings them half the time. The lyrics—some by Gordon, some by Kathy Acker—have a wanton innocence that can degenerate into Warholian down-and-out. In "Life Is Boring" Gordon says, "I read *TV Guide* in the bathroom for an hour and then I telephoned the weather."

Punk rock is a veritable celebration of dumbness. To wit, these vibrant lyrics of the Ramones' song, "I Don't Wanna Walk Around with You":

I don't wanna walk around with you
I don't wanna walk around with you
I don't wanna walk around with you
So why do you wanna walk around with me?

Randy Newman, like William Wegman, postures at ignorance, but you feel the sharp mind underneath. He *chooses* to arrest his thoughts at the point where a less sophisticated mind would get stuck and then illustrates the paradoxes of that state of mind. "We're Rednecks" is a case in point. So is "Davy the Fat Boy," with its ambivalent attitude toward fatness and friendship, and with lyrics like "Davy the Fat Boy, Davy the Fat Boy / Isn't he round? Isn't he round?"

A friend of mine, watching Linda Ronstadt record her latest album, asked why she "growled" several times in exactly the same place in the chorus of "It's So Easy." She answered, "We wanted it to sound dumb."

There is, of course, a definite charm to all of this. But we wouldn't be able to appreciate its charm, or be moved by its spareness, if we hadn't assimilated certain trends of the sixties and early seventies, when we learned to distrust words. Some of us, in fact, are only now beginning to move away from a total rejection of verbalness and toward the use of words—but not many and not fancy. Words—and images—you can trust. Crude building blocks, crude construction. Back to the beginning.

Dumb art may seem less ambitious than the art of a decade ago—less aggressive than minimalism, not so hypnotic as pure repetition, not so Zen as naturalistic dance. It incorporates all of these into something that no longer claims, or seeks, to be interesting. "Interesting" is too cluttered, contrived, over-created. And, ultimately, it must be disappointing because there will *always* be something else that is more interesting. Knowing this, artists look for space and for silence, both as requirements for making art and as content itself.

Like sixties camp, this dumb sensibility has been building slowly, until suddenly it seems to embrace the opposite of what we thought we respected. And, like camp, it yields to a "lower" self in each of us, with the consciousness that that is exactly what it does, no more and no less. But the very simplemindedness that makes it less fashionable and less fascinating than camp gives it more potential for illuminating the thoughts and thoughtlessness of the mind. We learned from John Cage to let sounds be sounds; dumb art lets the mind be the mind.

III   The Eighties

The eighties was my busiest decade so there was less time to
write. I think I got more gigs as a choreographer because my
work became more defined. I had a voice, and it was part
of the zeitgeist. I was one of the downtown, "postmodern"
choreographers; we were each working to unearth our own,
like-no-one-else's movement. And it seemed like SoHo
was the center of the dance world, the center of the post-
Judson explosion of new ways to approach choreography. I
felt I had found a style of movement that spliced smooth,
turbulent, fluid, spiky, odd, classical, silly, all into one
continuous flow.

When Michael Kirby at the *Drama Review* invited me to
write about my process ("Containing Differences in Time")
for his Choreography Issue, he also included Sally Silvers,
Stephen Petronio, Stephanie Skura, and Yoshiko Chuma—
all of whom, I note ruefully and admiringly, are still making
dances today.

I was officially on the dance faculty at Bennington until
1984. I loved teaching, but I used to joke that an instructor's
schedule should be not a sabbatical every seven years, but
five years on and five years off. For composition class, I
liked dreaming up assignments that might unlock students'
creativity—which is why I agreed to review a book on
teaching choreography (*The Intimate Act of Choreography*)
for *Dance Research Journal* in 1985. Another reason was that
Sally Banes asked me to. She had just become editor of this
scholarly journal. Sally and I had edited each other's work at
the *SoHo News* in the seventies.

This period was also one of big changes in my personal

life. I'd had a disastrous breakup with sculptor Don Judd (whom I had met at one of Trisha Brown's galas) that plunged me into a yearlong depression. I forcibly pulled myself together to create new work for my concert at the Kitchen in January 1986.

One James E. Siegel came to that concert. After a rocky beginning (or rather re-beginning, since we had met briefly a decade earlier), we eventually fell in love, had a relatively short engagement, and tied the knot in January '87.

Shortly after Jim and I got married, I had an experience that made me realize how fortunate I was. I was just leaving an appointment on the third floor of a medical building affiliated with Roosevelt Hospital. I had been given good news: I could go ahead and try to get pregnant. A borderline ovarian tumor the year before had been surgically removed, and I had to wait a year to get the "all clear" before planning a family. I mean, I was forty; it was now or never. I was smiling from ear to ear and felt a new bounce in my step. In my excitement I took an elevator going up instead of down. The doors opened on the eighth floor, and there I saw Arnie Zane, a fellow choreographer who had AIDS, crying at a desk with a telephone. He had just been informed that the chemo wasn't working—a death knell for sure. I quickly quelled my own happiness to offer Arnie support. What could I do? I was just told I could give life, and he was just told he would lose his. We hugged, he cried on my shoulder, we left the building together. It was heartbreaking to hear him say, "I know I complain a lot, but I love this life and I don't want to die." (A short version of this account appears in "Living with AIDS," in Section V.)

A few months later, I was at a tech rehearsal at P.S. 122 for the memorial service for dance writer Barry Laine, also an AIDS casualty. I was to perform a duet that Barry had liked, and Arnie was to give a spoken tribute. Arnie and I were sitting next to each other, waiting, as performers do during a tech rehearsal. Again, it was another cross-fade of my happiness and his despair, and I now see that I was insensitive. "Arnie," I blurted out, "I'm two months pregnant!" I was a teensy bit proud that I could still perform in my condition. He just said, "You must have a lot of hope."

I did and I do, and my son was born in 1988. I cherished my time with him and stayed home as much as I could. I felt lucky to have a child so late in life. My previous relationships, with both men and women, had not exactly been heading toward marriage or parenting.

The year Nicholas was born saw the deaths of three dance artists I knew: Arnie Zane, Robert Joffrey, and John Bernd. In the years that followed, many more of my colleagues were felled. Ultimately the epidemic demolished a big swath of the male population of the dance world. I didn't write about AIDS until later (see "Living with AIDS," in Section V), but the plague affected all our lives in the eighties.

Bausch, Brecht, and Sex: *Kontakthof* by Pina Bausch

The Kunsthalle, Basel, Switzerland

February 28, 1983

New York Native, March 28–April 10, 1983

In the last couple of decades of Pina Bausch's life, her work was full of pleasure, so it's easy to forget how disturbing the earlier pieces were. This review certainly brings that back to me. I happened to be in Basel, performing my own solo in a gallery at the same time that Tanztheater Wuppertal Pina Bausch was there. This was in 1983, a year before the company came to the United States to launch its long association with Brooklyn Academy of Music. So, it's just possible that this is the first review of her work published in the States. At the time my romantic relationships had been with women for a few years, so I fit right in with the skeptical stance on heterosexuality of the New York Native, *a gay biweekly that folded in 1997.*

A note about Josephine Ann Endicott: She left a searing imprint on my memory, but I never saw her dance again. She had stopped performing in 1987, so I was happy to see her in the documentary film Dancing Dreams, *coaching teenagers for a special performance of* Kontakthof. *I recently discovered that she grew up in Australia with a close friend of mine, and I obtained the photo directly from Endicott.*

I had heard about Pina Bausch's dance-theatre work but had never seen her, so when my recent visit to Basel, Switzerland, concurred with her Swiss tour, I took advantage of the opportunity to see her performance. The work was amazing in its craft, its looniness, its integration of movement, text, acting and film—and its brutality.

The piece I saw was created about two years ago and is called *Kontakthof*, which means court dance or arena of contact. It consists basically of ten straight couples going through a cycle of seduction, molestation, and separation with a few ghastly pleasures in between. The set resembles both a courtroom and a large gymnasium—the kind where they have high school dances and force the boys and the girls to dance together. *Kontakthof* starts with the twenty performers sitting in a row at the back of the stage. One woman walks downstage to do a series of clear and snide gestures: brush hair, show teeth, let stomach hang out, suck it all back in. The other performers then follow her lead. Though it's fun to see how each person is more bizarre than the last, the first dancer consistently holds one's attention throughout the piece. She is an unseemly mess of a woman: sordid, excessive, and absolutely riveting. Her name is Josephine Ann Endicott and,

Josephine Ann Endicott in Pina Bausch's *Kontakthof*, 1983: sordid, excessive, and absolutely riveting. (© Ulli Weiss)

without really being a protagonist, she is more active than anyone else. I've been told that Bausch introduces an idea to her group and then watches each person's interpretation. She decides whose bit will be kept and whose will be thrown out. The fact that Endicott has the most bits in the performance attests to her being the truest representative of Bausch's vision. She is rash and witty, Brechtian in her self-mockery and energetic decadence.

Like actors in a Fellini film, Bausch's characters look waxen and elaborately repressed. In fact, repression seems to be both the mode of expression and the subject matter of *Kontakthof*. The women do a diagonal procession where tortured feet jam into spike-heeled shoes; the company performs a ritual of progressively distorting their posture in one grotesque way or another. But the most oppressive behavior emerges from their biological (heterosexual) urges. Throughout the piece, sexuality is compulsive and manipulative, shameful and necessary. With smug faces they tweak, squeeze, and wrench their partners' body parts, and accept the same in return. They seem impelled to be horrible to each other. A man brandishing a toy mouse ghoulishly dangles it in the face of one of the women; she lets out a resounding scream and runs off. This happens repeatedly until finally she is too depressed to respond.

What gives the piece its complexity is the device of having one action comment on another. One couple marches downstage to observe and applaud another couple wrestling with each other. A film (by Theo Kubiak) about ducks traveling in groups serves as an indirect comment on human activities. Two women in pink perform a ballet/vaudeville routine that hovers around the main action while a man doggedly follows them with a microphone—commentators being commentated. This doubling up adds humor, campiness and self-consciousness. Needless to say, I missed a lot by not understanding German, which was the main language used in the occasional monologues and taped songs. But there was one moving episode that everybody could understand: Nineteen people were sitting in a row downstage while the twentieth held a microphone first to one person then to the next, as all continued talking non-stop. We heard, one at a time, each person talking in her/his native language, and thus learned of the remarkably diverse backgrounds among the group: British, Swedish, French, Polish, German, and American. Each time a monologue was funny, a different patch of audience laughed.

The image that stays in my mind as typifying *Kontakthof* is this: a man, lying on his back, drops a small, round tabletop on his stomach, thus triggering a hearty, frenzied laugh. When his laughter dies out, he lifts the tabletop up a couple of feet, takes a breath, and drops it again.

The Structure of Seduction

Village Voice, May 28, 1985

In May of 1985 I was still wallowing in heartache over sculptor Don Judd, who had ended our relationship abruptly a few months before. I was a wreck . . . in a funk . . . wearing the same flannel shirt every day for a year. I tried to understand how I'd fallen so hard. Making pronouncements on the nature of obsession probably helped me to feel that I had some control over it.

By this time the Village Voice *had a column called "Performance," similar to the* SoHo News*'s "Concepts in Performance," in which the writer could do a roundup piece rather than a single review. I believe this was the only time I wrote for it.*

It's funny for me to come upon my parenthetical reference to Joan Armatrading here. Her song "(I Love It When You) Call Me Names" is now on my iPhone, and I'm still trying to figure out what she meant. I suppose that when I wrote this piece, in the midst of my voluptuous misery, Armatrading matched my sense of rage within desire.

Love and art have this in common: you're always a beginner. And this: the simultaneous wish for, and fear of, exposure. It requires innocence to fall in love and courage to stay in love. You surrender first and think later. Later is when the danger sets in—the very closeness and visibility that were irresistible have thorns waiting for you.

In performances by Robert Longo and Karole Armitage, a sense of danger comes through. In Longo's revival of *Sound Distance of a Good Man* (1977), we see a projection of a man's face looking up to the sky with a stone lion behind him. A woman sings an aria to the right of the screen, and two men to the left in a muscular embrace move fluidly on a rotating dial. The men are engaged in what seems to be both a passionate embrace and an arduous struggle. And again, in *Surrender* (1979), we see two people, this time a man and a woman, in office/party clothes, dancing closely. Every step, every reach, every swing, is both affectionate and hostile.

In her book, *In a Different Voice*, psychologist Carol Gilligan notes that female children tend to see distance between two figures as dangerous, whereas male children see closeness as dangerous. This danger, wherever it is perceived, shows up in Longo's work in the twin aspects of abandon and despair.

If Longo shows simultaneous pleasure and pain, Armitage shows alternating pleasure and pain. Her new duet with Joseph Lennon, $-P=dH/dq$, maps the approaches, positionings and challenges of a seduction. Charles

Atlas's outlandish costumes are as alluring as a striptease, though with a less obvious goal. He's designed a sequence of progressively ridiculous and illuminating accessories, culminating in stilts that not only raise each dancer but provide an elaborate encumbrance—perhaps the ultimate statement on the precarious balance and inevitable separateness within a relationship.

Armitage matches Atlas's outlandishness by getting into bizarre confrontational poses—take an action and hold your breath till you see what the other person does. Like, "When I wrap my leg around your hips and push your shoulders, what do you do?" In the time it takes to flick a spiked heel or turn a head, the stance changes from adoration to indifference, surrender to dominance. No moment of pleasure is free; no act of assertion is victorious.

The structure of seduction is similar to the structure of learning: you get pulled in bit by bit until you reach a deeper knowledge and then you are either satisfied for a while or insatiable. It's the insatiability that makes you learn a new language, stay in love, or make some art. If out of control, this extreme curiosity or love or fear turns into obsession, which is what performance artist Jerri Allyn deals with in her readings. Obsession is an infinite feeling looping back on itself because it has nowhere to go. Obsession is a response to the quest for love that goes further back to the quest for a geographical/emotional/aesthetic home—the search for mental comfort in the face of severe disjunction. In *Raw Meet*—in which Allyn reads quickly from a notebook, accompanied by prerecorded voices—love is worship and it is also addiction. Allyn goes into detail about her smoking habit, incredulous that she is a captive of the habit. It makes her behave badly, dropping ashes on people's rugs, alienating herself socially—"Cigarettes come first." Likewise, in *Anonymous Portrait* (1983), she is incredulous that she is a victim of love, the cynic turned romantic.

The feeling Allyn calls "some kind of letting-go-of" is accompanied by a racing awareness of how it reduces her: "My favorite thing is to sit and stare stupidly into your eyes and blubber on and on about how much I need you, want you, love you. The rushes, the weak knees, the flashes, the words sounding funny." In her new piece, *Love and Worship*, she compares the weakness one feels in love with the yielding to religion, the wish for something higher, something that subsumes you and obliterates the need for thinking.

In love, one is ready for any adventure, any demand, any challenge. (Joan Armatrading: "I love it when you call me names.") In Johanna Boyce's *Ties That Bind*, Part 2, Jennifer Miller and Susan Seizer talk about their relationship—how they met, how they view each other, what they know of each other's past. They are ready for anything. Seizer holds Miller down when Miller tells of the confusing experience of electrolysis at sixteen. Miller plays

Seizer's stern father in the retelling of her coming out. Seizer plays Miller's mother dying of cancer. The innocuousness at the beginning of the piece ("She's a Gemini, can't you tell") and the end ("We plan to travel as a juggling act this summer") effectively sandwiches the intensity of the secrets they share.

The return of love as a subject matter for art is not an aesthetic regression. It can be treated unsentimentally as a "problem" in the formalist sense of opposing forces that need to be resolved. It's not saying much to point out that love and sex have classically been the raw material of art. As Rilke says, "Artistic experience lies so incredibly close to that of sex, to its pain and its ecstasy, that the two manifestations are indeed but different forms of one and the same yearning and delight."

The Intimate Act of Choreography by Lynne Anne Blom and L. Tarin Chaplin, University of Pittsburgh Press, 1982

Book review, *Dance Research Journal* 17, no. 2 & 18, no. 1 (1985–1986), a project of CORD, Congress on Research in Dance

I would never have given this book a second glance. But Sally Banes, who was the editor of Dance Research Journal *at the time, persuaded me to review it by saying I could use the book as a springboard to write about whatever it brought to mind. And what it brought to mind was teaching. I always loved teaching dance composition. I would devise an assignment and notice how it became the key to unlock a student's creativity. But other students needed other keys, and I enjoyed finding them. I was completely against a one-size-fits-all approach, hence my strong reaction to this book.*

> *If only you'd remember before ever you sit down to write that you've been a reader* long before you were ever a writer. *You simply fix that fact in your mind, then sit very still and ask yourself, as a reader, what piece of writing in all the world Buddy Glass would most want to read if he had his heart's choice. The next step is so terrible, but so simple I can hardly believe it as I write it. You just sit down shamelessly and write the thing yourself.*
> —*J. D. Salinger,* Seymour: An Introduction

When choreography seems overwhelming, I try to think of Seymour's letter to Buddy. Of course, making art is not as simple as Seymour implies. But his passionate advice posits a direct relation between vision and effort. It is about desire. Although *The Intimate Act of Choreography* admirably attempts to provide guidelines for teaching and studying, it omits desire as a motivating force. This review examines the usefulness of such a book and observes some of the aesthetic discrepancies.

A textbook on art—in this case choreography—that leaves out desire is informative in the same way that a step-by-step sex manual is: it is so thorough that it precludes any sense of freedom. The intimate act of making art, as with making love, requires a desire so intense that personal discovery is inevitable. Thus it is tempting for me to say that anyone who *needs* to read such a book will never become a choreographer. Although authors Blom and Chaplin claim to "provide situations, in the form of improvisations, where learning results from experience," they weigh the book down with overly literal instructions that ultimately flatten the imagination instead of free it. Here's an example:

IMPROV: CANDLE

A candle, a flame . . . flickering. The candle has many wicks. Some of the flames may be sparkling or sputtering. . . . The wax is melting, heavily, sluggishly. The shape changes, softens. . . . Work with the flickering in one part of your body and the melting in another. As the candle melts it takes on many different shapes—long and elegant, gnarled and scary. A drop of wax starts to roll down the candle, spills, picks up speed, then rolls onto the floor and hardens. . . . (p. 128)

Too much information. Having taught choreography at several colleges and studios, I prefer to maintain a delicate balance between information and independence. To be realistic, I should say that the book is geared to students who are attracted to dance and want to plunge in but aren't anywhere near practitioners. If they don't have some sort of guide, they are left out in the cold, and may resort to a *Saturday Night Fever* version of creativity: the Travolta character, when asked if he made up a certain step, says, "Yeah, I saw it on TV and then I made it up." If the readership of *The Intimate Act* had access only to TV, that would be one problem. But the book is aimed at students—and teachers—in a university setting, which has other problems. The university traditionally disseminates knowledge that has been notated and developed over centuries. The ephemerality of choreography doesn't lend itself to a stable kind of scholarship. Analysis and evaluation of dance are highly subjective. Many colleges are reluctant to support programs that look like trends: they want to know something is here to stay before they pass it on as knowledge. On the other hand, academic training can be more geared to the individual than a professional situation, which necessarily molds the dancer for a specific purpose (the Joffrey Ballet, the Alvin Ailey Company, etc.). One of the ideals of a liberal arts education is to expand the individual without regard for commerciality.

The Intimate Act reflects both positive and negative aspects of dance/art within a university setting: it gives permission to experiment and also tries to standardize definitions and goals in an attempt, I would guess, to bolster choreography in the eyes of academia.

Choreography, like education, is ideally the meeting of the present moment with consciousness of the past. Trisha Brown has written that "my continued interest as a choreographer is the employment of a structured scheme and how that interfaces with kinesthetically motivated dancing." Past decisions meeting with present energy. With this in mind, she choreographed *Set and Reset* (1983), a twenty-two-minute piece that has been called unforgettable by people all over the world.

If there is an absolute art, it is the extended moment when one first encounters a painting and does not think to ask any questions at all. They seem to all have been answered—or to be superfluous.—Robert Storr, Art in America, *March 1985*

Set and Reset seems to rise off the ground, demolishing questions as it progresses, forming a magical coherent experience for no visible reason. It has an element of the sublime that is rare in contemporary art.

Should a textbook on choreography refer to the possibility of the sublime? Probably not. Probably it is good that choreography is portrayed as a set of exercises designed to expand students' range of movement and sharpen their sense of shape, rhythm, and sequence.

In this way, *The Intimate Act of Choreography* is encouraging to the beginning student. But it manages as well to be condescending—to both the student and the art. With its conscientious definitions, clearly laid out plan, and overly helpful instructions, the message is "You can do it: here are all the elements and a logical guide to see you through. Just pay attention and put it together." I would think that even the most traditional fields of knowledge—math, history, literature—are abused by such an attitude.

The authors don't tell you what it really takes to choreograph. Maybe nobody can. If pushed to the brink, however, I would blurt out these three things: (1) a connection to the medium so strong and persistent that you can't help *thinking* in that medium, (2) a mind powerful enough to handle the paradoxes of order and chaos, simplicity and complexity, stability and change, past and present, and (3) a balance between fear and faith—the dare to oneself right up against the acceptance of oneself. The act of choreography is not only intimate and therapeutic, but radical.

I am torn between thinking this book pernicious and thinking it perfectly harmless. Pernicious because, if successful, it will perpetrate hordes of young choreographers who are innocently ambitious in the same way that some trained dancers are. A shallow, even if well-earned, sense of mastery results in a mere display of talents—"I can do this and I can do that"—that lacks a motivating force. Harmless, because the really inspired students, desire being the teacher, will find their own paths anyway, while the others who read it might learn more about dance and swell the ranks of the informed audience, and there's nothing wrong with that.

In a recent exchange in the *New York Times Book Review*, poet Andrei Codrescu holds that "If anything can be taught, it is the difficulty of the questions surrounding . . . art." Codrescu's letter was triggered by an article by novelist John Barth on teaching creative writing. Nowhere in Barth's article or in the letters of response is it mentioned that a textbook would be, or ever has been, helpful in teaching "creative writing." In my ongoing plea to have dance taken as seriously as the other arts, I would make a parallel statement saying that textbooks are nearly useless in the teaching of dance. One can learn to choreograph only by doing it, but one can absorb the seriousness of it through contact with an experienced teacher and stimulating colleagues. Louis Horst was a demanding and provocative teacher, but when his books *Pre-Classical Forms* and *Modern Dance Forms* were used by other teachers, hundreds of paint-by-the-numbers studies were composed. (I know: I was in one of those classes in 1967.) Bessie Schönberg, whose students have included Jerome Robbins, Meredith Monk, and Lucinda Childs, never used a textbook. Robert Dunn, in his legendary pre-Judson workshops, recommended books to read, but never gave assignments from a book. When anybody thinks of inspiring classes, a textbook is not what comes to mind. Albert Einstein, in talking about how he learned the Mozart violin sonatas, said, "I believe, on the whole, that love is a better teacher than sense of duty."

Along these lines, *The Intimate Act* does well to include "The Teacher's Addendum." The first point here is that the teacher must "establish an atmosphere in which the students can trust themselves, you and each other." The descriptions of privacy, responsible playfulness, constructive feedback, honesty, and camaraderie, help to define the atmosphere that becomes the foundation upon which the class develops. Honing students' perceptions about each other's work stimulates their own work and vice versa. It is not easy to build the trust that makes this possible. "The Teacher's Addendum" holds that

> the choreographer's whole life, personality, and education form the matrix from which she creates. The teacher's role is to help one little part of that complex matrix become well defined and integrated, and this is only made possible by providing a context in which what's being done is relevant to the student. (p. 216)

The book also contains articulate discussion on the stuff of choreography. The definitions of abstraction and form are thoughtful, clear, and applicable. The definition of "organic form" is so fine it could stand alone as the single idea of the book: it is the Zen quote, "You have allowed the cloth to weave the cloth."

Thus the book's practical advice about the classroom and its definitions are more considered than its lessons in craft. This makes me wonder whether one coauthor wrote the definitions and the other provided the how-to instructions. In any case, there is an inconsistency in their teachings that borders on hypocrisy. Time and again the authors espouse open-ness, nonformulaic composing, a "follow your intuitions" approach. They give a wide range of disparate examples of choreography, including the work of Trisha Brown, Merce Cunningham, Laura Dean, Martha Graham, Doris Humphrey, Murray Louis, Camelita Marracci, Meredith Monk, Alwin Niko-lais, Steve Paxton, Anna Sokolow, Charles Weidman, and Robert Wilson. Yet, even with thoughtful definitions and the broadest possible spectrum of ex-emplary choreography, the book presents dance as a set of finite possibili-ties. Perhaps this should not worry us because the brightest students may use the book only to rebel against. Delineating the possibilities makes one crave something beyond, and therein lie invention, newness, and the indi-vidual worldview. But the suggested exercises are so literal, so prescribed, so stuck to old standards—the Egyptian Freize, the Mother and Child, the Candle—that it makes me want to say, How about an assignment to make a continuous phrase that is *not* lyrical, a study that is *not* unified, a dance that is *not* a dance?

Blom and Chaplin's view of choreography as a closed set is clearest in the issue of phrasing. For all the open-mindedness of the examples, the taste remains aligned with the hierarchical phrasing of ballet and modern dance, complete with high point, stillness, and other conventional devices, such as the "powerful diagonal." The writers seem not to have absorbed that Cunningham has split the atom of conventional phrasing, that Yvonne Rainer's *Trio A* (1966) introduced a more democratic treatment of material, that Brown has redefined a concept of "organic" based not on musicality (like ballet), nor on breath (Duncan, Humphrey, Graham) but on her own unique logic. These changes, which have gradually happened over about twenty-five years, are at the heart of the shift in dance from "modern" to "postmodern." Though the writers acknowledge this new possibility in their choice of examples and their liberalness in general, their preference for rise-and-fall dynamics and theme-and-variations format is obvious. In asserting that the hierarchy of a phrase—build-up, climax, stillness—is as necessary as form itself, they promote a conventionally manipulative relation to the audience. In discussing choreographic "pacing," they say: "To achieve this, you tease, connive, invite, take pertinent side roads, introduce intrigues, develop nuances" (p. 121). And in the "Pure Percussive or Pure Sustained" study, they advise, "To keep it from becoming boring, remember to incorpo-rate changes in speed and in amount of energy used" (p. 81).

This attitude ensures that the choreographer/performer is master/slave to the audience. It aligns dance with entertainment rather than with art. This seems regressive to me. The general direction since Judson Dance Theater of the early 1960s has been to assume an active, intelligent audience that can handle complexity and doesn't need to be manipulated.

In the end, the book is not surprising. With all the new information available since, say, Doris Humphrey wrote *The Art of Making Dances*, Blom and Chaplin have spelled out all the possibilities they could imagine, which ultimately is not much more than Humphrey could imagine. But Humphrey's book has an eloquence and economy that shows more respect for students and practicing choreographers, perhaps because the dance world itself was more intimate at that time. With all its talk of discovery through improvisation, *The Intimate Act of Choreography* makes discovery unlikely. A more subtle, less detailed approach would be more fertile.

However, I would guess that this book is good for some situations. For a dancer with no experience in choreographing who finds herself having to teach it, *The Intimate Act* could provide a starting point for generating assignments. And, as I have said, the definitions of *form*, *abstraction*, and *organic*, and the classroom advice, are valuable. Of course it's preferable to let a class come up with its own collective definitions. If a class is well run, a natural identity forms over time, and the teachers, as with the choreographer, "allows the cloth to weave the cloth." In this case, no book is needed.

(A note on the pronouns in this book: I appreciate the use of "she" in some places and "he" in others, thereby avoiding the awkward "s/he" or "he or she," and having the fairness to imagine either gender in all situations.)

The Holes in *Tin Quiz*

Movement Research Performance Journal 17, Fall/Winter 98/99

While working on Tin Quiz *with the young dancer Donald Fleming in 1982 and '83, part of the process was getting to know each other in the studio. I gradually realized how brilliantly spontaneous Donald could be—and I wanted to draw on that gift to make a duet. I remember too that Donald was the first person I heard mention* AIDS. *When he uttered the word during a warmup session, I thought he meant the little chocolate candies that were supposed to help you lose weight. I learned a lot from him. I wrote these notes in 1986 or '87, mostly for myself. When we reprised* Tin Quiz *for an anniversary event of the Danspace Project in December 1998, I dug them up and published them in* MRPJ.

I like a structure that holds a piece together but also pulls it apart. If the fabric of the piece is woven so tightly that there are no holes, a deadness sets in. If the threads can be separated enough to let something else come through, the piece lives longer, both as choreography and performance. Arriving at the right relation between open and closed, void and solid, unknown and known, is an achievement.

Architect Robert LeRicolais, in *Structure Implicit and Explicit*, discusses the structure of bone texture, and extrapolates:

> But if you think about the voids instead of working with the solid elements, the truth appears. The structure is composed of holes, all different in dimension and distribution, but with an unmistakable purpose in their occurrence. So we arrive at an apparently paradoxical conclusion, that the art of structure is how and where to put holes.

In *Tin Quiz*, which I made and performed with Donald Fleming at Danspace in 1983 and later elsewhere, there are two holes where the choreography opens up to let in the present. One is the arithmetic quizzing, in which we hurl addition, subtraction, multiplication, and division problems at each other while improvising on prescribed paths. The other is the final section, in which I pose a series of four questions to Donald, each of which he has to answer before moving a few steps toward stage right.

I think up the questions during the day of the performance; Donald thinks up the answers under the gaze of the audience. This requires a huge amount of trust in each other and, for Donald, the gathering of all his psychic alertness.

Some of the questions are straightforward opinion questions. Others are what I think of as fiction questions because they locate an area of fantasy or near-reality, and require the answer to traffic in this area. At many moments during this ten-minute duet, we both had to swallow our surprise.

We have performed the piece about ten times. I was so wowed by Donald's quick wit in answering my questions that I started to keep a record of them. The following were all fiction questions except the last one:

April 1983

WP: When you were a token seller for the Transit Authority, did it drive you crazy being underground eight hours a day?

DF: Fortunately there was a grate just above my booth and I could see a little daylight coming through on nice days.

December 1983

WP: The last time you lost your apartment keys, was it because of that feeling of your mind being somewhere else?

DF: No, just the keys were.

March 1985 in Washington, DC

WP: Don't you sometimes wish we had a Pentagon in New York?

DF: It sure would make protesting easier.

March 1985 (rehearsal)

WP: Is it frustrating to know you're way behind the others in your conga drum class?

DF: I make up for it by being good in the samba class.

May 1985

WP: How did it come about that your brother grew up in Brazil?

DF: There was a Brazilian family living across the hall. My brother spent a lot of time over there. They were going back to Brazil. They drove there in a van and took my brother with them. They never brought him back.

June 1985 in Boston

WP: When you were writing your mystery novel, why was the first chapter the most difficult to write?

DF: Because I couldn't resist giving it all away in the beginning.

WP: Do you think every question has one best answer?

DF: At least one best answer.

Containing Differences in Time

Drama Review 29, no. 2 (T106), Summer 1985 (published by MIT Press, NYU/Tisch School of the Arts)

This was my only real attempt to describe my choreographic process, which was usually way more fraught than I let on here. Regarding the making of Standard Deviation, *all I say here about my doubts is that I considered separating the two parts into two different pieces. In actuality, I agonized over the decision for weeks. I was happy with the tone and choreography of each of the two parts, but I couldn't figure out the relationship between them. Every night I obsessed over the question: Are these two pieces or one? I was normally anxious at the beginning of making a piece, but with* Standard Deviation *I was anxious all the way through. I was afraid my whole concert would be a failure if I didn't make the right decision. My creative instincts, or rather my conceptual instincts, seemed to have flown the coop, leaving me no roadmap. Even when I finally decided that they were two halves of the same piece, I kept wondering if I'd made the right decision. I was sick over it. Later, in my composition classes, I sometimes gave the assignment to make a piece that has two radically different halves. I was still trying to solve the problem years later.*

Another thing I didn't admit to in this account is that the second half of Standard Deviation, *which we performed often on its own, was inspired by the break dancing I was seeing in the subways. I loved the springy precision, urgency, and camaraderie, all infused with a streak of rebelliousness. I tried to get those qualities into my body as I made the phrases.*

Note: The current names for Lisa Bush and MJ Becker are Lisa Bush Finn and Mary Jane Levin.

When I look at a phrase I've made in the studio, it either looks like nothing, or it looks like something. I can use both. Mainly I look at it to get clues as to how to go on. I go on by asking, "What do I want more of and what do I want less of?" which is on the way to asking, "What makes this phrase consistent within itself?"

When it looks like something to me, it's because of context or physical involvement. By context I mean what comes before and what comes after it, the "it" being either a split-second or a whole section. I used to spend a lot of time coming up with a single movement—the goal was to find what is both new and natural. This effort continues, but I also take advantage of the vocabulary I've established for myself—loose-limbed or stiff-limbed walks with sudden yielding in the joints, sometimes harsh against the floor or self, sometimes airy, arms not too often fully extended but used to im-

Standard Deviation, a work of mine from 1984, with
Lisa Bush, MJ Becker, and me. (© Lois Greenfield)

pel or sustain momentum, same arm and leg pairings to counter automatic opposition; off-balance moves with recovery by folding or twisting; rhythms of faltering or shivering or just going about one's business or interrupting one's business.

Now I pay more attention to how it all goes together. For the continuing line to be right, all the dots along the way have to be right (in the subjective sense of the word). You can't get too excited about each dot because as you add on the other dots, the first ones look very small, but you have to care about each dot as you make it. When you rehearse or perform the phrase, the challenge is to be cogent as well as fluid, to be a hundred percent with each dot but not dwell on it. You must forget all the past dots but somehow let them build momentum.

By involvement, I mean clarity of image. When I'm working with a dancer, usually Lisa Bush, I may say a few words about a movement, but sometimes I don't have to. I can just show it and she understands—I mean she does it so that I like it on her body. The other day I was working with Mary Lyman, who felt lost during one movement in between others—flat hands, table-height, press down suddenly while right foot jabs the floor. She yelled to me, "*This*, and what's *this* thing right here?" I did it myself (like singing to oneself) and then said, "It's like a stamp, like you're sealing something shut before you can go on."

The image is both a mental impetus and a memory peg; it may be verbal or visual or kinesthetic. It is the link between mind and body, but it is tiny and elusive, and the next day it may be lost. Sometimes you can find a new image to hold it together. But occasionally a whole chunk of, say, twenty seconds loses motivation—that is, loses the logic of how one image sweeps or jolts or fades into the next. This is more likely to happen when I'm working alone, and the symptom is that I keep forgetting it.

As I mentioned, my concern used to be mainly to find new movement. This was necessary in order to undermine the phenomenon of dancing on-stage, which has a history of narcissism. I do not like it when you can tell the performer is thinking, "Look at what a good dancer I am." In the absence of a demanding idea or situation, that kind of vanity degenerates into bland glistening muscularity.

I love dancing because it is full and gets to every corner of me. I am not interested in dancing that is less than that. People often talk about abstract and literal as being opposites, but I don't think they are that different. When you watch movement and do it a lot, you don't separate it into gesture and decoration or form and content. A gesture that has conventional meaning—

for example, waving—could have as much visual and kinesthetic informa-tion as an abstract gesture could have conventional meaning.

When I come upon a conversation between deaf mutes in the subway or the street, I pay attention. The density and fleeting shapes are beauti-ful—like seeing thinking written in the air. I like knowing that they under-stand each other completely while I understand almost nothing. I don't get frustrated; I *like* the difference. It is a clear area of misunderstanding, as opposed to most art and language where one person (the viewer) thinks she understands another person (the artist), but probably doesn't.

The little stretch of misunderstanding widens when you use gestures not conventionally understood, so it becomes clearer that meaning is a *range* and not one identifiable thing. And yet, amid the ambiguity, there will be one thing that gets everybody excited or annoyed or moved. There's a kind of understanding operating, but it is an understanding closer to absorption than recognition. Absorption in a kinesthetic language is the meeting place between choreographer and audience.

In my sign language pieces I've tried to simulate the speed, intimacy, and sense of legibility of American Sign Language. For *A Ststoryry: Impos-sible to Tell* (1981), I used two passages from a story by my friend Sophia Healy, who is a writer and a painter, as a score. To resist the temptation of smooth connections, I made an alphabetical list of the four hundred–some words and assigned a gesture for each. I did it very fast, using a known ges-ture if it came up and an obscure gesture if it was based on an unconscious association. Then I learned them in the order they appear in the prose. In the final piece, I perform the gestural sequence at the same speed that the reader tells the story, so that the effect is a two-way translation. To get up to that speed, I had to rehearse the sequence until my body knew it without my mind prompting, which could maybe be called the speed of language.

I sometimes use a related structure I call "inserts—hasty version." After working on a duet I made using this device for Paula Clements and Kyle de-Camp in 1980, Paula wrote:

> I remember one section in the dance that defies mental cooperation. We had first learned a series of single gestures, then later inserted our own intermediary movement between each of these. Eventually we ran through the whole thing without completing any of the sequential move-ments. While doing this, it is impossible to think of what you're doing because by the time you start, you're already doing something else. Each ensuing shape severs the last so quickly that all you can do is abandon counting, memory or expectation, and trust to a kinesthetic sense. Game-

lan players constantly know both where they are and where they were. Each time they play a note, they have to mute the last one. As one hand goes ahead with the music, the other must, at the same time, silence the reverberations of what has just been played. Without this sort of double thinking, I always felt a delightful discombobulation. My body was going through the moves at such a clip that my mind could only skip along a couple of beats behind.

I have an ongoing interest in making duets. Just as any two points determine a line, any two figures determine a duet, whether a chair and a table, earth and sun, or Fred and Ginger. In my duets, the starting point has been the choice of two very different people; sometimes I'm one of them. My sense of who the two people are creates not only the fabric and tone of the piece, but the possibilities for shifting imbalances as well. I try to avoid both the automatic symmetry and the dominant/submissive modes that duets easily fall into. I liked Contact Improvisation, a duet form initiated by Steve Paxton in 1972, because its essential facts—weight-bearing and disorientation—give rise to a mutual dependency, which cuts down on narcissism.

I consider all duets romantic. In an early version of *Line Up* (1977), Trisha Brown made a duet that combined Elizabeth Garren dancing the first "solo" of *Locus* while I did a version made through written instructions. As I danced it, I felt Elizabeth's slipperiness as surely as if we were touching. If it had been a ballroom dance, I could have said that I felt her gentle swaying motions under the palm of my hand.

I consider all duets political in that they have the potential for breaking conventional roles and coming into an area of better understanding. I agree with Adrienne Rich, who says, "The possibilities that exist between two people, or among a group of people, are a kind of alchemy. They are the most interesting things in life." The effort to communicate is the only possible source of reasonable coexistence.

———

I have a few rules for the making-up process:

1. Don't repeat anything unless it comes back by itself, pushing its way into the phrase I'm making. By not depending on repetition, the choreography underscores the fleetingness of the genre.
2. Follow the line of the phrase *as though it already exists*. In bed at night, I go over it mentally, and in the studio I watch it or do it and scan it for any wrong move. Like listening to a good story, you know when something is forced, or the pace is wrong, or a new character is introduced too early.

3. Use what's already there—the space and the dancers. Often I give a phrase with holes in it for the dancer to fill in. This presupposes a two-way trust and a kinship of energy/style. Seeing what the dancers come up with, either by filling in the holes or by making mistakes or associations, is a pleasure and a relief.

A few years ago, I began to include elements other than dance and music, like verbal texts and video, in an attempt to clutter the space. I was tired of the purity and remoteness of dance concerts. I wanted the performers to be more immediate and the viewers to have more to contend with. The verbal material also leads the viewer more literally through time.

For *Standard Deviation* (1984), I collaborated with Cathy Weis on the video images. Part I (thirteen minutes) is a duet for Paula Clements and Harry Sheppard with two TV monitors and an Advent projection screen. Part II (seventeen minutes) is a trio for MJ Becker, Lisa Bush, and myself with three video segments shown on the Advent Screen. Music written for the trio by Andy Blinx and Don Hunerberg runs through the internal video segments, connecting the whole second half in one spasmodic flow.

The first challenge of *Standard Deviation* was to make something in which the two halves are radically different from each other. How could two sections be entirely different but part of one piece? There were times when I gave up and considered them two separate pieces. For linkage material, I used a tiny bit of movement that came up in the trio for the duet, and I used strains of the Russian language in both halves. The links were strictly private; they were too subtle to be noticed on first viewing.

The other challenge was to incorporate video without splitting the focus or diluting the energy. Cathy and I wanted the video to be an interruption yet not an interruption—a nonliteral, bilateral extension of the dance. It throws your eyes off to the right, where the large screen is, but loops the energy back into the dancing. During the video bits, there was no dancing and vice-versa.

s.d. begins with a segment on the screen, a staged argument between a pro-capitalist Soviet man and a pro-communist American woman (Sally Banes) that starts in Russian and degenerates into both languages. (One of the things Sally and I shared was a fascination with Soviet life and ideas.) The ensuing duet with Paula and Harry is androgynous, tender, matter-of-fact. It contains a gestural conversation that takes place in front of two TV monitors, which open like a book to show the Cyrillic alphabet on typewriter keys and children's hands wiping away crayon marks as soon as they're made. Later we see Harry's figure on the screen dancing in a circle, blotted out by darkness every few seconds, while I read a quote from Tamara Karsavina about a performance in which Nijinsky did a spectacular suspended leap and disappeared from the stage. Then the real Harry leaps into the space, improvises a solo of Harry being Harry or Harry being Nijinsky, and Paula rolls on to do a final solo. Before that, the image of Paula has rolled on in another version in darkness: a car tire with a small TV monitor embedded in its center, showing Paula's face. As the tire rolls back out, the face miraculously stays upright while the tire-with-TV is turning. (This was my collaborator Cathy Weis's ingenious invention.)

The trio begins with another short video segment. Then the stage lights bump up. With the first two hits of the cowbell of Andy's score, Lisa, MJ, and I blink our eyes twice before launching into the dancing. The movement and shapes are hard-edged, and there is a rough but easily discernible relationship between the material we all do. The music provides a driving continuity and, like the dancing, seems to be clogged with rocks or pebbles. There's a brief section in which three relatively innocent people (non-dancers) enter and partner us according to written instructions. (The "three new people" change every night; they have had one fifteen-minute rehearsal.) They have a nicely uncertain performance manner next to our confident, churning-out-the-phrase style.

The way I started work on the trio was to make a phrase and show it to Lisa and MJ and ask them to do their personal variations of it. This is an idea I've used before: it means incorporating misperceptions and miscoordinations into the phrase as well as intentional deviations. I decided to keep composing this way until it led somewhere else. The day that Lisa's and MJ's variations slid into linking arms was the day the piece took off. After that, the joinings, separations and orderings seemed to fall into place. Non-arduous decisions were made by all three of us. The various schemes I used for organizing movement became less significant, and the yield from them fit into a context. Although the video and dancing interrupt each other, and the movement is self-interrupting, the piece as it goes from event to event seems not to be manipulated but to just occur. This is accomplished with the aid of the music, on which I worked closely with Andy Blinx. Andy mapped out all the events in time (naming them in his way, which was a small revelation to me). We had worked together before and share an understanding about abrupt and gradual changes in time.

The span of eight performances we had been invited to do at Dance Theatre Workshop (DTW) was another time problem. The usual commitment is four, unless you go on tour. I wanted to keep the piece alive by having an element that was not fully under my control. I also wanted to include people in

Instructions for Three New People
For Standard Deviation

February 1984

You will begin the piece backstage left and wait till about six minutes into the piece until MJ leaves the stage and comes to get you.

1. Enter in single file behind your partner. (Lisa Bush, MJ Becker, or W. Perron will be designated as your partner.) Do what she does. The six of us form a horizontal line on a track upstage.
2. When your partner arrives in place and all six are in, we all face front. Now the moves get more complex and you'll be looking to your right to be able to see and imitate your partner.
3. When she starts jumping straight up and down, partner her in some way.
4. When she returns to the complex movements, wind her up like a doll from behind.
5. When she starts running forward and backward (downstage and upstage) stay close to her while you are also turning yourself.
6. When she starts "Wonder Woman" (to be demonstrated), do whatever you think is the opposite of what she's doing.
7. When she jogs downstage at the end of "Wonder Woman," follow her, but DO NOT GO TO THE FLOOR when she does.
8. Instead, do what you remember from what you've already done while you drift upstage back to the original horizontal track.
9. After we do the "Mermaid Falls," we stand up by making sudden jerks. You will react to each jerk of your partner as though it is an electric shock.
10. When we start "Puppet Stiffs," which travels a little more in space, you walk side-to-side according to the horizontal directions of your partner, but staying in the same horizontal track. Slide past the other two new people when necessary. Stay accurately in the same right-to-left place in the space as your partner. There will eventually be a pile-up stage left.
11. Black-out. Wait a few seconds to get oriented, then exit. Wendy exits with you. Lisa and MJ stay onstage.
12. After about six minutes, the piece ends. Let the three of us take a bow, then you join us for one bow.

This whole section lasts only three minutes, so everything is pretty fast. Have fun. There is no such thing as a mistake, except laughing.—Wendy another way, less intense than the long haul, as I had been included in performances of Yoshiko Chuma, Johanna Boyce, and Daryl Chin. The "three new people" was a solution to both problems, plus it had the added benefit of giving us new faces backstage each night.

I approached the duet completely differently and much later. I only knew that I wanted Harry and Paula to dance together. Harry is buoyant and baroque, with an infectious energy; Paula has a kind of exotic, laconic quality. I kept thinking of the duet as a moonwalk; I didn't want to give in to the dreamy feeling I got when I pictured it. To work against that, I made specific tasks for them to do—like the gestural conversation, which was built on a passage from *Waiting for Godot*. Another task is the "Help no Help" section, in which Paula staggers around and Harry hovers over her, but when she finally falls, he disappears. There's a two-minute section that takes place in a tight square of light that is both plain and beautiful. It is a series of helping/hindering motions, still task-like, but very focused on each other. Having no music, the duet has no obvious continuity, and the decision of how to connect things was nerve-wracking for all of us.

The problem with the duet is that it is still in sections. A section just means you come to the end of an idea. I like to push myself further, to make each ending a beginning. I admire the seamlessness of some people's work: Trisha Brown's, Susan Rethorst's, Sally Silvers's group work. One thing follows another (as Yvonne Rainer used to remind herself). When I watch dancers, this is the most pleasing aspect—time passing. I like seeing how the choreographer and dancers conceive (of) time.

Shoot for the Moon, but Don't Aim Too Hard

VanityFair.com, April 2010

J. D. Salinger's books have always been my favorites to read and reread. I decided to write him a letter in 1982, knowing full well of his reclusive nature. But like many of his readers, I felt I knew him—or knew Holden, or Buddy, or Zooey, or Phoebe. It was a pleasant shock to receive a letter in reply. At the time, I thought the reason for his warmth toward me was because I told him about my family, complete with suicidal brother. But it may equally have been because I was a dancer. I do think he had a special place in his heart—and in his stories—for dancers, a place of innocence.

At some point when we were hanging out, I promised him that I would never say or write anything about him publicly, and he trusted me. That was just part of the bargain of knowing him. So it was with all kinds of ambivalence that I sought to publish this little memoir after he died. I asked myself (and my husband) the question: Does a promise extend beyond death? Ultimately I thought it would be a good thing and might dispel some of the damaging effects of other, more intimate stories about Salinger. I wanted to offer up my experience of him as a basically decent, if wildly contradictory, person. So I decided to write down—keeping my own mixed reactions to him intact—my memory of that friendship.

One nice follow-up: I recently met a Columbia student who wrote her senior thesis on the role of dance in Catcher in the Rye *after coming across this story when surfing the web.*

This is the only part of Section III that was not written in the eighties, but is about the eighties—just as I put my memoir about the sixties into "The Sixties" even though it was written much later.

The first thing I noticed was the look of fear in his eyes. We were meeting at the Drake Hotel in Manhattan, and for a moment I thought I had spotted the wrong guy. But he was the only man standing alone in the lobby.

I had written him, and he had responded within a week that my letter was a "tonic," that he wanted to "plunge into daily, if not hourly, correspondence," and that he wanted to see me dance. He signed the last page with initials only, and typed over them, claiming that he was paranoid about writing his full name. That was December 1982, when I was thirty-five and on leave from my job on the dance faculty of Bennington College in Vermont. Five months and several letters later, we were finally meeting.

When I read *Catcher in the Rye* in the sixth grade, I felt that Holden was just like my brother Tommy. The massive dissatisfaction, the restlessness, the inability to behave as expected, the brilliant spins of sarcasm, and the urge to puncture the pretensions of others were the same. And this: the constant lying, which sprang partly from evasion and partly from sheer excess of imagination. I'd been drafting letters to J. D. Salinger in my head for a long time. And then, six years after my brother killed himself at age thirty, I finally wrote.

I had an older brother, too, who was Seymour-like. This scholarly brother (who also went to college at fifteen) took Tommy and me under his wing, sharing his love for poetry, theater, and music. And redheaded Phoebe was like one of my two little sisters. So I had an eerie sense of familiarity with Salinger's characters. But I also loved the way, when you're reading him, you can burst out laughing in the midst of melancholy. In my first letter I tried to put into words what his books had meant to me.

I think Jerry responded out of sympathy, but also because I was a dancer (and had no ambitions to be a writer). After all, Bessie and Les, the Glass parents, had been vaudeville performers. And whenever Holden dances in *Catcher*—either breaking into a tap routine when horsing around or slow dancing with his kid sister—his depression lifts a little. Salinger seems to hold a special place for dancing as he does for childhood: they are two realms that are not lousy with phonies.

I don't know what I was hoping for when I sent off that first letter. After a few back-and-forths, the expectations built up on both sides. Even though Jerry was my parents' age, I was wondering what he looked like and waiting anxiously for his letters. But after lunch at the Drake, I was both relieved and disappointed to find him not particularly attractive. So it was all set in my mind that we would just be friends. And yet the next day I was hoping he would call and excited that I might see him again. I thought he was a beautiful soul trapped in an awkward body and personality. I speculated that perhaps he became a recluse because readers who cherished the wit and soulfulness of the author J. D. Salinger would be disillusioned when they met the man.

I was all over the map about this guy. "I don't know what I want from my correspondence with him," I wrote in my diary. "I do know I want to be able to talk with him. Not once, but all the time." I stayed up nights writing more letters that I never sent—that were unfit to send. Even the rough draft of my first letter had been too gushy ("Thank you, thank you, thank you forever"), and a friend of mine had scaled it back.

That look of fear disappeared when Jerry was on his own turf. He was comfortable in his house, on his grounds, in his community in Cornish, New Hampshire. We once went to see a film on the nearby Dartmouth campus. He had arranged to connect with a woman there and exchange homeopathic remedies. He wasn't timid or antisocial at all—except that he was partially deaf and happy not to hear what most people were saying.

In fact, I was the timid one, and that made him angry. One afternoon when we walked in the wooded area near his house, his dogs—two or three of them—trailed behind us or scouted ahead. I heard a hideous crunching noise, and realized that one of the dogs was chewing something. I asked what she was eating, and Jerry said, "Oh, Rosie just caught a chipmunk." Seeing me recoil, he scolded me: "Don't let it press your buttons." He wanted me to be more disciplined, tougher, more Zen-like.

Another evening we were watching a television program in which a preppy young man turned out to be a murderer. There was nothing redeeming in this show. It seemed to me not only violent but stupid, and I asked Jerry to change the channel. He was disgusted by my squeamishness and forced me to watch it, implying that it would be good for me. I have to admit I get panicky with media violence, and I was a wreck by the end of the show. I later promised him that this "TV phobia episode" would never be repeated. But I was surprised that he would waste his time or mine on such an unedifying show. I think he was so incensed by my avoidance of violence—I didn't know then that he had fought on the front lines during World War II—that he was determined to rub my face in it.

We also had arguments about politics. He said he hated the Soviet Union because he never got paid for *Catcher* being published there. He said Communism was "the opiate of the intellectuals." Since I was a Russophile, I told him how much I loved the Russian spirit anyway. He also denigrated some of the contemporary women writers I admired, saying they were competent but too concerned with their careers.

But we had some nice times, and one of them was when he set up his projector and large movie screen—much bigger than the usual home screen. In the days before DVDs, before VHS, the only films people showed in their living rooms were home movies. No one actually owned a copy of a Hollywood feature. But Jerry did. He had a large collection to pick from, and we watched *Knight Without Armour* (1937), all cozy under blankets (in separate chairs). That night he offered his daughter's bedroom for me to sleep in and was a perfect gentleman. He never made any move remotely like a pass. Still, I had a restless night: I dreamt that Jerry looked like Marlon Brando and that we were being chased and held at gunpoint like Marlene Dietrich and Robert Donat in the movie.

After that weekend, I started missing him. In my diary I called him "my knight, my fantasy man. . . . What I want most is the opportunity to get sick of him." But I didn't want him to get sick of me. I tried not to do anything that would get me labeled a "dope," a "phony," or a "cliché." It was a strain. A week or two later, I wrote, "I don't want to throw myself at him, but I'm deathly afraid he won't see me again or even write to me. I think we are soul mates. Is that completely far-fetched?"

Jerry was tickled by the fact that my aunt and uncle lived in the next town over, Cornish Flat, and he once picked me up there in his jeep. We had dinner at a local restaurant, and he polished off the meal with a big piece of chocolate cake. Later, at his house, after using the bathroom, he announced that he had gotten rid of the cake. "I'm not going to let that poison stay in my body," he said indignantly. And yet he kept stashes of chocolate bars in the refrigerator door.

He almost came to see me dance twice. In one letter, he volunteered to attend a performance of my solo in Sherbrooke, Canada, but then wrote, "Not sure." It was the only time he was not sure of anything. Although he liked the idea of my being a dancer, he was appalled when I would stretch my head and neck in a public place, which was an unconscious habit of mine. Dance, to him, was something totally innocent. (Remember what a good dancer Holden's sister was? And Jane Gallagher, the sad girl in *Catcher* who wouldn't move her kings out of the back row, took ballet lessons.) When I told Jerry that I liked watching Merce Cunningham because you could see him thinking when he danced, he stated categorically that dancing and thinking were two separate things. That pretty much put a pall on any further conversations about my line of work. He did express interest in the hoofer "Honi" Coles, however, and I offered to get us tickets to see him in *My One and Only*. Jerry declined. Undaunted, I sent him Arlene Croce's book on Fred Astaire and Ginger Rogers.

Jerry didn't make it to Sherbrooke, but I had friends drive me down to Cornish so I could visit him afterward. He showed me the Royal typewriter he used, which he had bought in 1948. He also pulled out the safe where he kept his current manuscripts. He said he wrote every morning, starting at six or seven. He drank only liquids until 11:30, when he would take a break and eat oatmeal. I don't know if he spent the rest of the day writing. I do know that his fictional characters were more real to him than flesh and blood. In discussing writer's block, he said he was "far more likely to block up about living people." He was endlessly interested in where his fictional characters would take him—in awe of them, really. He marveled at how patiently a fictional character waits, sometimes years, for a writer to "re-seat himself."

The next morning we drove to the local airport in Lebanon and took a small plane to New York. He asked the flight attendant if we could sit in the front seat, where there was more legroom, and she said no—at which point he said, "I hate everybody." He said it helplessly, not hatefully. I don't often have headaches, but I got one on the plane, and Jerry showed me how to press a spot at the base of the thumb to get rid of it. When that didn't work, he offered me a little homeopathy pill. When I balked, he in*sist*ed that I take it.

Although he was heavy-handed about many things, he could be light-hearted too. In the cab from LaGuardia into Manhattan, just before I got out, he tapped the sole of my shoe with the tip of his umbrella and said, "We'll see each other again." Sometimes he called me "Old Haircut," because on one visit I had just gotten a too-short trim and was self-conscious.

In his letters he referred to himself as an insufferable crab or boor. He apologized elaborately for denigrating artists I admired (Leonard Bernstein, Gertrude Stein, Meryl Streep), but he still railed against them. When he began a sentence with "When I was younger and nuttier," I was amused to note that he believed he had made some headway in the normalcy department.

I used to carry chopsticks with me because I didn't like using metal utensils. Once, after a meal at a restaurant, I asked him which of us was more eccentric. Without missing a beat, he said something like, "You, hands down." We had a good chuckle over that one. But he wasn't nearly as playful in person as he was in his letters.

I loved all four of his books and had read them many times, so I was always asking him questions. I once asked him something about the scene in *Seymour: An Introduction* when Buddy is playing marbles and Seymour tells him to try not aiming so much. Jerry replied that he didn't remember what the final version was, which surprised me. Maybe he was brushing me off because he just didn't want to talk about his books. When I asked him if he was from a large family, he told me he had only one sister, six years his senior. Then it seemed even more amazing that his sibling scenes were so stirring.

In my first letter, I asked if there was any new fiction in the works. He answered that he would publish, but didn't know when. In person, however, he told me he hated the whole process so much—he claimed it would interfere with his work—that he would not publish again in his lifetime. He didn't want his son, Matthew, to be burdened with the task after he died, so he was looking for a wife. (It then dawned on me why he was so enthusiastic to meet me.)

He talked with great affection about the characters he was continuing to develop in his new work—they were all the same wunderkinds we know from the Glass family. He said, for instance, that he "gave" Boo Boo an interest in astrology. I think Jerry really followed his own advice, which was: "Once you've found a treasure, you just keep going."

I could never tell him how much I loved his writing. Whenever I travel, I have to practically force myself to pack a non-Salinger book, because I would always rather reread *Catcher, Franny and Zooey, Nine Stories*, or *Raise High the Roof Beam, Carpenters and Seymour: An Introduction* for the twelfth time. Even to myself, I couldn't articulate why they meant so much to me. But with my last reading of *Catcher*, just after Jerry died, my sense is that it is all about loss; it makes one feel intensely about the loved ones who have passed on. Holden *seems* to be going through a rebellious adolescent phase, but his behavior, his malaise, stems from the death of his brother Allie. He loves the person who has left this earth, and he can't bear anything that's still here. Except for another sibling, his kid sister, Phoebe. When she brings her suitcase to meet Holden because she wants to run away with him, it just kills me. In all Salinger's writing, the greatest love scenes—and love thoughts—are between siblings.

We sometimes talked about romantic love—in an abstract way. On his wall I believe there was a quote that read, "Love is a journey into the unknown." He had a nice definition of love: it's when the mere sight of a person makes you happy. He didn't really believe in love on this earth, however. (Maybe the word "unknown" was code for "extraterrestrial.") But when I asked him if he had any regrets, lack of love was the first thing he mentioned. In the case of a possible relationship between us, I think any glimmers of romance faded early.

During that period, while on leave from my teaching job, I was trying to decide whether to go back to Bennington or to stay in New York and choreograph. Jerry was not the best at listening to a personal dilemma, but he said something I'll never forget: "Why don't you just shoot for the moon."

Sound familiar? In *Seymour*, Seymour tells Buddy that the two questions he will be asked when he dies are these: *Were most of your stars out? Were you busy writing your heart out?* (Italics are Salinger's.)

We rarely talked about literature, but he recommended two of his favorite novels: Turgenev's *A Sportsman's Sketches* and *The Old Wives' Tale*, by Arnold Bennett. And he jotted down on a piece of paper two other books: Buber's *Tales of the Hasidim* and *Chichikov's Journeys*, by Gogol, translated by Guerney.

He also gave me three slim books on or by Bhagavan Sri Ramana Maharshi, a guru whom he called "the real thing." He wanted to cultivate my potential for "non-duality," but he was not a stellar example of it himself. He seemed to feel very separate from other living beings and was compulsively critical about almost everything. The only non-dual part of him was his ambivalence about certain things, like movies. He bashed them yet couldn't live without them. I could see the contradictions at the core of his being, but I still sort of loved him. One of my diary entries said, "Jerry doesn't have beautiful eyes, but he wrote those beautiful books."

His spirituality came through in a more poetic way on the page than in his didactic push for nonduality. I wasn't crazy about Zooey's long-winded explanations about the Jesus prayer. But I responded to the little epiphany of his telling Franny that their mother's chicken soup is consecrated—and to the big epiphany at the end, that "Seymour's Fat Lady" was really Christ. It brought the divine down to earth. And Salinger brought the divine to art. In *Seymour*, he talks about the painter and the poet being the only ones who are true seers.

In one letter Jerry complimented my writing, but when I thanked him for encouraging me, he said he hadn't meant that at all. He meant something "with less woof in it"; he surely wasn't wishing publishers and readers on me. And yet he damned performing more than publishing. The arts that are done for immediate applause, he wrote, are "the most terrible of all." Knowing you're good at something tainted the purity of it.

Our correspondence trailed off in late 1983, soon after I got involved in a real romance. A couple of years later, when I was in Vermont and planning to drive over to Cornish Flat to see my relatives, I called his home. A woman answered, and when Jerry got on the phone, I asked if I could visit the next day. Instead of making up vague excuses, he simply said he didn't feel very "visitable." I didn't try to find out if that was a temporary or permanent condition. I always meant to write him one last time to say that I still loved every sentence he ever wrote (and published). But I didn't. I never bothered him again.

IV The Nineties

Over the years I became increasingly bothered by how critics handle (and possibly abuse) their authority. When I wrote "Beware the Egos of Critics" in 1991, I wanted to drive home the point that critics are as subjective as artists in what they bring to the public. No matter how much a writer tries to clean the slate before the curtain goes up, each has a certain perspective.

But of course I was a critic too. I was contributing occasionally to the *Village Voice* again (including my first international ballet reviews—on the Paris Opéra Ballet and the Kirov Ballet) while still working on choreographic projects.

My life changed irrevocably in 1995. In an inexplicable accident, my husband got up off the sofa in our living room, crashed into a wall, and fell to the floor, hitting his neck on the sofa leg. He sustained a spinal cord injury that paralyzed him from the neck down for about a week; it then "resolved" into permanent nerve damage all over his body. He could walk, but he was so impaired that he had to go on disability. I spent about six months doing nothing but helping him at home. Then, because I had to support my little family, I worked part-time at the peace organization that I had been volunteering for, Physicians for Social Responsibility. And I got short-stint teaching gigs here and there.

I also produced a full-evening work sponsored by the Lincoln Center Festival in 1997. For this piece, I pulled together seven young dancers, four of my previous performers who were now downtown "stars," fifteen students from the LaGuardia High School of Performing

Arts, and eight subway musicians. As I said earlier, I was becoming a gatherer as much as a choreographer.

And something else affected me in the nineties: I learned how to use a word processor. Miraculously, when I worked on a computer I did not get the pre-spasm burning in my upper back that had plagued me when I used a typewriter. So writing became physically more doable, thereby pointing the way to a future. As my dance career was waning, my journalistic career was waxing.

This happened in a decisive way in 1999. I was rehearsing with Sara Rudner, Risa Jaroslow, and Wendy Rogers for the twenty-fifth anniversary of the five-hour piece we had made together under Sara's baton, as it were. Thrilled to be working with them all again, I threw caution to the winds and made a "stomping variation" of one of the phrases. After that session of jabbing my legs into the ground, my back went into spasm (no surprise), so I spent much of the remaining rehearsal time lying down. I was so disgusted with myself, and so in love with this project, that I resolved to participate in another way. Hey, maybe I could write about it! I called my old pal John Rockwell, who at that time was editor of Arts & Leisure at the *New York Times*, and asked if I could write something about Sara and our mini reunion. He loved Sara's dancing too and accepted the idea on the spot. Thus began a fruitful association with the *Times* where I could pitch a story and have it taken seriously.

Beware the Egos of Critics

Village Voice, April 9, 1991

This tirade was part of a series initiated by Voice *theater editor Ross Wetzsteon called "Crritic!" In his opening salvo, Ross said he chose that title because that word, spelled this way, had been the ultimate insult—one notch beyond "Cretin!"—uttered by Estragon in Samuel Beckett's* Waiting for Godot. *He went on to talk about the growing unease between critics and artists. It was the first time I saw anyone say in print that the critic's attitude "refuses to acknowledge the power critics possess." He started the series as a way to open a dialogue.*

I had been stewing over the situation with dance critics for some time, so I jumped in and offered my two cents—even though the series was aimed at the Off-Broadway theater community and not necessarily at dance people.

When I wrote this in 1991, I felt more identified with performers and less with critics, so I was angry at "the critics." But now that I write and edit reviews regularly, I can understand both sides—though I still believe, like Ross did back then, that many critics do not own up to the power they wield. (More on that topic in "A Debate on Snark," Section VII.)

The critic always has the last word. There is no time, no place, no etiquette for an artist to respond. Your performance is a fleeting memory, but the critic's work is in black and white. Not only does it last longer, but it may well reach more people. If the review contains a distortion that gnaws at your insides, you learn to live with it. If it contains a factual error, that goes down in history.

In the seventies critics were often called parasites. Being a reviewer at the time—I wrote regularly for the *SoHo Weekly News*—I defended critics. The challenge of putting one's responses into words is stimulating, and the really good critics go beyond that: they give us a glimpse of why a performance can be relevant or revelatory. Criticism of the arts is necessary, and I don't think critics are parasites on artists any more than historians are parasites on wars. But after twenty years of choreographing, I have this to say: nothing I have done is more difficult than choreography. Existentially and intestinally, it is quite a different project than writing criticism. The charge of art is to create something from nothing. Critics can be edifying, educational, and even inspiring, but they have not dedicated their lives to the mind-boggling task of making art. So the condescending tone that some critics take is entirely, but entirely, inappropriate.

If a critic wants to be catty or careless about a movie star or rock singer, their opinions can be cute or malicious or eloquent, but it stops there. Sinead O'Connor might confess to feeling hurt by critics, but her career doesn't suffer. The dance world has drastically different economics. There is very little money and very little sponsorship because there is very little audience because there is very little familiarity built up in our education. A negative or mixed review can squelch interest from all quarters. Most critics, as Ross Wetzsteon suggested ("Crritic! A Proposal of Modesty," *Village Voice*, January 29), do not own up to their role in the making and breaking of careers. In dance, the bottom line is that our field is economically too marginal to withstand continually bad public relations.

Naturally no critic wants to do PR. The value of their work lies in their independence of mind. But there are other circumstances that make inroads into this purist stance. For instance, if a choreographer is dying of AIDS, or if a little-known international troupe has a culturally significant history, a fair-minded critic will weigh these factors. It is good and healthy to see a critic write a compassionate, socially aware review. I submit that part of that social awareness could be a recognition of the precariousness of dance and dancers in our society, a society where everything must be bought to be measured. Whether the critic imagines her/his primary responsibility to be to the public, the artist, the art form itself, or his/her own fulfillment, it behooves the critic to approach the subject with more tolerance, depth, and pleasure than we've been seeing.

It sometimes seems that critics today are out for the kill. Certain critics who may be fed up with the field go to a performance they know they won't like so they can sink their teeth into tender flesh. Every couple of years, for instance, a critic for an uptown magazine goes downtown and cleans up, lashing out at everything in her path. To the victims, it seems like a wilding attack—unprovoked and inevitable. To the readers, it may seem searingly honest. But do the readers know the critic's state of mind? Do they know that the critic is working on a book and resents being pulled away? Do they know if a critic is annoyed with his seating arrangement, or if a relative was rejected at an audition for the choreographer being reviewed?

There is no objectivity in looking at art, which of course is one of the infinitely wonderful things about it. Critics know this and revel in their individuality, just as we do. But the power of print brings with it the illusion of objectivity, and this must be dealt with honestly by each critic. Dance seems to be more subjective than other arts, not only because its métier is human movement—so personal and so much room for interpretation—but also because it is ephemeral. Dance leaves no traces that can be researched or pondered. Yes, there are Labanotation scores and videos, but both are sketchy documents. No museum or library can house choreography itself. An art, literature, or music critic can go somewhere and read the books, see the paintings, or hear the music. But a dance critic has to depend even more on instincts—and memory.

The narcissism of performers is well known. We have our different brands of it, and it's up there on the stage in our flesh and joints, in our every move. The narcissism of critics is hidden, safely tucked away. But it's there, in between the lines of the review, shaping their opinions. Early on in an artist's career, she or he realizes that a review is often more revealing about its writer than about its subject. In some circles, dancers spice up their pre-rehearsal chatter with potshot analyses of the critics' personal problems.

Here are some of the ways that a critic's ego can get in the way:

1. Because they don't want to admit gaps in their knowledge, they assume a familiarity with the work that is unwarranted and misleading.

2. They want to be important, so they construct an opinion that will cause a stir. They can loudly debunk a highly respected artist or blow the horn of discovery on a new young presence. Both tactics tend to produce unbalanced reviews and the critic has to eat his or her words in subsequent reviews.

3. They cannot afford to doubt themselves in print, so they ignore complexities that don't lend themselves to verbalization. (This is not the same as simplifying or reducing to accommodate editorial needs.) You almost never see a critic thinking out loud in print, "Maybe there was more to it than I thought, maybe I should go back a second time."

4. They engage in critic wars. They sometimes respond more fiercely to what their personal enemy has said in print than to what they see in performance. The more Critic A waxes sublime over Artist X, the more Critic B treats X like scum, and vice versa. Both extremes are, of course, unjustified, but they serve to fuel the competitiveness. And the artist becomes a pawn in their wars.

The pronouncements of reviewers sometimes seem so random to me that I've developed a hunch—and I hope someone writes in to say I'm dead wrong. Here's my scenario: knowing the economic necessity of filling a large house like City Center or New York State Theater, a critic feels pressure to praise, or at least to minimize the weaknesses of a company performing there. After a few nights of this, she/he, perhaps unconsciously, feels a bit of a relief. The next company, in a smaller venue and with less at stake financially, is expendable. I don't have to be nice, the critic thinks, there isn't that much riding on it, and I want to show that I have standards.

My plea is that critics write a balanced review in all cases. Further, I think, it's necessary to address the dual nature of dance: dance is a thing of the moment, and dance is a thing of history. Or, more crudely put, dance is both entertainment and art. So the questions "What was it like?" and "What does it contribute to the field?" must both be answered.

Some critics can only write primarily in historical terms, others can only say what happened at the moment. Some write well if they can find an all-encompassing metaphor but are incapable of describing style or texture (they don't know that the "how" in dance can be more telling than the "what"). Some write only in consumerist terms (does *New York* magazine *demand* crassness and negativism from its writers because that's how they sell magazines?). It's a continual disappointment for a serious choreographer to be described to the public by any one of these critics. Daniel Nagrin once told me he thought reviews should be written by committee. Considering the blind spots of some critics, I think that's a good idea.

I realize that dance criticism is an embattled field—that there are struggles with unenlightened editors, limited space, few opportunities. And, to be sure, there is that "resounding silence" of the performing artists that Wetzsteon recently mentioned in this space.

The "Crritic!" series can begin to take the edge off that silence. I envision a continuation of this series, to be published on a regular basis, perhaps entitled Critic Watch, in which individual artists can respond to individual critics. They could correct errors, address distortions, express appreciation, or initiate dialogue. And then no one would have the last word.

Trisha Brown on Tour

Dancing Times 86, no. 1028, May 1996

I had written an advance article on Trisha Brown for the New York Times Arts & Leisure section that was ultimately "killed." The assignment fell between two editors who didn't communicate clearly with each other. That was the first time I approached Arts & Leisure (well before John Rockwell was its editor). They had accepted the pitch and made the assignment with a warning: "Ask Trisha the hard questions." I guess they weren't hard enough because the story was pulled at the very last minute. I was devastated. So when the venerable editor of London's Dancing Times, Mary Clarke, asked me for a feature pegged to Trisha's tour of England, I was more than ready to comply. David Vaughan, author and archivist at the Merce Cunningham Dance Company, who had recommended me to Clarke, encouraged me to "cannibalize" the article that never saw the light of day.

During the heyday of the Grand Union, the legendary dance improvisation group of the early seventies, Steve Paxton would occasionally take up the microphone, and, very softly, tell the story of Trisha the Wild Child: "Trisha grew up in a forest; she made friends with the coyotes, slept in trees, and could foretell the weather. By age seven, her teeth were broken and stained with blackberry juice." The story was embellished differently each time, and as was the custom in the Grand Union, it was sheer fabrication based on solid suspicion. Trisha Brown's connection to nature, her prescience, and her relish for adventure have served her well as a choreographer.

When Brown improvised in the sixties, it was not uncommon to see her stop dead in her tracks and drop to the ground, hurtle through the air, or sit still so long that she seemed to disappear. She was, in her words, "practicing not knowing what I was about to do." She seemed able to be rebellious and peaceful in the same moment. Her choreographic project addressed how to preserve these moments, or, put in a more general way, how to adapt the essential wildness of improvising to the slightly tamer art of choreography.

The solution, for Brown, lay not in the accepted theme-and-variations format of mainstream modern dance. As part of Judson Dance Theater in the early sixties, she experimented with game-like rules, the collapsibility of the body, and ways to involve the audience. In the seventies she focused on simple clear structures that allowed her to build a movement style and vocabulary. Her "equipment pieces" defied gravity while exploring physical mechanics and perceptual illusion (e.g., using harnesses to walk on the wall) so that the viewer feels like she's looking down on people walking on

The exhilarating *Set and Reset* (1983) with Trisha Brown in the foreground.
This photo is from the 1990s. (© Chris Callis)

a sidewalk far below. She was always looking for ways of subverting expectation. Her love of the outdoors took her to rooftops, lakes, and trees, where she ingeniously fit the human figure into the landscape. In each case she was attended by rapturous, incredulous, and small audiences. Witnessing a performance of this kind, one's sense of place and possibility was inevitably expanded.

In the eighties Brown became known for her collaborations with artists of international stature: Laurie Anderson, Robert Ashley, Nancy Graves, Don Judd, Robert Rauschenberg, Lina Wertmuller. She welcomes the artistic interference. "These are always fateful, riskful situations," she says. "It makes a larger picture. There are two or three of us and we're carving up the culture one way or another, independently and together. That's larger than what I would do on my own."

Brown met with some controversy in this step to expand. There are those who prefer the intimacy and single focus of the earlier work in galleries, lofts, and outdoors. But she has not lost her sense of place: she and her collaborators approach the proscenium stage as an architectural or philosophical challenge. For *Set and Reset* (1983), Rauschenberg replaces the wings with transparent fabric so that the dancers are visible backstage, thus asking the question of when they are, and when are they not, performing.

In the ensuing years, Brown enjoyed a steadily growing audience, consistent critical acclaim, and an international touring schedule that places her in the top five most sought-after American modern dance companies. She has won two Guggenheim fellowships, a MacArthur Foundation Fellowship (known as a "genius award"), a *Dance Magazine* award, the Brandeis Award, two New York Dance and Performance Awards (the "Bessies"), and the Chevalier des Arts et des Lettres from France.

Even more impressive is her continuing influence on the dance field. Her loping, swooping movement style has been imitated endlessly in downtown New York and in Europe. She cultivates a soft, relaxed stance, offering a new look to rival the pristine verticality of Cunningham and the stylish versatility of Tharp. The bodies of her dancers are just as ready to spring into the air as to collapse to the floor. In the seventies younger choreographers tried to emulate her simplicity, wit, and repose; in the eighties and nineties they're going for the physical fluidity and daring, and a structural complexity that hovers on the edge of chaos. It is the general consensus that Brown, with her exquisite articulation in the joints and the unusual path of an impulse traveling through the body, has given us a new prototype of virtuosity. As dance critic Mindy Aloff wrote in *The Nation*, "Trisha Brown is a source, a foundation." In downtown New York there are many classes and workshops that mine this new virtuosity. This winter, the Trisha Brown Company moved to bright new studios in midtown and started consolidating occasional workshops into a schedule of ongoing classes. [Update: Weekly classes are now held at Dance New Amsterdam downtown.]

Having danced in Brown's company for nearly three years, I have a certain familiarity with her preoccupations, but I've learned never to assume what her next move will be. Since I left the company in 1978, I've been surprised over and over by her new directions. It has often taken two or three viewings of a new work for me to absorb the newness and relate it to her previous repertoire. When I heard she was doing a piece to Bach, and working closely with the music—I was surprised once again. And yet, it made sense to me. I feel that Bach's spirituality emerges from the small changes between the notes—no heroics or bombast, just a radiant interest in what happens next. I have always felt that Trisha is the Bach of dance. When I finally saw *M.O.* (for "Musical Offering," but also for "Modus Operandi," 1994), the sound of the harpsichord seemed to imprint itself on the dance, giving it a formal, almost restrained quality compared to her usual freewheeling look. But about halfway through, the appearance of one new dancer changes everything. She seems to be lost, wandering through the dance, looking every which way. The dancer is Diane Madden, the same one who jogged figure 8s endlessly through *For MG: The Movie* (1991). Eventually there is a prolonged moment of stillness and silence that coincides with an almost beatific brightening of the lights. Madden's character, perhaps a mother looking for her child, seems suddenly to accept everything and wash the whole stage in her acceptance. It's an intense moment, but if you spend the dance trying to figure out the relation of the dance to the music, you'll miss it.

Brown's 1994 solo, *If you couldn't see me*, is danced without ever facing the audience. It is a gently willful piece that presents an opportunity to see the workings of the body as remapped by Brown. Seeing dance from the back is usually the way dancers learn choreography. We can see more clearly her idea of movement traveling along the natural pathways of the body, and we see her finding new seams to fold on. It's also an opportunity to imagine, as Steve Paxton wrote in a letter to Brown that was published in *Contact Quarterly*, the upstage space in front of Brown as a "dimensionless depth." *If you* has the conceptual simplicity of her earlier work coupled with the loose-limbed elegance of later works.

The exhilarating *Set and Reset* (1983), on the other hand, is built not on a single idea, but has many layers. Although the typical Brownian rigor holds it together, I see it as a sublime anarchy of people and ideas. Laurie Anderson's alluring score gives it momentum and something else—a kind of nostalgia. I could swear there's a point when a mother's voice calls her child to dinner. The dance is so dense with elusive movement that I had to see it several times before I realized that it is embedded with simple actions like running and walking. With the ghostlike set by Rauschenberg, the slippery partnering, and the mercurial group formations, one can watch *Set and Reset* through a different lens each time.

Brown has her own ideas of how to view her dances. "I would like my audience to look through the dance to see the dance. I'm playing with where the energy is going. I'm purposely deflecting and re-entering the focus." This device can add to the excitement but also to the difficulty of viewing her work. Because some people do find her work difficult, I asked Brown if she could give any clues for people seeing her work for the first time. She said, "It's like seeing a very fine fabric. If you look closely you can see a particular thread that's present throughout, but you don't see it at first because it's not as bright a color or placed in as broad a patch. Everything is in full view, but woven in such a way that you have to really look to see the pattern."

Also woven into her dances are references to her previous work. In *Set and Reset* she quotes from *Walking on the Wall* (1971). Before the dancing starts, one dancer is held high and horizontal by other dancers who enable her to mimic walking on an imaginary wall. And *If you couldn't see me* has its antecedent in the role of the dancer in *For MG: The Movie* (1991) who stands still with his back to the audience for the entire twenty-two-minute dance.

Brown's performers are galvanized by a heightened sense of readiness. In an interview in the *Drama Review*, she told Marianne Goldberg that performance, for her, "exists in the paradoxical state of diabolic concentration and a feeling of outgoingness. You screw something down so tight that when it's locked into position and the stage manager says 'Go,' everything is solid and tight and gleaming like metal. From that moment on it's breath and corpuscles and instinct." Spoken like a true daughter of coyotes.

American Dance Guild Concert Review

American Dance: The Official Publication of the American Dance Guild 40, no. 4 (Summer 1996)

For a few years I produced radio programs for WBAI, the Pacifica, listener-supported community radio station in New York City. Usually I interviewed artists, but I also occasionally wrote reviews and read them over the air—not my favorite way to do radio. This particular review later saw print in the American Dance Guild's newsletter. The theme of aging as a dancer is something I touched on before and will again.

There's a new trend brewing in the dance world and it's a very positive one. It's the trend toward accepting and even celebrating older dancers. On June 8, the American Dance Guild produced a concert called "Breaking the Age Barrier." All of the thirteen dances on the program, which was part of a three-day conference at NYU's School of Education, were choreographed and performed by dancers near or over the age of sixty.

The evening was a revelation not only of the rich resources we have in the dance world, but of the magic that can be created, not with the energy and virtuosity of youth, but with the deep knowledge of the expressive possibilities that come with age.

Although there were wonderful duets and group dances by Gus Solomons jr, Richard Bull, and Alice Teirstein and Stuart Hodes, I want to talk about some of the solos, because they distilled a certain character in each case. And, in each solo, the dancer and the dance were perfectly melded.

Carmen de Lavallade did a solo called *Willie's Ladies Sing the Blues*, which she made with Geoffrey Holder. De Lavallade was Alvin Ailey's first professional dancing partner—before he started his company, just to let you know how long she's been around. She's still drop-dead beautiful. Every little motion—the curling of a hand, the stretching of a leg—is so fully felt by her that it's fully understood by us. She has a juicy sensuality that she shapes with great control. She recited a text that takes a modern, sassy view of Shakespeare's women characters, reinforcing the proud, volatile womanliness that she projects with every fiber of her being.

Jamie Cunningham is impish and hilarious while looking for a lost contact lens in a piece from the seventies that is every bit as funny as I remember it, but with an added reference to a friend who died of AIDS. When he gets up from the floor to do a spoof of the *Dying Swan*, he's both playful and ethereal, and he's so willing to be vulnerable that I felt my eyes tearing as I was still laughing.

Deborah Jowitt, who writes on dance for the *Village Voice*, stood tall, perfectly at ease, and a little bit mischievous. Her talk-and-dance solo encapsulates her personal dance history, complete with instantly recognizable takeoffs of Anna Sokolow, Pauline Koner, and Martha Graham. Talking about her love of dancing, her eclectic dance experiences, and the frailty of her body, she said, "Perhaps I hadn't counted on aging." Mmmmm . . . I think I know what she means. She ended the dance by talking about Steve Paxton's idea of the "small dance," which is done by concentrating on the most subtle movements possible. She stood still, or so it seemed, and said, "I am dancing . . . right now." As the lights faded, we realized that there are many ways to dance.

Beverly Blossom's new piece showed how she can create a wacky kind of drama with nothing but a stuffed monkey and superb timing. She handled the monkey the way a ventriloquist uses a dummy. Her movements were spare, and when she turned her quizzical face to the audience, she held us with her deadpan stare.

The extremes of the concert were mapped out by Frances Alenikoff on the joyous end and Claudia Gitelman on the somber end. Alenikoff is in her mid-seventies and still dances in her own inimitable style—small, impulsive, elastic movements, with deep shivers of the body. In this piece she tells a story of a close brush with death, and to show how glad she is to be alive, she revels in the pleasures of her own body, like languid stretching and full-bodied laughing. She goes so over the top with her indulgences—sucking and chewing outrageously on her fingers and arms—that I think, if this were a different era, she might have been taken for a witch.

Claudia Gitelman was her dead opposite. In a stark piece called *Mother Destiny*, she enters carrying a bundle of long sticks on her back, like she's shouldering the weight of the world. She lets the sticks down, one by one, each in a different way . . . with love and longing in her arms. She continues her task until all the sticks are laid out in a big fan pattern, and then she trudges off. A job done, no glory, no thanks. Considering the title is *Mother Destiny*, the vision is dark and chilling.

The solos of these dancer/choreographers brought each artist into clear focus, and in doing so, created a specific portrait with universal appeal. Each characterization was pushed to the point of being an archetype. If Claudia Gitelman was the martyr, Frances Alenikoff was the hedonist. If Jamie Cunningham was the wit, Deborah Jowitt was the philosopher. Beverly Blossom was the absurdist, and Carmen de Lavallade was the woman who's all woman. But what made this evening especially moving was the dance spirit that each of these performers has, still burning like an eternal flame.

Love Is the Crooked Thing: Paris Opéra Ballet

Metropolitan Opera House, Lincoln Center

June 24 through July 3, 1996

Village Voice, July 30, 1996

When I started writing for the Voice *again, I wanted to challenge myself to write ballet reviews. I guess I was still smarting from what Doris Hering had said about my writing years before. I was grateful to Elizabeth Zimmer, who was editing the dance reviews at the* Voice, *for trusting me enough to let me cover this age-old, purely classical company— which I had never seen before.*

The Paris Opéra Ballet sets itself the double challenge of upholding its 335-year history in classical ballet and propelling itself into the future. *La Bayadère*, a Petipa ballet from 1877, seen here in a 1992 version by Rudolf Nureyev, the company's former director, is a three-hour marathon in which lavish sets and costumes outweigh fairly standard choreography and staging. But Isabelle Guérin, who plays the temple dancer Nikiya, is terrific. With her waterfall arms and supple legs and feet, her rich phrasing and sure dramatic instincts, she provides the emotional center of the performance. (Her costar, Laurent Hilaire, comes alive only when he has hard steps to do.) Although her utterly natural demeanor and convincing passion pull us through the story, the weak choreography does not blot out questions like "If this dance is set in India, why is there no hint of India in Minkus's music and only the most superficial flavor of India in the dancing?"

Le Parc, on the other hand, is stark, ominous, and ultimately satisfying. A product of the French experimental choreographer Angelin Preljocaj in 1994, it tethers a postmodern outlook to strong classical technique. Using various Mozart string and piano pieces and a cast of twenty-six, it progresses from social flirtation to sublime love. Thierry Leproust's set, an abstracted version of formal French gardens, includes three flat towers upstage against a threatening sky, and several slatted cages on high stems in the wings. The second act disperses these cage-trees, creating a geometrical forest that can be read as the cold, forbidding environment where seduction takes place in the era of AIDS.

A quartet of "gardeners" introduces each act. Wearing leather aprons and sunglasses but looking as if they have never touched soil, they set the tone and guide the action. Like the cubic trees, their arms move in geometrical shapes and rhythms. With hands alternating between fists and limp wrists, they embody both warrior and hairdresser, dancing to chilling sounds (ticking and trickling) by Goran Vejvoda that leave traces of unease on the Mozart that follows. Preljocaj brings an edginess to Mozart's phrasing by breaking the lines of the dancers' bodies.

The dancers have fun in the first act, both men and women wearing the same period costumes by Hervé Pierre—flared waistcoats, leggings to the knees, and pilgrim shoes. After elaborate seduction rituals, they tear around the stage in a wild game of musical chairs. Later the women wear doll-like dresses over huge crinolines. In a daft, wafting sequence, each one falls to the floor, deflating like a marshmallow beneath its burnt crisp. In another scene the women, in fetching underclothes and bare feet, wander into the "forest," each finding her own cage-tree. The men crawl in on all fours, obedient dogs or prowling bears, heralding the power of the women and promising an animal sensuality.

The star couple, Elisabeth Maurin and Manuel Legris, dance a wrenchingly ambivalent duet. He touches her and turns away; she slips away and he turns back, ardently caressing the empty space where she's been. Maurin is distrustful, hurting with desire. In the opening of the last act, the gardeners (maybe they are therapists now) tend to her desires, lifting and swirling her through her dreams. Finally, Maurin and Legris melt into each other again and again, finding ecstatic moments in their new intimacy.

Le Parc is carefully crafted and inventively staged. The Opéra dancers bring out its humor and daring beautifully, sustaining Preljocaj's jagged magic throughout.

Marmalade Me by Jill Johnston, Wesleyan University Press

Book review, *Village Voice*, February 24, 1998

In the late sixties I occasionally read Jill Johnston in the Village Voice. *Though I appreciated her out-there imagination, her writing seemed incoherent to me. It wasn't until I read the first edition of her collection,* Marmalade Me, *that I was captivated. She made no attempt at "objectivity" in her observations, but rather reveled in her subjectivity. You always knew her state of mind. As a dance writer, she gave license to be wild. I couldn't write like her, but she set a stellar example of someone who allowed her own circumstances and feelings to seep into her writing rather than putting distance between herself and her subject. She also gave vivid accounts of the legendary Judson Dance Theater in the early sixties, which I had become very interested in. In fact, I asked her to write an essay for the catalog I produced for the Bennington College Judson Project in the eighties and worked with her directly on it. Her sharpness, exquisitely articulate ambivalence, and her compulsion to tell were all still at a height. When* Marmalade Me *was reissued, I rushed to buy it—even though I still had my dilapidated copy from the original printing.*

Readers of Jill Johnston's columns in the *Village Voice* remember her as both a quintessential voice of the sixties and a brilliant dance critic. Wesleyan University Press has just issued a revised and expanded edition of *Marmalade Me*, her collection of review-searchings published in 1971. In edgy, trippy prose, she plunges into the Village scene: the dreamlike happenings, the innovative dance performances, and the flowering of gender politics. Seeing beauty in the ordinary, hypocrisy in the social elite, she applies her defiant poetic vision to everything in her path.

An extraordinary document, the new *Marmalade Me*, with an introduction by her worthy successor Deborah Jowitt, reaches back to 1960 for new material. Now the book truly spans the decade, shedding light on the work of Paul Taylor, Anna Sokolow, Gerald Arpino, Katherine Litz, Jimmy Waring, and José Limón, as well as Merce Cunningham, Yvonne Rainer, Steve Paxton, Deborah Hay, and Meredith Monk. An expertly Kafkaesque review of Martha Graham foreshadows Johnston's ability to give rhapsodic form to her disorientation later on. Her championing of the seminal Judson Dance Theater helped define an era. She identifies a subtle but monumental shift in philosophy—namely that Rainer and Trisha Brown rejected dynamic phrasing in favor of a continuum of movement. This is part of what she calls the "new demanding realism in the dance art of the Sixties."

Eventually her unabashed celebration of the heady dance/art experiments of the period devolved into a celebration of her own wacky, hip, androgynous life, replete with a psychotic phase. Her mental break(down/through) propelled her into a stream-of-consciousness style that may seem disconnected, but is actually followable, cohesive, and studded with searing or joyful insights. She mailed "Critics' Critic," a lucid assault on the boundary between critic and artist, spectator and performer, to the *Voice* from a mental ward. Happily, performance criticism has never been the same.

Looking Back on the "Embodiment of Ecstasy"

New York Times, Arts & Leisure, June 13, 1999

This feature story, written in advance of an anniversary event I was part of, had the biggest real-life impact of anything I've ever written. A musician named Christopher von Baeyer, who had been Sara Rudner's sweetheart in college, read it in his Sunday New York Times *in Seattle and decided then and there to recontact Sara. Thus their love affair blossomed after a thirty-four-year hiatus. They have been living together ever since, bringing each other much happiness. This joyful union, as fate would have it, is reciprocal. In the late seventies, Sara and I went on a grant-writing outing to the home of Jim Siegel, the director of finance and development for the Joffrey Ballet, who had offered to assist Sara in starting a foundation. He was kind, helpful, and intelligent, and it was easy to see from the way he stooped down to help his two little children into their coats that he was a good father. That memory was with me ten years later when we met again, started a relationship, and married in 1987. So when Sara told me she had gotten together with Christopher (who, sadly, died in 2013), I felt like we had, inadvertently, been each other's matchmaker.*

And by the way, at sixty-nine, Sara still dances with the same miraculous qualities that I tried to describe here.

A few years ago I was watching a revival of Twyla Tharp's *Deuce Coupe* (1973) at City Center. This landmark work took on the Beach Boys' music with sass, and thrust Ms. Tharp's rugged postmodern dancers onto the stage with Joffrey Ballet dancers. It married high art and rebel art by featuring, as the set design, a group of teenagers spraying graffiti on a scroll upstage. As I watched this scaled down and paler version, I mentally debated the wisdom of reviving a piece that was vital at an earlier moment in time.

And then Sara Rudner entered. A sunburst of energy, she sashayed and shimmied across the front of the stage, melting my concerns, dissolving my questions. Sublime and earthy at once, she radiated a personal connection to the dancing and to everything around her. She reveled in the music, giving the song "Got to Know the Woman" new meaning. I was helpless to do anything but follow her with my eyes, dance with her in my heart.

I've known Sara for years. In 1972, my dancing partner at the time, Risa Jaroslow, and I asked her to choreograph for us. Sara had danced lead roles with Twyla Tharp's first group for years and was looking to conduct her own experiments. While fulfilling a grueling touring schedule, she choreographed on us and with us whenever she was in town.

Sara Rudner in her
33 Dances on her
33rd birthday, 1977:
Baryshnikov talks about
"the awesome beauty of
her stare." (© Nathaniel
Tileston, *Dance Magazine*
Archives)

Our work eventually incorporated Wendy Rogers and culminated in a four-way collaboration under Sara's direction in 1975. Originally a five-hour event, *Dancing-on-View* will be recreated on Saturday in a four-hour version for the Danspace Project's Twenty-Fifth Anniversary Silver Series at St. Mark's Church.

I watch Sara in the studio and try to analyze the mystery of her astounding dancing. Certainly she does not possess beautiful line, exquisite leg extensions, or soaring leaps. But every ounce of her body commits to the movement; all systems are go; she is doing what she was meant to do. Even the most pedestrian of moves are charged. In our new collectively made "stroll," we take the first four walking steps, and Sara has already imbued the movement with tantalizing rhythm and style. When I dance near her, her assurance grounds me and her enthusiasm warms me, so that I feel a chill when she steps aside and I'm dancing alone.

Although her presence is rock solid, her movements are mercurial. Like a great actress, she transforms with every feeling, every phrase. But the spell she casts is not theatrical. It is a pure dance spell, rooted in a bone-deep pleasure of motion and a lusty willingness to follow her own impulses.

Carolyn Brown, who was a principal dancer with Merce Cunningham for twenty years, recently mused about Sara's dancing: "She is the embodiment of ecstasy. Like the religiously inspired whirling dervishes, she seems to be possessed by something beyond herself." In a phone conversation, Mikhail Baryshnikov, who has performed one of Sara's solos, glowed with admiration: "She is the most extraordinary dancer, a powerful performer." Then he added quietly, "And this awesome beauty of her stare—her eyes, they take you somewhere. Very hypnotic."

Sara started dancing in her living room and on the streets of Brooklyn. As a child, she had so much energy that her parents sent her to a local dance school, where she learned interpretive dance and baby ballet. As a Russian history major at Barnard College, she took dance courses and joined the dance club but swam laps ("for my mental health") as much as she danced. Her twenty years with Twyla Tharp, during which she helped develop the Tharp style, included appearances in Milos Forman's films *Hair*, *Amadeus*, and *Ragtime*.

From 1975 to 1982 she also directed the Sara Rudner Performance Ensemble, and she won a New York Dance and Performance Award (called a Bessie) in 1984, the first year it was offered. Over the next ten years, although she continued to perform, her right hip joint deteriorated to the point at which she had to ask her son to tie her shoes. Sara had a bad year in 1994: she underwent a hip replacement, her father died, and her marriage broke up. It took two years to get back to dancing fully. This fall, she begins a new job as director of dance at Sarah Lawrence College.

The reason Sara originally chose to do a five-hour performance was that she didn't want to clip the creative sprawl of dancing to fit into the standard theatrical format. "The dancing in our lives is ongoing," she said recently. "And this way the audience isn't captive; they can make their own intermissions."

True to her vision, Sara will not present a finished work on Saturday. Instead, "Dancing-on-View 1999" is a tossed salad of mostly new and some old material. It is a retrospective, not of the forty-odd works Sara has choreographed, but of the dancers she has worked with. Added to our reunion group of four will be sixteen younger dancers, all women.

We don't recall much of the original choreography of *Dancing-on-View*. Wendy Rogers remembers starting the performance before the audience filed in. Risa remembers the exhilaration she felt at the end of the five hours. Sara remembers the camaraderie we shared and the vulnerability of showing the work in progress.

And I remember this: every time I rang the buzzer at the Canal Street loft where Sara lived and danced, she poked her head out the window to drop the keys down with the most inviting expression on her face. She looked like a child who can't wait to get to her favorite playground. Twenty-four years later, we are revisiting that playground—with gusto.

The Power of Stripping Down to Nothingness

New York Times, Arts & Leisure, November 7, 1999

The growing presence of butoh in all its intensity and strangeness has enriched the international dance scene. Watching one of these performance was like being inside a dream that could turn into a nightmare at any moment. I decided to go on a search for what was "authentic" butoh and why its slow-motion imagery packed such a punch. I needed to hear an array of voices. This piece also asks questions that come up when any culturally specific dance form takes hold and spreads: Where did tap dance (or flamenco, or Contact Improvisation) come from, and who is entitled to do it? I was lucky with the timing because a spate of butoh performers was reaching New York just as I pitched this to the Times.

When Sankai Juku first performed at City Center in 1984, audiences were transfixed by its brutal images, its haunting beauty. It grabbed something fearful and nightmarish from inside us and reflected it back with a new intensity. Four men, covered only with white powder, dangled upside down from high above, tied at the ankles like pieces of meat. They descended slowly, backs arching, arms coiling, flaunting their closeness to death. (The next year, one dancer did fall to his death during an outdoor performance, prompting a yearlong hiatus in their work.)

Tony Micocci, former executive director of City Center, ranks the first time he saw Sankai Juku among the top five theatrical experiences of his life. "You're being torn," he said, "you feel like your soul is being looked at. Although the aesthetic is very elegant, you feel completely ripped open."

Since 1984, butoh-influenced groups have proliferated internationally, attaining some measure of familiarity and acceptance. Maybe they can't shock us as they first did, but we go back to their performances again and again to learn about our bond with nature and our place in the universe.

Butoh (shortened from "ankoko butoh," meaning "dance of utter darkness") grew out of the American occupation of Japan as an effort to resist the Westernization of Japanese culture. It drew on the ancient forms of Kabuki and Noh, especially in their embrace of the grotesque. Tatsumi Hijikata, the primary originator of butoh, was known for his transgressions into vulgarities and violence, as well as his meticulous, riveting dancing. His spirit is refracted in three current butoh leaders, all of whom will appear in New York City in the coming weeks. Ushio Amagatsu brings Sankai Juku to the Brooklyn Academy of Music Wednesday through Sunday in *Hiyomeki*

Sankai Juku in Ushio Amagatsu's *Hibiki* ("Resonance from Far Away") at Brooklyn Academy of Music, 2002. (© Jack Vartoogian / FrontRowPhotos)

("Within a Gentle Vibration and Agitation"); Min Tanaka will do late-night performances at P.S. 122 on December 3 and 4, followed by a two-week stint at P.S. 1 in Queens; Kazuo Ohno, ninety-three, will dance a new solo at the Japan Society on December 9, 10, and 11.

The challenge of butoh is to reveal the nakedness of the soul as well as the nakedness of the body. Last month Ohno led workshop students in Venice into an improvisation aimed at understanding the devastation of the bombing of Hiroshima. "The atomic bomb destroyed everything," he told me through an interpreter. What he tried to elicit from the students, through dance, was "How we find the first life growing from that destroyed place."

We tend to think of butoh as exclusively Japanese, but there has always been a kinship with Western artists. Ohno's teacher, Takaya Eguchi, had studied with Mary Wigman, Martha Graham's counterpart and leader of expressionist dance in Germany. For musical accompaniment, Tanaka favors jazz; Ohno favors Chopin; other butoh artists have used Bach, flamenco or bagpipes. Sankai Juku's dangling action has something in common with the gravity-defying feat of Trisha Brown's *Man Walking Down the Side of a Building* of 1970. And Ohno, inspired by Allen Ginsberg's reading of "Kaddish," once danced for him at a party.

Anna Halprin, the mother of American experimental dance, feels this kinship, too. Last year, when reconstructing her seminal work *Parades and Changes* of 1965, she hired Oguri, a butoh group in Los Angeles, to perform it. One section requires the dancers to dress and undress with ceremonial slow motion. She wanted the movement to evoke reverence for the nude body instead of lust. As she said in a recent telephone conversation, "Moving really slowly is the hardest way to move, and they did it beautifully."

The Eastern sense of time flows differently from the Western. One of the reasons the dancer/choreographer Le Minh Tam admires Sankai Juku, whose name means the School of Mountain and Sea, is that it brings back his world as a child in Vietnam. "Time does not dictate your life in Asia, but is part of an aesthetic continuum," he said. "Sankai Juku's dances are slow enough to let things evolve. It doesn't bore me to see something slow." One of Tanaka's practices is to lie on his back in a stream, feeling the direction of the flow, the rocks, whatever comes rushing below him, and try to be completely passive.

Melinda Ring, a choreographer from Los Angeles, remembers Tanaka's nature imagery in workshops. "He did a series of monkey images; we became the monkey who hugs, and then the monkey who is hugged," she said. Although there are similarities between butoh training and the release work used by many downtown dancers, Ring finds that butoh encourages an abandon she does not see in the United States. "They push the limits of the body," she said. "Dancers here are so careful."

This abandon brings to mind rock 'n' roll for Roxanne Steinberg, an American dancer and the wife of Naoyuki Oguri, director of the Oguri group. She finds the potential for expressiveness, made powerful by the communal force that characterizes rock, is here, too.

Butoh training can strip you of everything—technique, habits, self-esteem. Participating in Tanaka's Body Weather Laboratory can mean going into the mountainside to test survival skills. This can lead to powerful experiences. The Montreal dancer/choreographer Jocelyne Montpetit recently recalled her participation in the premiere of Tanaka's *Rite of Spring* on his farm in Japan in 1989. As typhoon rains lashed out, the group danced in the mud, bonding with each other and with nature. "Life was strong and dangerous; everything was melting inside ourselves; we could smell the earth," Montpetit said.

Like all art forms that grow from a particular subculture, the spreading of butoh inevitably involves some dilution. In the last few years, this Asian art form has been used by dancers and theater directors in a variety of ways. Dawn Akemi Saito, who has brought butoh to plays directed by Joanne Akalaitis and Lawrence Sacharow, is currently performing a solo with spoken text at the Kitchen. Maureen Fleming, who has an international following, creates erotic, surreal transformations of the body. In a work by

Poppo and the Go-Go Boys you might see someone smashing melons while a piglet sleeps, or twenty gold-sprayed dancers writhing in hedonistic ritual. Laurence Rawlins provides a shamanistic presence in a dance by Ellis Wood, pouring water over another dancer's head. Oguri dances atop a photocopier, the sound and light radiating a techno-heartbeat from the earth upward.

So what is authentic butoh, and who is entitled to do it? Koosil-ja Hwang, a New York choreographer from Japan, says: "Butoh grows in Japan and needs the water, the entire cultural environment of Japan, for its authenticity. And it is from a different time, before TV."

Others, however, say that butoh is not the exclusive domain of Japanese dancers of a certain age. Rawlins, who is part African American and part West Indian, thinks that butoh has been successfully transplanted and is there for the taking. "If someone has an affinity, it's what you do," he said. When he first took Natsu Nakajima's butoh workshop, he recalled, "I realized that butoh was always inside of me." Now he considers himself a post-butoh dancer. Eiko, of the acclaimed partnership Eiko & Koma, resists using the term *butoh*, claiming that it limits audience response. "Once the word became available there's no way to stop it," she said recently. "But now, we don't use lots of energy to kill the word."

Brechin Flourney, who studied butoh in Japan, started the San Francisco Butoh Festival five years ago. Since then, artists from Japan, Europe, and Latin America have performed each year to ever-expanding audiences. Filmmakers, writers, scientists, and martial arts enthusiasts fill the houses for workshops and performances over a three-week period. The festival has engendered so much activity that several local groups, with names like Collapsing Silence, performed in the festival last summer. In New York City, Ellen Stewart of La Mama E.T.C. has nurtured butoh artists since she brought over Kazuo Ohno nearly twenty years ago.

One of the appeals of butoh is simply this: the female side. Hijikata often said that one reason he danced was to find within himself the body of a sister who had disappeared into prostitution. Ohno glories in female roles, and members of the all-male Sankai Juku often wear long gowns. Power and vulnerability coexist in the muscles of these dancers. Butoh seems to embody the Jungian notion that man contains woman and woman, man.

Whatever is the opposite of fast food and shopping on the Internet is butoh. It calls to us to dig deep inside and risk our psychic safety doing it. A form of dance that celebrates perpetual change, butoh revels in all that is treacherous, ludicrous, pathetic, or heroic. Like the American avant-garde of the 1960s, it shuns conventional rules for making art and, by shedding all the outer layers, forges a new path to beauty.

The New Russia: Sasha Pepelyaev's Kinetic Theatre

Dance Theater Workshop, New York City

Dance Insider, December 1999

When I started visiting the Soviet Union in the eighties, I happily sated my curiosity about the land of pure ballet. But I saw no modern dance. Someone explained to me that this form of "free expression" did not exist there. It was considered too American and therefore corrupt. You weren't even allowed to utter the words "modern dance." Even Isadora Duncan–style dancing, which had been carried on there continuously throughout the century, had to be done in secret and call itself "rhythmic gymnastics" or "musical movement."

But after perestroika, a whole movement of experimental dance broke open in Russia. It didn't come from modern dance or ballet but from traditions in physical theater, mime, circus arts, folk dance, and gymnastics. What I did not know when I wrote this review was that Charles and Stephanie Reinhart at the American Dance Festival brokered exchanges with some of these artists, including Sasha Pepelyaev, which helped foster experimentation in Russia.

Sasha Pepelyaev's Kinetic Theatre, which opened the citywide New Europe Festival October 13 at Dance Theatre Workshop, stole my heart. Knowing that anything experimental in Russia can barely get started let alone survive, I was curious. The group of three men and three women are all young, adventurous movers with crew cuts. In *One Second Hand* they wear drab suits; the women wear black bras under suit jackets. They are not lush, elastic dancers; they do not have adorable size differences; the movement is not extra-release-y or particularly breathtaking. But there is an astringent magic in this group.

The men are rangy movers and possess an engaging intensity and freedom. The women are stony, almost zombie-like. I've seen those faces in Russia, in the wastelands that pass for department stores, where some shop girls are stuck for life (pre-Perestroika). The groupings and partnerings are very physical, slightly absurd, and have a beguiling humor. A man growls on top of a woman as she smushes his face with her fingers. He doesn't mind; he just gets more into his animal self. It's not sexy sex; it's sex from a funny dream. Things happen that are odd or straight from someone's subconscious, but all these things get pulled along by a terrific kinetic momentum. A blunt tango breaks up into a chaotic argument. The lifts glide into rolls, which tumble into lifts again. The dancers are stubborn and scrappy with each other. Not from competitiveness it seems, but just from a constant and brutal knowing of life.

The tender moments are rare and hard earned. Nothing in *One Second Hand* is predictable, and yet it all fits together in a jagged way. If they weren't speaking Russian, I wouldn't know what country they are from—except I would know they aren't American. There is no smugness, no gratuitous muscularity, not a shred of complacency. The psychic ground is not solid but shifting. Every bit of fun has its emotional cost.

One Second Hand is made for an intimate space. It begins in the dark, and you see only glowing lights growing in number from right to left. This could be the beginning of a hypnotic image-y type piece, but it isn't. They speak softly in English—maybe it's an interrogation at an immigration center: "Who shot Lincoln?" "What is the capital of Maryland state?" But then we hear, "How many seconds are in a day?" The talking soon shifts to become mostly in Russian. Maybe because we are not meant to understand everything, the text adds texture without asking for interpretation. However, I heard "Yeshcho raz" repeatedly, and I know that means "One more time." So for me, it reinforced the obsessive quality of the dance.

Some of the sounds didn't need translation. "HA HA HA, oyoyoy, HA HA HA, oyoyoy." The movement phrases were repeated enough times in different contexts that when the men and women exchanged phrases, I could tell. A favorite scene: facing front, a man and a woman wave their arms out of sync, he more frenzied than she. They are signaling through the flames.

The lighting, by Vyacheslav Korjavine, cuts through with a bold bright glare, turning each tableau inside out. The music, recorded except for live violinist (and composer) Alexey Aigi, is hard-edged, mostly with a deep beat, adding to the humane harshness. Text fragments are from Lev Rubinstein and Robbe-Grillet. The dancers are Tatiana Gordeeva, Darya Buzovkina, Katrin Essenson, Roman Kislouhin, Konstantin Surikov, and Taavet Yansen.

When I saw the Kirov (Mariinsky) Ballet this summer, I felt I was seeing the best of Czarist Russia. Here I felt a fresh energy from a Russia no longer part of the Soviet Union. Sasha Pepelyaev and his dancers, some of whom are from Estonia, are struggling for a new vision, one not afraid to face the past and future. That this group can exist at this time in a country making only minute changes in its ballet repertoire, represents an enormous cultural and artistic leap forward. This is an exciting time to see them.

v From 2000 to 2004

This section covers the period from when I started to work for *Dance Magazine* until I became editor in chief.

In January 2000 I was asked to speak on a panel about how women are discriminated against in dance and how the men get all the breaks. I had been so angry about this in the seventies that I had co-written (with choreographer Stephanie Woodard) an exposé of male privilege in the dance world. It was published in the *Village Voice*; we used, as a headline, a quote from a high school dance teacher: "When a Woman Dances, Nobody Cares." Twenty-five years later, even though the attitudes that devalued women persisted, I found myself less involved this time around. I didn't even want to be on the panel. My own career as a choreographer was pretty much over by then. Also, I realized how fortunate we women in dance were: for the most part, we escaped the threat of AIDS that loomed over our male peers. In the eighties and early nineties, it seemed like every few weeks we'd hear of another casualty. During that period my anger just naturally dissolved.

When the panel, which was part of an APAP (Association of Performing Arts Presenters) conference, was over, the publisher of *Dance Magazine* approached me. She asked if I'd be interested in the newly created position of New York editor of the magazine, which had just moved its main office to Oakland, California. Since I had a fondness for editing, I thought I would take the offer until a good teaching job came along.

As the part-time New York editor, my beat was dance in New York—what could be better? That had really always been my beat. My appetite to see dance was with me long before becoming an editor—or a critic or even a choreographer. During the four years in that position, I continued to contribute to the *New York Times* while also writing for *Dance Magazine*. I enjoyed longer pieces because I could delve into a subject in depth and incorporate other voices. Writing features was more about listening than forming a quick opinion, as in a review.

On staff at the magazine, I chafed under my second editor in chief, perceiving an undercurrent of distrust, even though she was three thousand miles away. I resolved that if I were ever to have a leadership role, I would do things differently. I would be more direct in my communication, and I would foster an atmosphere where staff editors felt comfortable putting forward ideas and participating in decisions. I would try to bring out the best in my coworkers.

The terrorist attacks of September 11, 2001, struck just as my story on Eiko & Koma appeared in *Dance Magazine*. Because their work hints at surviving disasters, the timing seemed uncanny. (I describe my experience of that horrific day in the introduction to that piece, which is about their collaboration with Anna Halprin.)

Two years later the magazine, now under new management, relocated back to New York and the position of editor in chief opened up. This was my chance to put my ideas of leadership into effect. Knowing how time-consuming the job would be, I asked my husband and son whether it was okay with them if I applied for it. Since Jim was still on disability and we needed to save money for Nick's college—and since my teenage son wasn't eager to have me around every minute of the day—the decision made itself.

In February 2004, I was named editor in chief. As it happened, the appointment caught me in the middle of making a solo for the ballet dancer Martine van Hamel, and I could barely find the hours to finish it.

My new position was so stimulating that I no longer missed

teaching. I found that editing had something akin to that other love of mine. Just as I had given my students an assignment and waited with anticipation to see how they fulfilled it, now I gave assignments to writers, some of them quite young. When a story came in that surprised me with its craft and depth, I felt I had received a great gift.

Seeing Balanchine, Watching Whelan: Some Thoughts on Balanchine and Wendy Whelan's Double Smash

New York State Theater, January 7, 2000

Dance Insider, January 8, 2000

On my first visit to New York City Ballet as a critic, I hit the jackpot with Wendy Whelan. She had a kinetic sizzle that transcended the conventional pretty-girl ballet aesthetic. It made me sit up, pay attention, and learn her name. At the same time, I reacted against the triple dose of Balanchine and vowed never to attend an all-Balanchine program again. (I do, however, enjoy the work in smaller doses, and I rush to see Serenade, Prodigal Son, *and* Symphony in Three Movements *whenever I can.) But Whelan infused the Balanchine courtliness with a thrillingly contemporary energy.*

Not being a member of the Church of Balanchine that many New York dance critics belong to, I resolutely claimed my independence with this mixed response. In a way, I was posing as someone from a different planet who is unaware that Balanchine worship is the proper position to take. Or maybe I was just reviewing it as the modern dancer I was. But also I see in this the beginning of my self-education about Balanchine, determined to develop my own take on this creator of American ballet.

When I leave an evening of Balanchine ballets, I want to go out and make a messy ballet. The amount of order he employs is too much for my blood.

From the *Tschaikovsky Piano Concerto No. 2* (1941) to *Mozartiana* (1981) there seem to be endless rows of girls framing the principal figures. Structurally, Balanchine uses the devices of canon and right-left repetition rather liberally. Symmetry prevails. For those of us who see more Merce Cunningham than Balanchine, the look of his dancers can seem very Cunningham-esque—vertical, quick-legged, eating through space, but keeping to a contained base otherwise, able to change direction on a dime, and rarely yielding to each other. These two choreographic giants also share a knack for making scintillating trios within a large work. But Balanchine's trios are symmetrical, whereas Cunningham's are more like what you might see on the street, but with a sense of constantly finding new relationships. With Cunningham it's more fun to cull the order from the chaos. With Balanchine, it's all too easy to figure out what he's doing structurally. I think one reason that Balanchine is considered a god by ballet-goers is that you always know where you are with him. If you can get yourself inside his orderly world, you see the subtleties within it very clearly, and that is a reward.

This program was an excellent opportunity to see different aspects of Balanchine. The Tchaikovsky was originally entitled *Ballet Imperial* and was done as a tribute to Petipa, whereas *Agon* is an entrance into modernism. *Mozartiana* is a meditative oasis choreographed shortly before his death. *Tschaikovsky Piano Concerto* reminds one of Petipa with its rows of girls (in ballet, no one is called a woman or man) framing the leads, and the gracious curtsies used as commas for pausing to remind us of how courtly ballet was for a couple of centuries. Everything is orderly and contented and hierarchical. The girls bow lovingly to their queen. I cringe to think that Balanchine made this piece to show off the "purity" of European ballet to the countries of South America during American Ballet Caravan's tour there in 1941. Thank goodness he streamlined the scenery and costumes in 1973, using Karinska's soft chiffon dresses instead of the originally stiff imperial tutus.

The ballet isn't much, unless, as I've hinted, you adore wall-to-wall symmetry. So when Wendy Whelan, dancing the lead for the first time, makes her entrance—luxuriously, energetically, extravagantly billowing thither and yon—she saves an otherwise unremarkable piece of work. She is an impetuous creature, a white swan-type—edgy, not quite human, threatening to elude the grip and support of her escort at every dive.

Charles Askegard is a gallant, patient foil to her wildness, but is almost left behind. He is more at home with a string of "girls," generously unfolding an arm to give them a hand, while they loop around behind him, ebbing in the breeze. This is a beautiful section, and Balanchine allows you to see it so many times that you might not crave to see this particular ballet again for a while. Another thing that reminded me of *Swan Lake* is that, even though the ballet has been cleansed of story, when Whelan leaves the stage, a dimness settles on everything and there is a hint of bereavement in the prince. He looks to one line of girls, they turn away; he looks to the other line of girls, they turn away. Somehow in the midst of this plotless ballet, this device works, maybe because Whelan really does take the light with her.

Jennie Somogyi in a featured role is pretty great too. She swirls with sweetness and roundedness, and I'd want to see her do the main part sometime. But I'm too happy with Whelan to think of that now.

In the opening of *Mozartiana*, the central figure, danced nicely by Miranda Weese, is surrounded by four young girls. (These really are girls.) They all wear black. Weese does some praying gestures, lilting this way and that. But it doesn't feel very spiritual to me, maybe because there is no connection between the woman and the girls. They neither look at nor touch each other. The four girls seem merely decorative; maybe they are preparing for a life as ladies. The achievement here is to make black seem pretty and delicate. Damian Woetzel spins fabulously; his turns are low to the ground with rock-sure endings. The music, which is Tchaikovsky's tribute to Mozart, includes an exquisite passage for solo violin. Trouble is, at that moment, the dancing (or was it the choreography?) by the two principals is forgettable, so I practiced Balanchine's advice of closing my eyes to enjoy the music. This solo, played, I believe, by first violinist Guillermo Figueroa, was piquant, with a slight feeling of a gypsy violin. His rich tones carried many emotions, but onstage I saw only a steady-state cheerfulness. Later the four little girls return, this time jumping and skipping. Although the unison is a strain, their youthful burst of imperfect energy buoys the ballet.

Agon shows how Balanchine started breaking the line of the body, influenced perhaps by jazz (music and dance). A motif for the men was throwing themselves off-balance by thrusting a leg out so far in arabesque that it pulls them back on their heel so the standing foot flexes. There were turned-in knees and pelvic thrusts (one or two of those in *Mozartiana* as well, pristineness notwithstanding.) A trio for isolated body parts, danced by Peter Boal, Jennifer Tinsley, and Kathleen Tracey, brought a dash of humor. The tour de force, of course, was the final pas de deux, originally made for Arthur Mitchell and Diana Adams. The series of entwinings is so inventive that it makes us alert to who puts what hand where and how each stretch is completed. Whelan and Jock Soto create a real electricity here. (But if you see the video of Diana Adams with Mitchell, she is actually pretty soft and yielding in it.) With the atonal Stravinsky music, the choreography seems to be made expressly for Whelan. Her line is crystal clear, and she possesses a forcefulness that is especially effective when she seems to be going in two directions at once. She creates a pull between two destinations as well as between herself and her partner. Her suppleness is a bit scary sometimes, but it is never just for show. It is about stretching to her limits, and there is both satisfaction and challenge in that.

If *Agon* were a painting, art critics would say it has no "mass," that it is a collection of parts with no weight to the whole. Musically Stravinsky deconstructs any idea of a clear direction; it doesn't build to a climax like Tchaikovsky does. But it has another way of getting to you. One image I love is a curled-up position. This is how the duet ends, with the two leads clasping each other in a huddle instead of with a fanfare of the fantastic limbs they've been showing us. One of the men's sections ends similarly: with the four individually hunched over. This curved over, into oneself position, along with the broken lines and syncopated beats, is one of the ways Balanchine has gotten away from the grandeur and irrelevance of imperial ballet and made it modern.

Note: It was daring in 1957 to pair a black man with a white woman in *Agon*. They almost got kicked off the *Ed Sullivan Show* for this, but it was filmed in silhouette instead. Someday, I'd like to see a black woman do the *Agon* pas de deux with a white man.

Merce at Martha@Mother

Mother, New York City

February 29, 2000

Dance Magazine, May 2000

The popularity of Richard Move's nightclub act revealed the need — indeed the craving — that many of us had to relive, or maybe revise, the Martha Graham experience. I started studying at the Graham school at fifteen and was a scholarship student there my first year out of college. I'd moved on from my fascination with "Martha" long ago, but being at Dance Magazine *brought me back to an awareness of that powerful persona.*

Richard Move invited various guests for each performance. It was wicked fun to hear Merce Cunningham talking about Martha. I'm sure he had lots more stories. After all, it was Merce's rejection of Graham's theatrics that led us into postmodernism.

At a tiny downtown nightclub called Mother, Martha@Mother is packing them in for its hilarious send-ups of early modern dance. This is the fourth season that the Bessie Award–winning coproducers Richard Move and Janet Stapleton have presented a show that simultaneously reveres and mocks the mother of modern dance, Martha Graham.

Move's imitation of the modern dance goddess has already attained cult status. An experienced dancer, tall and statuesque, he captures her glamorous despair, but lacks the fierce torque in the center of the body that

Richard Move as Martha Graham: capturing her glamorous despair. (© Josef Astor)

Graham flaunted. His facial expressions are perfect—the grandeur, the fabricated modesty, the pride in suffering. When speaking, his voice is right out of Martha's honeyed narrative in the documentary film *A Dancer's World*. It is all very funny and somehow deeply moving. To be in a room crowded with others who let Graham under their skin is like, well, being with one's spiritual brothers and sisters. And what a delicious relief to laugh at it all!

The evening begins with Charles Atlas's collage of film clips from old musicals: dramas with stars like Barbara Stanwyck playing the part of someone named Martha, some kitsch Denishawn-like stuff, and Martha, in her waning years, going through the motions of *Acrobats of God*. The audience howls and mutters at these witty juxtapositions as it gets in the mood to see Move's impersonations. The night I went, special guest Isaac Mizrahi gave his camp rendition of her obsessive dedication to creating the perfect costume. The dancers, some of whom are members of the Graham Company, perform bits of her repertoire.

Into this heady mix comes Merce Cunningham, dancing a solo on a chair. His electric stillness is broken by a hand slowly lifting toward his face to support a tilt of the head. Using his eyelids as shutters, he gradually makes his eyes into slits and then opens them wide. His mouth too. Suddenly, he shifts his whole body to a three-quarter view, and the piece is almost over.

Then Move as Martha reenters and interviews Cunningham, who has plenty of stories from when he danced with Graham. For example, in one rehearsal she hasn't made up her mind whether his character is a preacher, farmer, or something else. She asks him to work on his solo independently and is delighted with the results. "Oh," says Martha, "Now I know how to finish the piece!" (*Appalachian Spring*, one presumes.)

In another story, the famously blind and deaf Helen Keller visits the studio and asks to touch a dancer in motion. Martha leads her over to Merce so she can touch his waist as he jumps, after which Keller declares, "How light, like the human mind!"

Pieces by Julie Atlas Muz, Kate Valentine, Donlin Foreman, Doug Varone, and Mark Baldwin were also presented. Other performers who have appeared in this zesty series include Mark Dendy, Sean Curran, Carmen de Lavallade, Maxine Sherman, Deborah Jowitt, and Jane Comfort.

Unfortunately, attorneys representing The Martha Graham Entities have filed cease-and-desist orders against Martha@Mother. Meanwhile, it seems clear that these loving lampoons help ensure the legendary status of Martha Graham.

Postscript: Since then, the Martha Graham Dance Company has embraced Richard Move as both a host and dance maker. Artistic director Janet Eilber commissioned him to make one of the first "Lamentation Variations" in 2007 and to restage his 2002 work, *The Show (Achilles Heels)* for the company's 2013 season.

Moving, Joyfully and Carefully, into Old Age

New York Times, April 2, 2000

With this story, I uncovered a treasure trove of mind/body wisdom. Asking dancers how they dealt with the aging body was far more interesting—and entertaining—than consulting medical professionals. It also helped me to remember why I still identified as a dancer, even though I was in the midst of transitioning from being a dancer who writes a little to an editor/writer who dances a little. This is when I realized that I still see like a dancer even if dancing is no longer my profession.

A couple years ago I was teaching a technique class in Athens, bringing my usual mix of youthful vigor and sorrowful limitation due to age. At one point I apologized for being old, and a chorus of Greek voices called out, "Oh no, you are very young." Without thinking, I responded, "You're right, I am young. But my spine is old."

Since then I have found out just how old my spine is. An MRI shows that the disc between the first and second lumbar vertebrae has oozed out and clings like ivy to the entire length of the vertebra below. In an attempt to stabilize the vertebrae, my back muscles go into spasm several times a year, sending me into bed for days. When not in spasm, I have trouble rising from a sitting position, not to mention dancing. In the studio, I take ridiculously frequent breaks simply to lie prone, and even when I am "dancing," I do not curve, jump, or stomp for fear of triggering another spasm.

So why go into the studio at all? The answer is a surprise to me because I have, in my middle years, become interested in many projects outside of dance, and have approached dance from other angles. But the fact remains that I feel like my most essential self only when I am dancing. I still feel the air on my arms in a certain way, the pleasure of cutting through space, of letting the movement well up from the center of my being, the torquing of the body that pulls me into another move, the lift, the glide, the yearning reach, the crouch-to-spring, the float, the pounce, the melt. The individual defining herself in a sea of possibilities.

I miss being in a studio and working with other dancers, all concentrating on movement. We understand that it matters how you choose to move. Each little nuance has meaning. Even if that meaning cannot be read from the audience, one is engaged in the creation of a language, and we mean to be saying exactly this and not that. I've lost that total immersion that provides the mental and physical readiness to dance. But I still *see* like a dancer.

Dancers see a netherworld of thought, motion, and energy invisible to non-dancers. We see subtle differences in how movement travels through the body and how pedestrian traffic travels along a sidewalk.

A dancer works for decades to bring the body and mind into some form of unity. One trains the body as an instrument, but an instrument that includes the mind. In thinking back to the class in Athens, I realize that my remark bespoke a split between my self and my body. Now, I am probably more like most people: I experience my body as separate from my spirit.

But other dancers who have continued into the far reaches of middle and old age have handled these limitations better than I. So I went on a tele-phone and e-mail pilgrimage to seek out their insights. What I found was that underneath each person's ability to sustain a dancing life lies a philosophy that welcomes change and honors the spirit as well as the body.

The former New York City Ballet principal Allegra Kent, a heavenly ballerina in her youth and middle years, danced the role of the mother in the Pennsylvania Ballet's *Nutcracker* last year. "I'm grandmother age, sixty-two, but if I move a little faster and more rambunctiously, I can play a mother," she said. Though she acknowledges the lessening of her range, she maintains that "the spirit, the love, the input, the thrill, are the same."

Like Kent, the dancer and choreographer Gus Solomons jr, sixty-one, feels speed is still available. "I'm dancing on momentum now," he claims. "You can do more on momentum than on muscles." Remy Charlip, a seventy-one-year-old dancemaker as well as writer and illustrator of children's books, is not too bothered by his shrinking range. "I can't jump or turn anymore," he admitted. "Of course, I would like to fly, but I do two-feet-on-the-floor dancing now." He feels nourished by his study of psychic healing, and redirects his energy by envisioning circles and figure eights within himself: "I am constantly rearranging my internal furniture." As he moves through his daily chores, everything becomes a dance.

For the legendary innovator Anna Halprin, dancing is still something to be worked up to. She starts a physical, mental, and emotional training several weeks before a performance. "I've never lost my passion for dance. The body, with its stored memories, holds so much knowledge and is so full of surprises." In her fifties Halprin was stricken with cancer; "enlightenment at gunpoint," she calls the experience. Now seventy-nine, she sums up her faith in dance: "I have worked on creating dance that anybody can do, and so aging and even illness have not gotten in the way of my dancing; they have only provided new possibilities."

James "Buster" Brown, one of the original Copasetics (the famed tap dance group), has maintained rhythm and syncopation, but at eighty-six he can't do the steps that require elevation. "You're only as good as your legs and your breathing," he said. But what keeps him going is that "I'm still in love with tap dancing."

Hellmut Gottschild, at sixty-two a pillar of the dance community in Philadelphia, describes his daily warm-up: "I do a thorough stretching and then springing movements to get the joints going, which takes about two hours. Then I can't start dancing because I'm tired!" In comparing age with youth, he mused: "When you're young, you shoot out energy in every direction. When you're older, you're reducing, reducing, reducing, to save energy. I guess people take that for wisdom. I also hope there's enough foolishness left in my work. I always wanted to be an old fool. I don't know if I've achieved that because I have too much good taste."

Frances Alenikoff, an outrageously elastic and juicy dancer at seventy-nine, does a holistic workout. "I love stretching combined with undulations," she said. "I do a movement and vocal meditation that goes into the cells, heightening inner awareness. I reach a point where the deliciousness of it makes up for the agony of preparing pieces to present in public." Five years ago Alenikoff contracted a rare tick disease, which robbed her of some of her capability, including falling to the floor and coming up. But her sense of possibility reigns. "Someday," she said, "I will be able to do it. It's a matter of paying attention."

The celebrated butoh dancer Kazuo Ohno, ninety-three, feels that dancing promotes well-being. "After dancing, I feel better," he said. "Even if I have some physical problem, after performing I often find myself cured. It's much more effective than seeing the doctor." In Japan, it is not unusual to see people perform into their eighties or nineties. According to the Japanese-American dancer Eiko, the technical manuals of traditional Noh theater give instruction on how to proceed when a performer dies or faints onstage.

But there are cultural reasons for this artistic longevity, too. It is still common in Asian countries for couples to live with their in-laws. For instance, Ohno lives with three subsequent generations of his family, including the son who partners him onstage. The Japanese reverence for a long life extends to the arts. Toshio Mizohata, Ohno's manager, describes it this way: "We feel the deeper things in older performers. It's like flowers and trees. The flowers of older trees, for instance the cherry blossom tree, are small, soft and delicate. We feel time makes some kind of shape. In the shape of the branches we can recognize an older or younger tree. After a long time, the tree makes a different shape, each branch is more different, more individual. We have a similar feeling for performers." Eiko identifies a spiritual element: "Because their bodies are not young, older performers carry something that is almost between this world and the next, that itself is artistic and transcending."

In Western countries, more dance groups are featuring older artists, and there is growing audience interest. Call it the demographics of the baby boomers, but there seems to be a new acceptance of aging as a fact of life. Groups like Netherlands Dance Theater 3, Liz Lerman's intergenerational Dance Exchange, the 40 Up Project, and Dancers Over 40 are flourishing. The new trio Paradigm, formed by Solomons with the dance stars Carmen de Lavallade and Dudley Williams, recently drew praise for its performances at Symphony Space. Last fall a program in San Francisco shared by Halprin, Charlip, June Watanabe, and Frank Shawl elicited tears and ovations from an audience of all ages. Martha Wittman, sixty-four, who dances with the Liz Lerman Dance Exchange, told me that audiences seem shocked at first to see old and young people dance together but ultimately find it inspiring.

An Improbable Pair on a Quest into the Past

New York Times, June 4, 2000

To me this was a miraculous coming together of two vastly different worlds—two worlds that I had inhabited at different times in my life. Although Mikhail Baryshnikov had worked with modern dancers from Martha Graham to Alvin Ailey to David Gordon, I couldn't imagine him cottoning to feminist firebrand Yvonne Rainer. Nor could I imagine that she would relish a commission from a ballet dancer. But in some ways they were each starting a new life—he as an impresario, she as a returning prodigy to the dance world.

From opposite ends of the dance universe come two superstars: Mikhail Baryshnikov and Yvonne Rainer. He from the purest, centuries-old classical tradition; she from the rule-breaking Judson Dance Theater of the sixties. He the prince of Russian ballet; she the high priestess of the American avant-garde. He known for his natural theatricality, she for her resistance to anything theatrical.

They are rehearsing together for a season of the White Oak Dance Project, of which Baryshnikov is founder and director as well as lead performer, at the Brooklyn Academy of Music from June 7 to 11. In addition to a new work by Rainer, there will be premieres by Mark Morris and John Jasperse and Trisha Brown's *Glacial Decoy* (1979). How did it happen that Baryshnikov asked Rainer, who had not choreographed a dance in decades, to contribute to this program?

In the last twenty-five years Baryshnikov has journeyed deep into the repertoire of American modern dance, while Rainer, in the last year, has returned to the dance studio after twenty-five years as a noted feminist filmmaker. Since its inception in 1990, White Oak has commissioned forty new dances from modern choreographers, starting with its initial resident choreographer, Mark Morris, and on through Lar Lubovitch, Maurice Béjart, Kevin O'Day, Neil Greenberg, and Lucy Guerin. Last fall Baryshnikov, fifty-two, came to Judson Memorial Church in Greenwich Village when Rainer, sixty-five, danced in a new version of her seminal *Trio A* (1966), a five-minute continuous phrase in which the dancers never look out at the audience. Planning a program for this fall featuring choreographers from Judson Dance Theater, legendary as the incubator of postmodern dance, Baryshnikov invited Rainer to choreograph something.

"When I came to see White Oak and met him, I was surprised and pleased that he was familiar with the titles and the personnel of my past work," Rainer said recently during a rehearsal at the Trisha Brown Studio near Columbus Circle in Manhattan. "He'd done his homework. I said I could give him *Trio A* and *We Shall Run* (1963). Then he said, 'Maybe you'd like to do a new piece.' I gulped. And then it began to obsess me. What would I do?" Separated by a quarter-century from her work in dance, she went home and riffled through her book *Work: 1961–1973* to gather bits and pieces from her past artistic life that could be rearranged. Harking back to the Dadaist method of fragmentation, Rainer chose a collage structure to contain the selections. Like much of her work in both dance and film, the ideas and images are presented not in a beginning-middle-and-end format, but in a series of radical juxtapositions of tasks, interactions, and spoken texts.

Ingredients for this collage, titled *After Many a Summer Dies the Swan*, are drawn from *Three Satie Spoons* (1960), *The Bells* (1961), *The Mind Is a Muscle* (1968) and *Continuous Project—Altered Daily* (1970). Actions may be simultaneous, deflecting attention from one another, or sequential. One section, in which dancers cushion one another's movements with pillows, has a goofy precision. In another, two women link arms around each other's waists as they repeatedly melt to the floor and rise, still attached. They are reciting, in falsetto, a Gertrude Stein-ish bit of text by Rainer: "That was so lovely." "Yes yes that was so lovely." "It was so lovely it will make me think about it a lot." "In fact we will write about all that thinking," and so on. Rainer advises audience members: "You kind of roll with the different elements that keep coming to the surface and disappearing."

Seeing Rainer and Baryshnikov in a studio together makes perfect sense. Both have short spiky hair, long torsos and arms, boyish bodies. When they kissed each other hello, they seemed to be exactly the same height, and their rehearsal demeanor has a similar balance of readiness and calm. They understand each other's physicality, and more, they seem to understand each other's state of mind. Rainer said, "He has this restless intellect that's led him into this sixties corner of dancing." He affectionately called her a "professional revolutionary," and added, "It's fun to see such passion in her."

While rehearsing the group sections, the six White Oak dancers—besides Baryshnikov, they are Raquel Aedo, Emily Coates, Roselynde LeBlanc, Michael Lomeka, and Emmanuele Phuon—have vivid personalities and dance technique to burn, but Baryshnikov shows slightly more relish for the movement than the younger performers do. A highpoint of the piece is sure to be "Valda's Solo," originally from Rainer's first film, *Lives of Per-*

formers (1972). Here, it reveals Baryshnikov in a different mood. He wears a velvet gown, and lets a red ball roll off his hand and drop to the floor. Not much happens, but it's riveting. While Valda Setterfield looked elegant and aristocratic in the film, Baryshnikov looks lonely and pensive, creating an aura of melancholy.

Far in the pasts of both Rainer and Baryshnikov are precursors to this collaboration. Baryshnikov started dancing with modern dance choreographers soon after he defected from the Soviet Union in 1974, including Twyla Tharp, Alvin Ailey, Martha Graham, Paul Taylor, Erick Hawkins, and Merce Cunningham. Even earlier, during his last year in St. Petersburg, he presented a program in which he chose and danced in works by experimental choreographers, including Mai Murdmaa from Estonia. She had him rolling on the floor—quite simple and grounded compared to what his audience expected of him. The photographer/writer Nina Alovert recently said: "From the beginning, he wanted to do contemporary dance. He tried to do every way of ballet which we've had in Russia. In 1971 he danced in *Creation of the World* by Natalia Kasatkina. It was everything not classical. It combined knees turned in and knees turned out. He danced it like a god."

Rainer remembers seeing Alicia Markova dance *Giselle* in the late fifties. "She was the only dancer I have ever waited for at the stage door," Rainer said. "I was totally transported." Much later, one of the many bits in *The Mind Is a Muscle* was something she called the "Nijinsky pose." In the new piece, she extends the cushion section with a kind of classical pas de deux with Coates, the most balletic of the White Oak women, partnered by Baryshnikov with pillows. She is using their virtuosity as a "found object," in almost the same way visual artists like Robert Rauschenberg used a bed or a tire as found objects in the sixties.

Baryshnikov traces his interest in Judson Dance Theater back to David Gordon, whom he invited to choreograph for American Ballet Theatre when he was its artistic director. Gordon created *Field, Chair and Mountain* (1986), in which famed ballerina Martine van Hamel was promenaded on point on top of a metal folding chair. Gordon said of Baryshnikov's being drawn to this experimental work: "His attraction is to dance with integrity. He's willing to back up his own taste and intuitions. He refuses to stay in the past. He takes other people's past and tries it on; he's an inquisitive guy." Trisha Brown has called Baryshnikov "a questing spirit."

His quest, at this point, is partly a search for what sits comfortably in the mind as well as on the body of a no-longer-young dancer who wants to keep dancing. Two years ago, Baryshnikov told Laura Shapiro of *Newsweek*: "I've gotten into minimalism in my dancing. In the first part of life you accumulate experience, and then at the end you try to get rid of what's not necessary."

Rainer started getting rid of the extras early on. In fact, it was her modus operandi as a dance minimalist. After working on *Parts of Some Sextets*, she wrote the now-famous manifesto, "No to spectacle no to virtuosity no to transformations and magic and make-believe no to the glamour and transcendency of the star image no to the heroic . . ." first published in 1965 in *Tulane Drama Review*. But in the new piece, she uses not only Baryshnikov's heroic image, but also a new text about transformation—an essay by Vladimir Nabokov about a caterpillar turning into a butterfly.

In defense of her manifesto, Rainer now says, "One of the functions of a manifesto is to clear the air, to start over or reexamine expectations." Here, Rainer and Baryshnikov join together in the postmodern project of reexamining, reconstructing, reanalyzing, and representing. He is reexamining his role(s) in the dance world and she is reconstructing and rearranging her works from the past. For Rainer, the challenge is to bring her quotidian, task-like dances onto a proscenium stage.

One of her few forays into such a situation was at the Billy Rose Theater on Broadway in 1969, when the producer Charles Reinhart invited several young, unorthodox choreographers to perform, including Twyla Tharp, Meredith Monk, and Rainer. Pat Catterson, new in New York at the time, remembers the effect that Rainer's *Rose Fractions* had on her: "I'd never seen anything like it. It was in that anything-can-follow-anything mode. In one part, Yvonne did Lenny Bruce's monologue on snot. In another part, dancers and nondancers were doing *Trio A*. It was unpretentious, accessible, egalitarian, and totally of the moment. They ended by doing it to the Chambers Brothers' 'In the Midnight Hour,' and the audience was on its feet hooting and howling. We all felt like we wanted to do that. After it was over, some audience members went right up on the stage and did it. When I got home, I did all the moves I could remember from it."

Rainer is enjoying her return to the dance world: "I love working with dancers. I've never been entirely comfortable as a filmmaker because I never shot my own film. I'm a techno-idiot, so much of it is out of my control. Here I feel like I'm back where I belong. It's like coming home, at least temporarily." She has the utmost regard for Baryshnikov's choice to delve into dances of the rebellious sixties. "It's unprecedented for a classical dancer to do this," she said. "And he's pulling in an audience that, in many cases, is unfamiliar with that history. So in that sense he is a revitalizing force in the dance world."

Last month while on tour, after two standing-room-only performances by

White Oak in Clearwater, Florida, Rainer faxed this report: "The first night we softened them up. Misha introduced me and I basically told them not to worry. They laughed at everything. The second night: no introduction, much more subdued response during the piece, but at the end, a combination of standing ovation and boos."

Katherine Dunham: One-Woman Revolution

Dance Magazine, August 2000

As a teenager I had loved Katherine Dunham's autobiography, A Touch of Innocence, for its eloquent writing before I knew anything about her as a dancer. I remembered that she grew up so poor she had to wear cardboard shoes. I never saw her dance onstage, but my mother told me what a beautiful, sensual dancer she had been—which you can easily glean from YouTube clips. For this interview, one of the Dunham technique teachers, Dana McBroom-Manno, ushered me into Dunham's quarters at the Atria, the fancy senior facility where she lived on the Upper West Side. Because of knee problems, she'd been wheelchair-bound for years. Her sentences would sometimes ramble, but every digression held a pearl. I enjoyed playing back the audiotape to hear her low, slightly guttural voice with its Midwest twang and ring of truth.

When Dunham talked with Dana and a couple of other colleagues gathered there, the glorious past of her touring company was still alive for them. They cackled over the memory of sacrificing a chicken in a Vaudun number, and they oohed and ahhed over the mention of the vibrant blues and greens that John Pratt, Dunham's costume designer and husband, had dressed them in for another dance. Everything about "Miss Dunham" (who died in 2006) was theatrical, yet not one bit artificial. She emanated wisdom and love.

All roads lead to Katherine Dunham. Well, not all. But sometimes it seems to be so. Jazz dance, "fusion," and the search for our cultural heritage all have their antecedents in Dunham's work as a dancer, choreographer, and anthropologist. She was the first American to present dance forms from the African diaspora on a concert stage, the first to sustain a black dance company, the first black person to choreograph for the Metropolitan Opera. She created and performed in works for stage, clubs, and Hollywood films; she developed a dance technique that is still taught today; she fought unstintingly for racial justice. She could have had her own TV show called "Dance Roots."

Dunham, ninety-one, lives in Manhattan, where she is undergoing physical therapy for her surgically replaced knees. Surrounded by former dancers, friends, and a bright-eyed two-and-a-half-year-old goddaughter, she regales them with stories, songs, and warm-hearted joking.

The young Katherine Dunham studied ballet with Mark Turbyfill of the Chicago Opera and the Russian dancer Ludmilla Speranzeva. When she was only twenty-one, with Turbyfill's help, she formed the short-lived Ballet Nègre (also called Negro Ballet). Soon after, she started the Chicago-based

Katherine Dunham Dance Company, which performed a mix of cultures including Russian folk dances, Spanish dances, and plantation dances.

In 1935 and '36, under the aegis of a Rosenwald fellowship, Dunham traveled to the Caribbean to research African-based dances. She soon choreographed pieces that reflect Haitian movements, for instance, the yanvalou, in which the spine undulates like the snake god, Damballa. But more than that, she absorbed the idea of dance as religious ritual. "In Vaudun we sacrifice to the gods," she has said, "but the top sacrifice is dance." Her dance *Shango* (1945), which depicts a possession ritual, hypnotized audiences during the Alvin Ailey American Dance Theater's "The Magic of Katherine Dunham" celebration in 1987.

Dunham also focused on American dance forms: "I was running around getting all these exotic things from the Caribbean and Africa when the real development lay in Harlem and black Americans," she says. "So I developed more things in jazz." In 1940, her revue, *Le Jazz Hot* included vernacular forms like the shimmy, black bottom, shorty George, and the cakewalk. That same year, Dunham collaborated with George Balanchine in choreographing the Broadway musical *Cabin in the Sky*. She recalls, "He took an Arab song and taught it to me for a belly dance." About their collaboration, she confesses, "He was a help, but I was pretty adamant about what I wanted to do. We had a wonderful time together."

In 1943, the international impresario Sol Hurok presented Dunham's company in *Tropical Revue* at the Martin Beck Theater on Broadway, adding Dixieland jazz musicians to boost its commercial appeal. The show became a hit, enjoying a six-week run. Dunham was a glamorous performer, and it is rumored that Hurok insured her legs for a million dollars. According to biographer Ruth Beckford, the dancer demurred, saying the amount was a mere quarter million.

Dunham's school in Times Square flourished for ten years beginning in 1945. Dana McBroom-Manno, who was a student there and later danced with the company, describes the Dunham technique as modern with an African base. "You use the floor as earth, the pelvis as center. You work for fluidity, moving like a goddess, doing undulations like the ocean. High leaps for the men. You elongate the muscles, creating a hidden strength. We use both parallel and turned out, so it's easy to go from Dunham into any other technique. The isolations of the hips, ribs, shoulders that you see in all jazz classes were brought to us from the Caribbean by Miss Dunham."

The school offered classes in ballet, modern (José Limón was one of its thirty or so teachers), "primitive," acting, martial arts, and more. Carmencita Romero, who danced in Dunham's early company and later taught

Katherine Dunham, 1940s: a great innovator and a great humanist. (Courtesy Special Collections Research Center, Morris Library, Southern Illinois University Carbondale)

dance history at The Ailey School, emphasizes the spiritual. "In Africa, all dance is based on animals, plants, the elements of the universe. . . . The Dunham technique gives you a feeling of release and exhilaration by letting the body go."

Among the students were James Dean, Arthur Mitchell, Butterfly McQueen, and Doris Duke. Donald Saddler, recently reminiscing, said Marlon Brando would come and play drums. Sometimes jazz great Charles Mingus would be there with a group of his musicians and play for classes.

Out of the school came a student group, directed by the legendary Syvilla Fort, that included Julie Belafonte, Walter Nicks, and Peter Gennaro. Belafonte—who met her husband, Harry, through one of the student performances—recalls: "We were taught the rhythms of the movements with drums and with song in other languages; for instance, Portuguese and Haitian patois. In class anyone could break into song at any time."

The Dunham company was an incubator for many well-known performers, including Eartha Kitt, Talley Beatty, and Janet Collins. In the 1940s and '50s, its heaviest touring years, the company visited an astounding fifty-seven countries. Audience response was heady. Dr. Glory Van Scott, who danced with the company in 1959 and 1960, says, "Everywhere we went, audiences went crazy. In Paris, we'd do our show and then go dancing half the night at the Samba Club. The audience loved us so much they would follow us there. It was unreal."

But the company encountered racism at home, and Dunham responded with defiance. In 1944, while touring in segregated Lexington, Kentucky, she found a "For Blacks Only" sign on a bus and pinned it to her dress onstage. Afterward, she declared to the audience that she wouldn't come back to a place that forbade blacks to sit next to whites.

In Dunham's *Southland* (1951), an impassioned response to the lynchings of Southern blacks, Julie Belafonte played a white woman whose false accusation of rape leads to a black man's hanging. "It was very, very difficult for me," Belafonte recalls. "I had to transpose my hatred of the character. . . . It was an acting problem. I had to overcome it in myself. . . . Everyone in the audience cried when we did it." [Update: Belafonte helped reconstruct *Southland* for Dallas Black Dance Theatre in 2012.]

Dunham has lived her credo that "all artists are humanists." For many years her home in Haiti, Habitation Leclerc, served as a medical clinic (as well as a tourist attraction, with its nightly drumming and dancing). Having given injections of vitamin B and penicillin to ailing dancers, she administered first aid in cases of parasites and joint diseases. Once a week, local doctors helped her to diagnose and treat patients in exchange for the medications that she could bring to them from New York.

During the racial troubles of the sixties, Dunham moved to East St. Louis, Illinois. Despite death threats and bomb scares, she helped a gang of black youths by giving them classes in martial arts, drumming, and dance. During that period, the police were picking up young black men as a matter of course. On one occasion, Dunham railed against this racial profiling, getting herself thrown in jail.

While in her eighties, she made national headlines by going on a hunger strike to protest the u.s. government's policy of returning Haitian refugees to face starvation and repression in their native land. She was supported in this effort by comedian Dick Gregory, filmmaker Jonathan Demme, and the Rev. Jesse Jackson, along with hundreds of other Americans. It was only at the coaxing of Jean-Bertrand Aristide, the deposed and later reinstated president of Haiti, that she ended her fast after forty-seven days.

Asked about her courageous stand, Dunham says simply, "You can't learn or acquire these things; I think they're just put in you from the beginning."

She feels it is an extension of her destiny to teach: "My guiding voices tell me I should teach, and that's what I've been doing my entire life." The Dunham technique is being taught all over the country. McBroom-Manno, who has taught it at Adelphi University, The Ailey School, and now at the 92nd Street Y Dance Center, says, "I teach Dunham technique as a way of life. Nutrition, African-based religions, and social conscience are all part of it." She remembers how, as a scholarship student getting free lunch at the school, she was required to learn the traditional Japanese tea ceremony. "We would be squirming and carrying on, but she wanted us to learn the serenity and silence of that tradition."

Dunham (or "Miss Dunham" as she is often called) is still concerned about Haiti. During a May 25 interview, she was gratified to hear that very day that Haiti had held free elections without incident.

But her thoughts linger on the art of dance. "Dance has been the step-child of the arts for a long time. I think now it's time for it to take its place among the other arts."

It is also time for Katherine Dunham to be honored as one of the great innovators in the field of dance and one of the great humanitarian artists in history.

Martha Clarke: Between Terror and Desire

Dance Magazine, October 2000

Not since my interview with Susan Sontag twenty-three years earlier did I have the sensation that every sentence my subject uttered was worth repeating. Martha Clarke was keenly in tune with her own psyche, and her fertile imagination spilled over in every direction. We laughed a lot.

Nobody knows what to call Martha Clarke's work. Is it dance? Is it theater? Is it music with images? Is it performance art? Critics try to define it; audiences want to know what to expect. But it's a losing battle, because she changes all the time, surprising even herself.

Her most recent creation, *Hans Christian Andersen*, is now playing at the American Conservatory Theater in San Francisco until October 8. With songs by Frank Loesser (from the 1952 Danny Kaye movie) and book by Sebastian Barry (*The Steward of Christendom*), it is a musical. But it's unlike any musical you've ever seen. Actors tell stories while dancers fly; the setting is otherworldly; no sunny, optimistic message is waiting in the wings.

If you heard Andersen's fairy tales as a child, you remember the pull between desire and terror that could haunt you long after the end of the story. Clarke, with her overflowing imagination and slightly sinister edge, is a perfect match for Andersen. Jane Greenwood's costumes and Robert Israel's set take you back to nineteenth-century Denmark, and Barry's script intercuts Andersen's poverty-stricken life with his hallucinatory stories.

A founding member of Pilobolus in the early seventies, Clarke later developed her own brand of physical theater that beguiled, startled, delighted and occasionally disturbed audiences. She would immerse herself in a time period to create a full-evening tapestry, interweaving imagery, movement, text, light, and music. Recognized as a ground-breaking artist, she has given us unforgettable pieces such as *The Garden of Earthly Delights* (1984), based on the paintings of Hieronymus Bosch; *Vienna: Lusthaus* (1986), which depicts a pre-Hitlerian erotic decadence, and *Vers La Flamme* (1999), a poetic merging of Scriabin's music and Chekhov's characters.

Spending an afternoon with Clarke in her Manhattan apartment, I learned about her past, present, and future while basking in her whimsical view of life and her hearty laughter. Clarke started out as a dancer but always thought in visual images. As a student at the Juilliard School in the sixties, she revered ballet teacher and choreographer Antony Tudor and composition master Louis Horst, but didn't feel the call of dance as a single art. "I actually wanted to leave Juilliard, but my parents wouldn't let me," she says. She railed against the business-as-usual aspect of dance composition: "I never was that interested in steps, but in gestures and movements that came out of a story or an emotional context. I didn't want to just put together turns and leaps and arabesques because I think they always look like turns and leaps and arabesques."

She was drawn to Anna Sokolow's work, and began as an apprentice in her company while still a student. After a few years she felt a vague sense of confinement: "At that time, modern dance called for a dedication and a lifestyle that cut off certain things, like rolling in grass. So I left Anna's company, had a baby, and moved to Rome, where I was a mother and a wife." In musing about her changing desires, she says, "I wanted to be a painter; now I'm doing musicals, and I want to do film directing. I just keep moving on some kind of dirt road of my own, and I'll probably circle back to making dances. But I still have some wanderlust."

That wandering has given her trouble with dance critics who like their dance straight up. But theater critics have heralded her work, calling it "hypnotic," "powerful" and "intensely erotic." Jack Kroll, writing in *Newsweek* in the eighties, pronounced her "one of the most exciting artists to emerge in the new 'performance' theater." Frank Rich wrote in the *New York Times* that with *Vienna: Lusthaus*, she "tapped into everyone's wildest dreams."

Indeed, Clarke says she often has flying dreams, and in *Andersen*, she's letting it fly (as it were). All eight dancers are rigged for flying in different terrains. "Thumbelina is in the forest, with fairies falling out of trees; the Ice Maiden floats across mountains; and courtiers glide on the floor in 'The Emperor and the Nightingale,'" she says. (Though Andersen also authored the dance talisman "The Red Shoes" and Clarke loves it, she didn't include it, because she feels the story has been explored fully by other artists.)

Although Clarke has directed actors and singers in recent projects, she prefers working with dancers. "I love their intuition, sweetness, their way of living, way of moving, way of seeing," she says. "When you work with actors, it's often much more analytical, a lot of conversation. Dancers have the uncanny intelligence of animals."

And dancers like working with her. Rob Besserer, who has appeared in many of her projects, describes her process: "It begins when you come in the door. She's already watching, for instance, how you flop into your seat, how you stand around in a group. She doesn't tell you specifically what to do—to the point where you can sometimes go crazy. She walks around you and eventually, from her notes and your suggestions, she orchestrates it.

It's sort of a sad moment when it has to crystallize. But in performance, you focus on the initial freedom."

The Andersen piece, Besserer says, is not all smooth sailing: "The flying hurts. Like riding a horse, you have to get back into it. The harness chafes terribly and pinches you. To change direction, you use your neck and head. If you try to use your legs for power, you're flailing." Then he adds, "Sometimes she likes that; she likes it when you're out of control."

Another brave soul who has surrendered to Clarke's artistic demands is Gus Solomons jr, who played an invented character in her *The Magic Flute*, a coproduction between Glimmerglass Playhouse and the Canadian Opera in 1994. Clarke had planned that Solomons would breathe fire for this part. But that didn't work out, so she asked if he could work with a live boa constrictor. Luckily for Clarke, snakes were Solomons's favorite animal. When I asked him about it, he exclaimed, "Lola, I loved Lola!" Turns out, he says, that a boa will kill you only if you're mean to it or take its babies. "Lola's tail was wrapped around my waist, and she was draped on my shoulder, and I was holding her neck. When I would hold her head away from me, she would hug my waist for more leverage. She was warm and felt good."

Clarke can't say exactly where she gets her ideas or images. But she does have a sense of their evanescence: "They're like wonderful birds—they pass through, and if I don't act on them immediately, they go. If I get on a riff and the muses are home, they can be very generous. And when I go dead, when it's not working, it's like being buried in a nailed coffin."

She admits that difficult times are sometimes fertile too: "There were years when making things would cause me enormous pain, and I didn't know how to alleviate the loneliness. Now I'm very grateful to that time. I went through fifteen years after my marriage dissolved and a very painful love affair, the kind that turns you inside out, and it was the same time I was discovering my own voice artistically, and they may have helped each other on." On the other hand, she is relieved to be more centered now: "Now that I am free of a love life, it's easier to create. I know who I am better. The world can turn down my art, but I love doing it. I'm irrepressible that way: As long as somebody offers me a job, I'm gonna work. When you have a lot of responsibilities, you never get quite the time as a creative person, like brewing the beer. You don't get the time to ferment when you're trying to be everything to everybody."

Clarke aims for the timeless as opposed to the topical. But in order to reach that timelessness, she goes for detail. "I often bring the clothing of the period on the first day of rehearsal," she says. "It affects the physicality of the work. In *Vers la Flamme* Margie Gillis wears a silk dress. She couldn't rehearse in sweatpants, because it has to do with how you hold your whole body back to get the skirt to swing. Every element in my work is interdependent. You can't take the dance steps away from the way you move in the cloth; you can't take the cloth away from the angle of the light; and you can't take the light away from the fade of a phrase of music. I see it as a kind of architecture in which these pieces are brought together."

While her architectural approach provides unity, constant change brings it to life. "My favorite thing is transitions," Clarke says. "In transition, you come carrying something and you suddenly receive something new. It's the things between things that I love. I've always loved spaces, I love the silence between words." This is the dancer in her speaking. And she feels that Andersen's tales are particularly adaptable to dance. "His motion imagery is so rich: Mermaids learn to walk with stabbing pain in their feet; a princess flies on a dog's back through the night; a man cuts off the wings of a swan and flies away," she says. "The stories are transformational. Metamorphosis is something you see; you don't talk about it. And that can only be done physically."

Clarke feels critics should be more open-minded. "I'm not self-consciously trying to break borders. I do what I do. But it's frustrating the way some people interpret it. Walls are breaking down all over the world, and we can't seem to do it artistically in America. Everything gets pigeonholed and labeled. It would be nice occasionally for the work to be seen for what it is."

The year Clarke won a MacArthur "genius" grant, 1990, was her worst year professionally. She felt humiliated—she can laugh at it now—by the response to *Endangered Species*, a piece based on her love of animals. The critics trashed it and the Brooklyn Academy of Music canceled it in mid-run. After a year of reflection afforded by the grant, Clarke found work in Europe, indulging her love of music and opera.

About her future, "I'm lucky I'm restless, because I don't think I'd be working had I stayed with choreography," she says, pronouncing it *chore-*eography. "Like a child blindfolded in the attic, I just keep stumbling on new adventures. I have a terrible fear of repeating myself. By going from dance to straight theater to opera to" . . . (she bursts into song) "musicals, I feel very fortunate."

Clarke deeply appreciates the producers who have stood by her year after year: Charles Reinhart, Lynn Austin, and Paul Kellogg. "I was beginning to be so grim, performing with Pilobolus. At the American Dance Festival, I came offstage and I picked up a match and held up a unitard, and Charlie said, 'Do you wanna do your own work next year?' In 1978, he gave me my first opportunity to spring from the Pilobolus nest. Lynn Austin of Music Theater Group produced me, and now I call her every weekend; she's like a mom. Paul Kellogg, who directs New York City Opera, really encouraged my career in opera. I get a little teary about it, but they have been so loving and believing, no matter what hills or valleys I was in professionally."

At fifty-six, Clarke savors the perspective that aging can bring. "Yes, I'd love to have a tight little body like an English bicycle again, but I'm more at peace with myself now. The most important thing to me is keeping an equilibrium. The people I see grow old with grace and inspiration are the people who keep challenging themselves."

Misha's New Passion: Judson Dance Theater

Dance Magazine, November 2000

As it turned out, Mikhail Baryshnikov's collaboration with Yvonne Rainer (see "An Im-
probable Pair on a Quest into the Past," Section V) was a prelude to a larger project.
Misha's Past Forward tour was similar to the Bennington College Judson Project I had
organized twenty years earlier in that both drew on the seminal Judson period of the
early sixties. My interest was ignited while working with Trisha Brown and seeing the
Grand Union; for him it happened a decade later while working with David Gordon at
American Ballet Theatre. Obviously, the ballet superstar's clout and visibility enabled
him to bring Judson choreographers to larger audiences. I had my doubts as to how this
downtown style of dance would play in big theaters, but kudos to him for trying!

Several dancers and choreographers were scattered in the seats of the
McCarter Theatre in Princeton, New Jersey, watching a dress rehearsal of the
White Oak Dance Project's new production, "Past Forward." Steve Paxton,
the legendary originator of Contact Improvisation, had just given directions
to thirty-nine volunteers from the community on how to perform *Satisfyin*
Lover, a piece he created in 1967. In this dance, people walk across the stage
one at a time, some of them pausing after a set number of paces, some of the
thirty-nine sitting on chairs that face front, a completely ordinary task. But
somehow, a sense of vulnerability and humanity comes through.

Mikhail Baryshnikov, one of those observing from the house, softly exclaimed, "It's so exciting!" Later he leaned forward to his fellow dancers and
whispered, "You see, it's different every time."

In strictly dance terms, what we were watching was anything but exciting.
The excitement lies in the fact that this piece is being done at all, and that
White Oak is celebrating the brazen and sometimes difficult work of Judson
Dance Theater.

At fifty-two, Baryshnikov could simply bask in acclaim as one of the
world's greatest-ever ballet dancers. But he continues to seek new challenges for his eclectic White Oak Dance Project. The current tour unites his
company with downtown-style gurus Paxton, Trisha Brown, Yvonne Rainer,
Simone Forti, Deborah Hay, David Gordon, and Lucinda Childs. Like Bob
Dylan's fabled seventies concerts with his famous poet and singer friends,
this is his own "Rolling Thunder" tour. His repertoire includes fourteen
dances by these choreographers, two of whom are included in his cast.

Over a carafe of cranberry vodka at the Russian Samovar in Manhattan, Baryshnikov discussed "Past Forward," White Oak in general, and the dances that absorb him now. He lights up when talking about the dance artists he has worked with, and is clearly both stimulated and humbled by great choreographers. An independent thinker, he doesn't wait for the press or anyone else to tell him who the great choreographers are. He follows his thirst to the well of artistic invention. At this moment, that well is the art-as-life minimalism that characterized much of the work shown at Judson Memorial Church in the early sixties, the breakthrough period of experimentalism that gave rise to postmodern dance.

Baryshnikov's interest in breaking the rules and defying expectation goes way back. In 1973, while still in St. Petersburg, he chose to dance in a work that required him to roll on the floor at a time when, of course, fans adored his high leaps and sparkling technique. Once in New York, Baryshnikov journeyed through the American modern dance repertoire, becoming ever more daring in his choices. He danced in works by John Butler, Martha Graham, Twyla Tharp, Lar Lubovitch, Paul Taylor, Alvin Ailey, Mark Morris, Merce Cunningham, Trisha Brown and many more. As artistic director of American Ballet Theatre from 1980 to 1989, he made controversial choices by inviting "punk" choreographer Karole Armitage and postmodernist David Gordon to create pieces for America's premier classical ballet company. He certainly has no allegiance to the traditional ballets he grew up with. If he were still in Russia, he says, "I would be dead by now. I was a bit reckless and it would be difficult to predict what I would have done. I definitely wouldn't have stayed for the classical ballet."

Getting to know Gordon was partly what set the superstar on his current path. The two have remained friends since their days at ABT. Gordon is contributing four ballets to "Past Forward"—*Chair/two times* (1975); *The Overture to "The Matter"* (1979); *For the Love of Rehearsal*, which is a new work to portions of Bach's cello suites, and a brief chair solo for Baryshnikov to Sousa's "Stars and Stripes Forever." In addition, Baryshnikov asked Gordon to direct the production. The choreographer wrote a witty introduction that Baryshnikov narrates (on tape) with the help of projected images: "In the sixties, Russia put the first man in space; Trisha Brown walked on walls. . . . Kennedy said 'No' to Russian missiles; Yvonne Rainer said 'No' to American dance conventions."

When asked what attracts him to the Judson artists, Baryshnikov answers, "Bravery! They were all truly experimental." Impressed with stories Steve Paxton told him about *Flat* (1964), a solo Baryshnikov performs in this program, he tells of the first time Paxton showed it in Dunn's workshop. Nobody said anything, Baryshnikov relates, but the feeling was, "What the hell was that?" He concludes, "He knew that there's something there that's never been done before. A long time before, Kafka, Beckett, Ionesco, and Sartre were a slice of existentialism of the highest order." The brand of existentialism favored by some of the Judson choreographers meant stripping the dancing of drama, embellishment, theatricality. In other words, it meant unadorned plainness, which can be hard for audiences to take.

Baryshnikov anticipates being challenged for his new direction: "Some people will say, 'Why's he doing this?' It's not decisions I make rationally. I listen to my heart and mind. This is the most interesting thing I can do right now, and I'm doing it." Although his decision is intuitive, it is supported by his knowledge of its historical value, Baryshnikov says. "Nobody seriously understood the influence of the Judson people on the present generation of choreographers. Mark Morris said, 'I'm telling my dancers Judson this, Judson that, and they haven't seen anything.' Now they can. Meg Stuart [an American choreographer active in Europe] said, 'Without Trisha and the others, I wouldn't even exist.' John Jasperse, Neil Greenberg, Tere O'Connor, Dana Reitz, Sara Rudner—they all got that extra chutzpah from knowing about Judson. It gave them hope, stamina, inspiration. That's why it's so important for people who are choreographing now to see this kind of work."

He speaks about *Single Duet*, a new duet created by Deborah Hay, with respect and affection. "Deborah is the queen of this kind of internal commitment in improvisation. Her approach is really far out. You're warming yourself up, just dancing together like children would do when they put the music on, for a substantial amount of time, to get yourself into the blood-flowing and mind-calming state. The word 'rehearsal' doesn't exist. She comes in with a very strong structure, because she knows exactly what she wants. It's very intense and exhausting."

Hay tells me, during the dress rehearsal, of Baryshnikov's progress in improvisation. "At first he wanted something to hold on to, but then he learned to let go. I have so much faith in his intelligence and his ability to observe. He sees everything. It's jaw-dropping, the amount of stuff he lets go of. He's sailing now."

In performance, the two portray a strange and fascinating pair. Hay, whose face is a cross between Martha Graham's and a butoh dancer's, exudes an internal authenticity—serenity through turmoil, one might call it. Baryshnikov, boyish and buoyant, strives to be her partner in oddness. As he moves, he seems to shape-shift from an old ballet master to a flamenco star, to a self-caressing exhibitionist, to a squirrel. Occasionally, they share a faraway look together.

He finds Paxton's solo *Flat* particularly challenging. It consists of walking around in a suit, striking four or five non-virtuosic positions, removing garments and hanging them onto hooks taped to his skin, and then interrupting the daily task of dressing with frozen moments. Paxton says that by the end, the viewer "knows something very intimate about the person that doesn't show through the clothes. He's covered up again, so it's like a secret has been revealed and concealed." The performer must make spontaneous decisions about what pose to strike and where to freeze the action.

Baryshnikov says, "You buy children's toys that say, 'Some assembly required,' but one thing they forgot to tell you is what order to do it in. You have to make a dance out of it. Steve cannot teach you what makes sense. You have to make it happen while you're actually doing it. The audience can see if it's premeditated. There is logic and there's absurdity. That's Steve. He's the most elusive person I ever met."

Paxton, like Hay, gives kudos to his student. At first, he says, "Misha would start doing something like unbuttoning the shirt or unlacing the shoe and forget that he was supposed to arrest the motion. I think he discovered a habit that he is learning to address, which is getting through something as quickly as possible and getting on to the next thing."

In Trisha Brown's *Homemade* (1965), Baryshnikov carries a projector on his back, beaming images of his dancing self around the auditorium. Explaining this solo, he is obviously moved that Brown would transfer such a personal piece to him. Brown says, "I gave him the same instructions I gave myself: to enact and distill a series of memories, the stories you tell when you know someone really well. He went deeply into these memories, like the last time he saw his mother as the train pulled out of the station." (His mother committed suicide when he was still a boy in Latvia.) One can easily see how much these moves mean to him.

Baryshnikov clearly revels in the presence of these seven artists: "They're all beautifully crazy. They're all insane and I salute that." Perhaps they give him the same sense of permissiveness that allowed them to find their unique artistic voices nearly forty years ago. He is delighted that some of them have chosen only to do new work, while others have reconstructed older pieces.

The kind of everyday actions—or, as David Gordon calls it, "behavior"—displayed in "Past Forward" can present a dilemma for the White Oak dancers, all of whom have strong ballet and/or modern training. At a rehearsal for *Scramble* (1970) at LaGuardia High School of Performing Arts in New York City, Simone Forti, renowned for her sensuous simplicity, instructs the dancers to "run across the floor as though to catch a bus." Typically, she brings cosmic principles down to earthiness: "A mass in motion tends to remain in motion. The universe is carrying you. See if you can taste that moment."

When Forti demonstrates *Scramble*, which is based on the simple action of threading in between any two people, her own pleasure in fulfilling the task is palpable. But some of the dancers are confused. In the talk session between Baryshnikov and the dancers afterward, Emily Coates, formerly with New York City Ballet, says, "I thought this was supposed to be pedestrian, but now it seems like you want it to be more dancerly." Discussion. Finally, Raquel Aedo, who has danced with Douglas Dunn and Dancers, comes to her aid by saying, "I feel that doing a task creates a state of mind."

While the White Oak dancers struggled with aesthetic issues, the community people who volunteered to perform were enjoying a rich experience. John Tucker, an executive search consultant who lives in Princeton, says, "It made me feel that we were in on some secret stuff. Because of the willingness of the directors and choreographers to share their thoughts and feelings about the work, we began to care about what we were doing. It was great, great fun." Amanda Loulaki, a dancer from Crete who joined in *Scramble* as well as Paxton's and Gordon's group pieces, says about Baryshnikov, "He is beautiful. He's such an inspiration because he's totally committed to research. He asks the choreographers questions, wanting to understand where the work comes from." Teresa Kliokis, a student at Marymount College, is ecstatic. "I got to meet him! I came in early for rehearsal, and he was eating. I didn't want to disturb him, but he shook my hand and asked me where I'm from. I said to myself, 'Oh my God, Oh my God, I can't believe this!'"

Audiences, however, have been ambivalent. About the standing-room-only event, McCarter impresario Bill Lockwood reports, "The audience was respectful but puzzled. They don't recognize the name of the choreographers, with the possible exception of Trisha Brown. Their whole dance experience is totally at odds with what they saw. This was like a bolt out of the blue." A few people walked out, and Lockwood later received a handful of letters claiming that this wasn't dance and that the publicity was misleading. (Still, scores of people flocked to the stage to get Baryshnikov's autograph after the performance.) Although Lockwood finds the project fascinating, he feels that White Oak needs to clarify to its audiences the what's and why's of the project.

That is just what is happening as the company readies itself for its fall tour. Charles Atlas, a brilliant media artist who has worked closely with Merce Cunningham, will assemble a video collage to give the program a historical context.

In Florida, where White Oak toured last spring with a program that included only one of these pieces, Rainer's *After Many a Summer Dies the Swan*, audiences had no such help. Baryshnikov describes their reactions to her piece, which is a collage of fragments of older works: "People were mesmerized. They were sitting, listening, watching, laughing, protesting, bravoing, booing. It's so encouraging. It's a theater of life; something is there they can relate to, and they are happy to discover in themselves those elements. Sometimes they do understand; sometimes it's total absurdity. But they are intrigued by it; they want to know more and sometimes it hits them right between the eyes."

But one may wonder: Can works from long ago—even groundbreaking works—that were made for a church or a gallery, have an impact on a proscenium stage? Obviously, a piece that was vital at a particular time is not necessarily vital many years later. And yet Forti says, "There is still much nourishment that audiences can get from these pieces."

About being artistic director and étoile of the White Oak Dance Project, which he founded with the help of Mark Morris, Baryshnikov says, "My life started ten years ago with White Oak. All my creative thoughts are related to White Oak and nothing else." He enjoys the communality of the dancing. "From the beginning of White Oak, I wanted to dance as part of the group. I never had a chance to, in all my years as a classical dancer. Dancing together . . . I like the shoulders of other dancers, I like that touch, I like that look, the communication, the dynamics. There's nothing sweeter than this. I always love doing it. Maybe from my childhood, because we danced a lot of character dances, international dances with sixteen other kids." He now finds himself wishing for a slightly larger group. "If I could afford it, it would be fun to have ten or twelve people. But we are really cozy right now with six people. I cherish that tightness and family feeling."

Another family is thriving because of the project. The Judson family, remembered by a few and influential to many, is being legitimized by a mainstream star. Jennifer Tipton, lighting designer extraordinaire, started her career by dancing in a piece of Paxton's at Judson. Now, designing lights for "Past Forward" she says, "In a way I feel like it's my family; that's where it began."

Reviewing "Past Forward" for the *Asbury Park Press* of New Jersey, Karyn Collins notes that she saw a member of the audience tear up his ticket and throw it toward the stage in disgust. But after observing the ups and downs of this program, she concludes, "The painstakingly detailed and carefully casual performances add up to a truly extraordinary experience." Perhaps Baryshnikov will find that, in presenting the Judson choreographers, he too bears the burden of bravery.

Living with AIDS: Six Dancers Share Their Stories

Dance Magazine, December 2000

When I joined the editorial team of Dance Magazine, *I was asked, What is the issue we are not covering? My immediate answer was* AIDS. *The disease had ravaged the dance community, yet not much had been written about it in the magazine. I was devastated when my friend Harry Sheppard died in 1992, and that was just one death of thousands. Working on this story immersed me in the sadness and anxiety we all felt. But it was galvanizing—and uplifting—to hear what these six dancers had been through and the courage they called upon.*

By 2000 there was some good news: people who had found the right combination of meds were living with AIDS *a long time. At least five of the six dancers I interviewed are still alive and thriving. (I don't know about the Broadway dancer who wouldn't let me use his real name simply because I don't remember his name.) By the way, if the lead sounds familiar, it's because you read a longer version of this scene in my introduction to Section III.*

I was riding in an elevator in a Manhattan hospital, and the elevator doors happened to open onto a ward in which a distraught young man was talking into the phone at the nurses' station. I recognized him as a fellow choreographer—Arnie Zane. I knew Arnie had AIDS, and I stepped out to say hello. He had just learned that his chemotherapy wasn't working and the doctors were telling him there wasn't much hope. He was crying, and I hugged him. That was all I could do. As we walked outside, he lamented, "I know I complain a lot, but I love this life and I don't want to die." A few months later, Arnie was dead.

That was in 1987. If this scene had happened today, there would be more hope.

In the eighties and nineties, the dance community was decimated by AIDS. We lost some of our most treasured elders: Alvin Ailey, Robert Joffrey, Rudolf Nureyev, and Michael (*A Chorus Line*) Bennett; some of our most promising youths: Edward Stierle of the Joffrey and Peter Fonseca of American Ballet Theatre; and mid-career artists like Arnie Zane (whose memory is preserved in the name of the Bill T. Jones/Arnie Zane Dance Company), Louis Falco, Robert Blankshine, Christopher Gillis, John Bernd, Harry Sheppard, and Ulysses Dove. During that period, it seems, we were attending as many memorial services as dance performances. We learned the meaning of community—the gathering together when the loss of someone you love leaves a big hole.

But thanks to improved medication, testing positive for HIV is no longer a death sentence. More dancers are continuing to live and dance with the virus. Others are still having a hard time. The fatality rate is slowing, but we cannot forget the devastation the disease still brings. I spoke with six dancers and former dancers who are handling the disease in different ways.

Dancer/choreographer Neil Greenberg, who teaches at the State University of New York at Purchase, tested positive in 1986. He's been basically asymptomatic, so he is living his life as usual, only cutting back on alcohol. Greenberg says 1993 was a hard year for him: his brother died of AIDS, two-thirds of the people in his HIV support group died, and he learned that the virus's presence in his blood had increased. Out of these tragedies emerged his *Not-About-AIDS-Dance* (1994), a powerful work that created a buzz in downtown New York. But in 1997 he landed in the hospital. "I had high fevers the whole week I was performing that fall," he says. "About a year later the doctors realized it was the medication that was doing that to me."

Now on new medication, he is thriving again. All along, he says, he has maintained a positive approach. "I tried to deny what all of the papers said, which was a ten-year maximum life expectancy," Greenberg says. "I refused to believe that and, as it turned out, I was right, for myself." However, he still struggles with the disease emotionally: "The whole AIDS-as-punishment thing is hard to get rid of in the deepest layers, and I probably haven't." In order to dispel some of the stigma that he grew up with, he makes a point of telling his freshman students at SUNY Purchase that he has the virus. After all, he reasons, it's part of their education.

Another dancer I spoke with performs every night in a high-powered Broadway musical. He has asked that his name be withheld, so I'll call him Jack. Jack got the bad news in 1996, the year that new medications came into being and many AIDS patients found "cocktails" of a variety of medications to be effective. Jack says, "My doctor told me right away, 'This isn't the end of your life. Don't drive your car off a cliff. There are medications that are helping people, and you should be able to live a normal life. It's a controlled disease like diabetes. You just have to take your pills every day.'" At first Jack balked at telling his fellow dancers. But, he said, "I've never had a bad reaction from people I've been working with, though it's scary at first. You're afraid that people will look at you differently. But I don't mind being out at work, because people have questions and they know they can come to me. I enjoy giving back whatever I can to people around me." He's been generally very healthy, but his doctors haven't always known what to prescribe: "One time, for a whole month, I couldn't leave the couch: vomiting, diarrhea, severe stomach cramps. It was very scary."

The knowledge of his HIV status actually motivated him. "It made me pull my life together and get my career going. I was happy doing revues and competitions, but I decided I wanted to make Broadway. Within three months, I made Broadway."

He feels comfortable in the dance world. "Being gay in the dance world is more accepted and you can be who you are. Because of that, people who are [HIV] positive can come out and share that also. When you get into TV or film, being gay is not OK. They may hire you to be a gay character, but they want you to be straight. If they were to find out you're HIV [positive], they would probably not hire you."

Of course, not only gay men get the disease. Stephanie Dabney, former star and unforgettable Firebird with Dance Theatre of Harlem in the early eighties, was diagnosed ten years ago. Her first thoughts were, "There goes my career. If I get too sick to dance, what am I going to do? How am I going to tell my brother and sister?" She spent all of 1996 in the hospital with recurring pneumonia, and the following year in nursing homes. "My fourth pneumonia was PCP [pneumocystis carinii pneumonia, a life-threatening infection for people with weakened immune systems], and my lung collapsed. I had a chest-tube pump in me for eight weeks. I remember the doctor coming into my room, surprised, saying 'Hi, I didn't think you would be here.' He thought I wasn't going to make it through the night! That freaked me out." She is now participating in an experimental program, a nine-month trial with an Italian physician. "Maybe I'll help him find the cure," she says. Friends encourage her to resume dancing. "I ran into [actress] Cicely Tyson, and she thinks I should dance again," she says. "But Arthur [Mitchell, DTH's artistic director] has young, healthy, and eager dancers now, and there's nowhere else I would want to dance besides DTH. I can't imagine trying to get in shape. I'd rather be remembered as the Firebird when I was young and healthy."

Sometimes nondancers would turn against her when they found out she had AIDS. "There was a woman in Atlanta whose position was to wine and dine the Somebodies," Dabney says. "I was the black ballerina who did Firebird, so I was in her in-crowd. But when she found out I had it, she wouldn't even return my calls."

Dabney, who has taught at Spelman College in Atlanta, thinks about the future. "I thought I'd want to teach again, but I'm walking with canes now.

Tanaquil LeClerq [the extraordinary Balanchine ballerina who was struck down with polio in 1956] was my favorite teacher. She used her hands and arms as legs and feet."

Another former dancer, Joseph Carman, is now a freelance writer. Carman, who has danced with American Ballet Theatre and the Joffrey, almost died four years ago before the new medications became available. He had been diagnosed in 1987 while dancing with the Metropolitan Opera Ballet. "I kept it secret in the beginning because there was such a stigma. That was the time when the *Post* was running headlines like 'AIDS Killer.' There weren't many support groups around. The year before I left the company, I told the ballet mistress, Diana Levy. The Americans with Disabilities Act had just been approved, which protects anyone in the work force who has a disability. It allows people with HIV to shorten work hours or to do a less demanding job. She was understanding and would ask me during rehearsal, 'Are you okay?'" The main thing for Carman was getting enough rest. Working on a new production, he'd sometimes be in the theater for twelve hours: "When things were bad, I'd break out in shingles."

In 1996, he was diagnosed with Kaposi's sarcoma (KS), a cancerous growth associated with AIDS. "It progressed slowly and then all of a sudden my immune system went like a house of cards. I'd wake up with two new lesions every day. It was terrifying. They discovered I had KS in my lungs. That usually means a year to live if you're lucky. The doctor put me in the hospital and administered heavy-duty chemotherapy. I call it 'slash-and-burn' chemo because it wrecks everything. For days afterward I would feel like crawling out of my skin. But it did get rid of the tumors."

An AIDS conference in Geneva had just demonstrated that protease inhibitors and the new "cocktails" were helping people. It was good timing, and Carman started a regime of the new medications. "My immune system slowly started to rebuild itself, and my T cells [white blood cells that help suppress disease] climbed from ten to over six hundred. It's truly miraculous." But it wasn't easy emotionally. "I thought I was dying, and then all of a sudden I wasn't dying. I was in shock for about a year. Physically, it took me four years to feel like myself again."

But Carman has been through a significant shift. "When you come that close to death, it changes the way you look at things. It's like a rebirth; it cuts the bullshit factor. For me now, the quality of life is important: eating well, walking my dog in the park, spending time with my boyfriend. I still do a juggling act with all my medications."

Carman feels that consciousness has been raised and there is less stigma about the disease. He is grateful for the concern of people in the dance world. But the past is a string of sorrows. American Ballet Theatre's 1977 video of *The Nutcracker* starring Mikhail Baryshnikov and Gelsey Kirkland used to be broadcast on TV every Christmas. He says, "I can't even watch it now because half the dancers in it are dead."

Chris Dohse, a dancer/choreographer/writer who is also a proofreader, is torn between submitting to the new medications and just letting himself slide downhill. "I don't know if I want to buckle myself into the regime of the new cocktails. I don't want to go through that ordeal." Dohse, who tested positive in 1987 when he was dancing in Washington, D.C., was put on azidothymidine, or AZT, in 1990. AZT inhibits the spread of the AIDS virus, but it can have debilitating side effects. "I felt terrible every single day of that year," says Dohse. "It makes you tired, nauseous, headachy, dizzy, and run-down. During that time they were finding that it works better if you take less of it. I got disillusioned and distrustful, so I don't believe anything the doctors say."

But for Dohse too, the news was at first a motivating factor: "Knowing I had the virus made me stop fiddling around. I stopped dancing for other people and started making my own work." Like Greenberg, he used his despair creatively. "I made a big dance for nine people that was going to be the final thing that I gave to the world. I kept revamping it. I didn't want to finish it because then it meant I was going to live, and have to make other work. This was supposed to be the everything-I-have-to-say piece."

He lost the few romantic figures in his life, which has left him with a sense of alienation. "Mostly I feel anger that I didn't get to go with them. They had these memorial services and dramatic narrative arcs, but I have to stay here and turn gray and have my teeth fall out and pay back my student loans. I'm lonely." Medically, he's not up for the new round. "They started saying I should take new medication to reduce my viral load. They said that to me in 1990 with the AZT. My blood data will improve but I'll feel awful." His T cells are under a hundred, and, after thirteen years, his viral load has gone sky high. Looking back, he says, "Eight years ago the data showed that thirteen years was the longest anybody had lasted before they started getting sick. I thought: Okay, I got five years left; I'll make a five-year plan. For eight years I had made six-month plans. I would have gotten a college degree back then if I wasn't going to die any day. I danced instead, thinking I'd go out in a blaze of glory. Little did I know I would keep lingering. I'm the boy who cried wolf because I've lived so long on this edge of despair."

Christopher Pilafian, on the faculty of the University of California at Santa Barbara, has found some measure of peace. He danced with Jennifer Muller/The Works from its inception in 1974 to 1989, eventually serving as associate artistic director. Now forty-seven, he says, "It's hard to tell whether what I'm feeling is a result of the virus or of the natural aging process. I'm a little more methodical, less rambunctious now." Four years ago, he improved his T-cell count tremendously with the new medications.

Pilafian feels fortunate to have colleagues who are sensitive to his condition. "When I was having a bad time, they were available to cover classes for me." He mourns the toll the virus has taken on the lives of dancers he admired as well as on his own. "The middle years are an important period in a dancer's life: you've still got your chops and also your independence. I would like to have seen what Louis Falco would have done, had he lived past fifty. If I weren't HIV positive, I might have focused on my work as a choreographer. Instead, I had to go into self-preservation."

In 1989, he attended a seminar that redefined AIDS not as a terminal illness, but as a manageable chronic infection. "To take the assumption of fatality off the diagnosis is very powerful. Now I'm doing things that support life: meditation, visualization, eating well, and watching the purity of things. There was so much fear about the available medicines at that time. To deal with that, I used what I knew from dancing: imagery. I began to visualize the medications as rainbows, waterfalls, and light."

"At the conference we were asked, 'What is this apparent misfortune bringing to you that is a benefit?' It gave permission to look at your life in a different way. You could imagine the endpoint being closer. Then starts the dropping away of the nonessentials, which is a sacred, life-sustaining process."

These six dancers are, like the rest of us, many-faceted people. One of those facets, surely, is tremendous courage. Another is hard-earned wisdom. All of them agree on one thing: the need to tell young people to take precautions. Anyone can contract the virus from sexual activity, and drug users can get it from using a contaminated needle. Although a broad range of treatments is now available, not every patient does well on them, and the side effects can be devastating. The ultimate message is one of prevention: inform yourself, protect yourself, and have only safe sex.

Updates, as of 2012:

· Joseph Carman, a senior contributing editor at *Dance Magazine*, has written about the performing arts for *Playbill*, the *New York Times*, the *Los Angeles Times*, the *Village Voice*, the *Advocate*, and many other publications. Now in stable health (and juggling many medications), he is the author of *Round about the Ballet* and also teaches various styles of yoga, including vinyasa, hatha, and restorative.

- Stephanie Dabney still lives in Manhattan. She's had kidney surgeries that are unrelated to AIDS and says her medications are keeping her alive. She's been following the resurrection of Dance Theatre of Harlem and will be visiting the DTH studio at the invitation of artistic director Virginia Johnson.
- Chris Dohse has worked as a copywriter and editor for several major pharmaceutical ad agencies in New York. His life performing, choreographing, and writing criticism has become an avocation. He is currently on disability, dealing with the effects of multiple medications and comorbidities.
- Neil Greenberg is a professor of choreography at Eugene Lang College, The New School of Liberal Arts in New York City, where he continues to choreograph and dance. Though he had a run-in with an AIDS-related complication (Castleman's disease of the lymphatic system), he's had a complete recovery and is living happily, with no viral-load, with his husband.
- Christopher Pilafian is director of dance and vice chair of the Department of Theater and Dance at UC Santa Barbara. In 2011–2012 he received tenure, coorganized a national conference, cocurated an exhibition, performed, wrote an essay for publication, and was appointed artistic director of the resident professional company, Santa Barbara Dance Theater. He's been in the same domestic relationship for almost thirty years.

Irina Loves Maxim

Dance Magazine, February 2001

I've always found that Russians, if they are not completely dour, have a sharp sense of humor. So it was with Irina Dvorovenko and Maxim Beloserkovsky, two of the most classically trained ballet dancers in New York. This profile was the first section of a five-couple story for our Valentine issue with the headline "Irina Loves Maxim . . . and other real-life pas de deux." I tried to keep their charming, Russian-accented English and witty exaggerations intact.

Seven years after leaving Kiev, Irina Dvorovenko and Maxim Beloserkovsky are rising stars of American Ballet Theatre. Their performances are charged with dramatic excitement, audiences can't get enough of them, and they are getting juicy lead roles. And, seven years after their wedding day, they are dancing together more and more; traveling together; helping each other through artistic, physical, and emotional highs and lows.

Dvorovenko, twenty-seven, and Beloserkovsky, twenty-nine, met as children at the Kiev Ballet School in the Ukraine. She went on to dance with the Ballet Theatre of Kiev, and he with the National Opera of Bulgaria and then the Kiev company. It wasn't until they were touring with a group from the Bolshoi, and were assigned to the same hotel room (because it was assumed they were a couple), that the shy feelings they had for each other blossomed into a romance. Now a unified team, they bring an old-world glamour and the purity of the famous Vaganova technique to ABT.

Recently they talked about their life together and their artistic goals. Hearing about their first performing experiences as children in *Sleeping Beauty*—the same ballet that enchanted little Georgi Balanchivadze at the Mariinsky Theatre some seventy years earlier—is like hearing a single stirring memory with two voices. Maxim: "I remember like yesterday. The first time you experience this light onstage . . . the power of this light . . . was unbelievable." Irina: "You see the ballerina close to you, and it was just like in a dream."

Once they became professional, they were frustrated by the limitations of ballet in the Ukraine. Maxim likens the conditions to a flower that has no water to grow. Looking back at the generation that preceded him, he says, "Twenty years the same, no new choreography, only Petipa, Petipa, Petipa." The official word was that the Russian defectors—Rudolf Nureyev, Natalia

Irina Dvorovenko and Maxim Beloserkovsky in *Giselle* at ABT.
(© Gene Schiavone, courtesy ABT)

Makarova, Mikhail Baryshnikov—didn't exist. "We were told that they got destroyed in the West; they're nobody." But then Maxim, still a teenager, saw pirated videos of Makarova doing *Swan Lake* with Anthony Dowell for the Royal Ballet, Nureyev dancing *Spectre de la rose*, and Baryshnikov in *Don Quixote*. It was a revelation. Says Maxim, "Something clicked in my mind that I have to try what's there." Economically there was no incentive to stay in the former Soviet Union. "The life was so miserable and you always have to fight for your food, for your money, for everything." Irina adds, "I remember how my parents [also dancers] spent all their salary for my pointe shoes."

The struggle for decent shoes has been a theme in their lives. Maxim explains, "We had an old wood floor, so it means a couple tendus or a couple pirouettes and you have huge hole in your shoes. We didn't have this marley." In order to extend the life of his shoes, Max learned how to carefully darn them with thick thread. Irina: "Every day sitting with needle. Oh, you should see how Max did the application on his shoes. He could put in museum." When at sixteen Irina won a silver medal at the U.S.A. International Ballet Competition in Jackson, Mississippi, she was wearing a new brand of pointe shoe called Grishko. After that, she was asked by Yuri Grishko to help him develop the ideal pointe shoe. She would try out different models and phone in the results, saying exactly how many minutes each pair lasted and helping to analyze what had gone wrong. (In the ten years since, Grishko has become a major dance supplier.)

In 1994, Maxim had a contract with the Hamburg Ballet, and was able to get a tourist visa to the United States from the American Embassy there. Irina followed soon after, but it was rough going at first. They had been stars in the Ukraine, but in the United States they were faced with a new language, a new culture, and only corps roles. They had to start from the beginning. At first there was no place for Irina in ABT, so she freelanced for a year and a half. Once they landed roles, they had to get used to the new schedule. "We never worked for seven hours a day, rehearsing three or four ballets in one day. In Russia you do a performance and then have three days' rest."

They started getting injuries. Maxim developed a bone spur that wouldn't let him stay on half toe, and Irina damaged a tendon in her foot. Both required surgery and rehabilitation.

Plus, they found the dance values to be different. Their Russian training stressed the integration of technique, musicality, and acting. Here, they found the emphasis to be primarily on technique. One of the reasons they like dancing together is they can embrace the wholeness, the sense of harmony that they equate with true artistry. Maxim says that when they dance as partners, "We say one thing, one language together." Irina says, "I trust Max; he knows me and he knows my body. He knows I could behave differently. If I skip something, he can handle it." They work hard to achieve the "sublime harmony and breathtaking stylistic unity" that Anna Kisselgoff praised them for in the *New York Times*.

Although they project a oneness in duets, they have distinct personalities. Maxim is the picture of ardor and nobility onstage, and Irina is impetuous, seductive, and slightly mischievous. When she veers close to him, sparks fly. She can be daring because he is her safety net. Part of their chemistry is the difference in temperaments and tempos. "There is always a feeling," says Maxim, "that we run a marathon and she's a little bit ahead. Her natural speed, even her simple walk on the street, is so fast."

If she has the edge on speed, he has the edge on coaching. He has an excellent eye, and he works with her in their living room—"a glissade jeté from one end of the room to the other"—to perfect the roles she does without him like Gamzatti in *La Bayadère* and the Siren in *Prodigal Son*. "The most important thing for me is that every step she does onstage, every movement of arms, eyes, and body, will be truly believable. If it's a little fake, that's it for me." He watches from backstage, calling out to her in Russian, "Breathe" or "Very good, darling" when she comes close enough to hear. If something goes wrong, he gets a "cold, wet feeling on my skin." At a recent performance of *Prodigal Son*, there was a mishap during her duet with the Prodigal, played by Jose Manuel Carreño. The Prodigal is sitting, and the Siren stands on his knees as he slowly lowers her—a tricky maneuver that Balanchine called "the elevator." The timing wasn't quite right and she fell off his knees, recovering so expertly that most of the audience didn't perceive it as a mistake. But Maxim, watching from the wings, sweated it out: "I lost three pounds immediately."

They are now completely comfortable at ABT, which welcomes international dancers. "We are part of the universe here," says Maxim. They feel fortunate to have as an adviser ballet mistress Irina Kolpakova, who was a member of the last class graduated by Agrippina Vaganova. Reached by phone, Kolpakova said she does not work with them on steps, but on style. "They are talented *inside*," she said. "But sometimes they have too much energy. I have to remind them they have to come back and dance the next day too."

Their busy schedule keeps them dancing as guest artists with companies like the Australian Ballet, Finland Ballet, Hamburg Ballet, and the Asami Maki Ballet in Tokyo during times off from ABT.

Romance upon romance is promised for Irina and Maxim during ABT's spring season. Artistic director Kevin McKenzie is casting them together more often, and they will be dancing *Swan Lake, Don Quixote, Cinderella, Giselle,* and *Onegin*. Regarding *Onegin*, Irina is looking forward not only to dancing Tatiana, but to seeing Maxim dance the role of Lensky in this Russian story. "I'm dying to see Max dance this role. I know already I'll be crying so badly because it will touch my soul really really deeply. It will stay for several weeks inside."

They are also keen to dance *Giselle* for the first time in this country. Back home, they were possibly the youngest couple—she was nineteen, he twenty—ever to do *Giselle* in Russia. Here in New York, they've waited years to attain the proper rank—both were promoted to principal only last August—and seniority to be cast by ABT.

Naturally, they often dance with other partners, and they pour their energy into those partnerships as well. But they always find time to express their tenderness to each other. "Sometimes," says Irina, "all day long we don't see each other. I have another partner. At the end of the day we kind of miss each other. It's so sweet, you know."

Update: After long careers with ABT, Maxim and Irina are no longer with the company but still perform as guest artists elsewhere. They have founded summer intensives in both Panama and New York, and Maxim teaches at Ballet Academy East in Manhattan. Irina recently performed in the "Encores!" series at New York City Center as the diva ballerina Vera Baronova in *On Your Toes*—and was a smashing success. Their daughter, Emma, born in 2005, studies ballet.

Twyla Tharp: Still Pushing the Boundaries

Dance Magazine, March 2001

This cover story came at a time of transition in Twyla Tharp's work. When I watched her rehearsal, it seemed like she was reaching a peak of a certain genre of dancing to music—or, shall I say, another peak, since In the Upper Room *(1986) had certainly been a peak. She was a master of "pure dance," and this was clear at the photo shoot, where she improvised for three hours straight, without even a sip of water. Soon after this interview, she took these same five dancers and made* Movin' Out *to songs by Billy Joel, which enjoyed a three-year run on Broadway. So not only did she trade in concert work for a Broadway show, but she turned away from pure dance toward narrative.*

The episode I open the story with happened about a year before I joined her "farm club," a kind of group repository of her repertoire, for six weeks. Twyla was such a huge figure to me and my peers in the seventies that I relished the opportunity this feature gave me to delve into what made her a great dance artist.

One of the few choreographers I ever said "no" to was Twyla Tharp, and boy, was I sorry later. In about 1970, Sara Rudner and Rose Marie Wright, Tharp's two main dancers and scouts, watched a ballet class I was taking given by the popular teacher Maggie Black. After the class, they approached me and told me that Twyla was looking for another dancer and would I come to the studio. I had seen only one work by her, *Group Activities*, which had seemed blunt and exercise-y to me. But I agreed, partly because I loved Sara's dancing from seeing her in class at Paul Sanasardo's. At the end of this one-person audition, Twyla said, "I think you can do it." When she called me at home to talk details, I declined the invitation, saying, "I feel uncomfortable in the movement." She snapped back, "You're supposed to feel uncomfortable!"

Not long after, she held an informal showing of her work that included *The One Hundreds*, danced by herself, Sara, and Rose. The vitality, precision, and sheer bounty of inventiveness were breathtaking. As each eleven-second segment unfolded in all its vivid glory, in a direct path from upstage to downstage, it erased the one before it. Spectators were totally focused on the ebb and flow, but came away with nothing except the feeling that they'd seen something new and untamable. This dancing was about sensation, impulse, timing, and camaraderie. For those of us looking for the excitement of "pure movement," this was it.

Robert Joffrey must have thought she was hot stuff too, because in 1972, after seeing Tharp at the Delacorte Theater in Central Park (I think it was *The*

Twyla Tharp: improvising during the *Dance Magazine* cover shoot.
(© Robert Whitman for *Dance Magazine*)

Bix Pieces), he commissioned her to make a new work for his company. The result was *Deuce Coupe* (1973), in which Tharp's rugged and brainy dancers joined the Joffrey dancers onstage, and history was made. Her brash, complex, gorgeous works kept on coming, and now Tharp, at the age of fifty-nine, has more than 120 ballets to her name. In just the last year she has made premieres for New York City Ballet and American Ballet Theatre, over-seen reconstructions of *Deuce Coupe*, and started a new company that plays the Joyce Theater February 20–25.

Tharp recently dropped by *Dance Magazine*'s New York office to talk about her new dancers and her hopes for the future. She is thrilled with the current incarnation of Twyla Tharp Dance. "I love my dancers," she says. Like a proud mother, she tells of their prowess in crossing the line between modern and ballet, even though they are primarily ballet dancers. They are Benjamin Bowman of the Fort Worth Ballet and New York City Ballet; Alexander Brady of the Joffrey Ballet and Miami City Ballet; Elizabeth Parkinson, formerly with the Joffrey, Feld Ballets/NY, and Donald Byrd/The Group; Ashley Tuttle, a principal with American Ballet Theatre; and Keith Roberts and John Selya, both previously with American Ballet Theatre. She wants only "great" dancers, so naturally I ask her to define the term. "Greatness—how do I see greatness? Ambition, sweetness, personableness. . . . I mean there's something absolutely connected, a commitment that goes beyond sincerity. English does not supply the right descriptions for greatness—you just feel it."

The two new ballets for this group are nearly opposites. The *Mozart Clarinet Quintet*, K. 581, is dreamy, playful, sublimely open and extended in the beginning, with daring partnering creeping up on you. *Surfer at the River Styx* is edgy, driven, grandly conflicted. *Mozart* is sweetly harmonious, full of light, while *Surfer* is dark, ominous, a modern version of the ancient Greek underworld. The program thus represents two sides of Tharp: the Apollonian and the Dionysian, the lyrical and the dramatic, harmony and conflict. The choreography plays with other polarities, too: long line vs. broken line, childishness vs. maturity, fluidity vs. abruptness, comfort vs. discomfort (as I had noticed years earlier), earth vs. air. Tharp reconciles opposites not by arriving at a midpoint, but by bouncing off the ends of the continuum. If it's arduous, it's really arduous; if it's silly, it's really silly. Like all her work, these two pieces demand the dancers to be fully alive every nanosecond and to merge ballet and modern dance seamlessly. From ballet, Tharp uses the strength and suppleness of the legs as well as the expansiveness of the upper body; from modern, the stirrings in the core of the body. Tharp herself brings the ability to create flow, no matter how disjunctive the movements are.

Keith Roberts recalled by phone the first time he worked with Tharp in 1988, when he was newly with ABT. "I thought she was crazy and really fun. The mood was completely different [from other rehearsals]. There were no absolutes—no right or wrong—just how you can explore what you're doing." Like Parkinson, Roberts dances in *Fosse*, doing eight shows a week on Broadway. "*Fosse* is a commercial venture that gives me job security," he said. "Twyla Tharp Dance is an artistic venture that satisfies my soul." All six dancers have been in ballet companies a long time. "Twyla is giving us the opportunity of taking everything we've learned and being free with it. We've been able to rediscover the feeling of why we love dance." About the two new dances, he says, "*Mozart* and *Surfer* are incredibly hard. It takes a lot of mental power to rev yourself up. I always ask myself, Can I get through this?" But, he says, "We're pushing the boundaries. She'll give us material and let us play with it. Can I turn more? Can I twist more, be more off the leg? She'll see something she likes and then it goes in that direction. We're collaborating with each other."

Roberts is not the only dancer who wonders if he can get through it. In a recent rehearsal of *Mozart*, Selya joked about how he couldn't catch his breath between sections. "It must be the altitude," he said of the third-floor studios at ABT. Anna Kisselgoff of the *New York Times* described his performance of Surfer as "nonstop, fierce bravura, delivered with mind-boggling stamina."

Shelley Washington, who danced with Tharp from 1975 to 1990 and now stages her ballets internationally, said, "People always ask me, 'How can you work so hard?' I work like this because Twyla works like this. Whatever I do, she's done it tenfold. If I work six hours in the studio, she's there two hours before me and four hours after. That's how you create energy and enthusiasm. Twyla's in the room before the dancers are in the room. She's there already. And it makes you want to be ready. It's infectious."

Like the great romantic ballets, Tharp's works turn dancers into heroes and heroines. Not because of the deeds of the characters, but because of the hugeness of what they endure, what they transcend. Think of Sara Rudner in *The Catherine Wheel* (1981), Shelley Washington in *Nine Sinatra Songs* (1982), Baryshnikov in *Push Comes to Shove* (1976), every dancer in *In the Upper Room* (1986), Kevin O'Day in *Everlast* (1989), Damian Woetzel in *The Beethoven's Seventh* (2000), and now John Selya and Keith Roberts in *Surfer*. Each of these dancers, and many more, comes through the experience bursting with a superhuman radiance.

Although Tharp has been known to be occasionally brusque in the past, Roberts says, "Twyla's incredibly supportive. Always listening, and valuing what we have to say. She doesn't try to dictate; she's very giving. I think what we give back to her charges her."

One of the settings where you can see her charged up is during lecture-demonstrations. On such occasions, she wittily explains how she organizes movement, how she makes use of mistakes in the process, and how she trusts her dancers. One gets a glimpse of the brilliance of her creative process. Tharp is well aware of this. "To see material being done—that's where I shine; the dancers shine onstage, but when I'm making work I'm in my element. So I figure I need an audience, and I think audiences enjoy it."

Tharp has always made efforts to involve a wider population. For the set design for *Deuce Coupe* she invited graffiti kids to "write" on a scroll upstage during the performance. Not only did this historic piece merge ballet with modern, but it merged concert dance with street art. She admits that her decision to use Beach Boys music reflects her desire for accessibility. "I must confess to having at one time thought, 'Wouldn't it be great to be completely accessible.'"

Tharp may use popular, jazz, or classical music, but her approach is never obvious. She does not match each musical theme with a recognizable movement theme, but she meets the music at its own level of complexity. Whether it's the sassy joy of the Beach Boys in *Deuce Coupe*, the driving metaphysics of Philip Glass in *In the Upper Room*, the unctuous romance of Frank Sinatra in *Nine Sinatra Songs*, or the grandeur of Beethoven in *The Beethoven's Seventh*, her choreography is never overshadowed by the music.

And yet Tharp says, "Music is a very big problem because, in some ways, I find working in silence to be the most gratifying and honorable because it allows an audience to see what the dancer actually does." She feels that the style of music has "an unbelievably overpowering flavor: it's like a cook who is going to put in an ingredient and it's going to take over the stew." Her first choreographic attempts were done without music. In *The Fugue* (1970), the boots stomping on the floor helped define the defiance of the three women (later three men) and the surging density of the rhythmic patterns. (*The One Hundreds*, which so captivated me years before, has no music.)

Tharp has almost a moral feeling about her early pieces. "When I started working, I wanted to go to a place where I felt I had a right to be, where I wasn't taking somebody else's material. . . . I was getting to something that was so pure and nonderivative that I could call it my own and start from there. In terms of the invention of movement, it's a matter of honesty. It may have been an illusion, but nonetheless it drove me to do a lot of work in the studio." She continued to be rigorous with herself. "Whenever I made a new piece, I demanded that I try to make it completely unlike any of its predecessors, which meant tearing everything apart, throwing everything out and starting all over again each time. It was kind of a horrific thing to do."

William Whitener, now artistic director of Kansas City Ballet, was a member of the Joffrey Ballet when Tharp, then known only in downtown circles, came along. "At the first rehearsal she carried a phonograph under one arm and a stack of Beach Boys records under the other. I was hooked, because that's what I had done in my living room as a child—dance to records." But other dancers had a different reaction. Says Whitener, "There was a section of sliding and skidding, and being close to the floor with knees bent that hurt people's thighs, and some of the dancers rolled their eyes. Within a few days there was a breakdown of those who were having a great time and those who were skeptical. They were worried about looking silly, and yet when you saw the Tharp dancers, they were funny, witty, unusual, delightful. At one point she made a statement that the people who didn't want to do it were free to leave, and some did." Whitener eventually left the Joffrey to join Tharp and danced with her from 1977 to 1988.

Her use of ballet dancers actually dates back farther than *Deuce Coupe.* Trained in ballet herself, but briefly a member of the Paul Taylor Dance Company, Tharp felt that any centered, well-trained, unmannered dancer could do her work. Rose Marie Wright, who danced with her from 1968 to 1980, had been a purebred classical dancer. She had performed with the Pennsylvania Ballet from the age of fourteen to eighteen, during which time she grew from five foot seven to six feet tall. Not surprisingly, she was cast in fewer and fewer roles. Years later, says Wright, PAB director Barbara Weisberger "confessed that she really didn't know what to do with me when I grew. Twyla did know what to do with me."

Coming from the ballet world, Wright noticed two differences right away. The first was a positive working atmosphere: "Nobody was fighting for parts. Everyone was treated equally and everyone respected one another." The second was that, in the intimate spaces where they performed, they were not expected to smile or "project." Wright had to figure out, on her own, how to cultivate a new demeanor. "I was so used to smiling that I didn't know how to perform the work. Then I realized that it was about concentration and working among ourselves. Eventually, I learned how to interact with the audience and with the other dancers."

American Ballet Theatre has commissioned more works from Tharp— about fifteen—than from any other choreographer. Artistic director Kevin McKenzie says, "She has unbelievable energy that homes in on individuals. ABT has always nurtured individual interpreters. She draws the best out of people, finds their uniqueness. She stretches your ability both musically and physically."

What is the most difficult aspect for dancers new to Tharp's work? According to Washington: "Plié, getting into the ground, earth, dropping their weight, total abandon. They need to have a strong center to release the extremities. And the speed. No one can quite believe the amount of steps per second."

Now is a time for consolidation in Tharp's life. As she approaches sixty, she is thinking about what will happen when she is no longer around. She is appalled by the legal battles that plague the Martha Graham Center. Her plans for the future include stabilizing her video archives, developing curriculum-oriented materials based on her repertoire, and offering videos and notes to dance departments to reconstruct her choreography "as though I were not here." Although she still gets to the gym by six every morning, submits to a personal trainer, and does a ballet barre, she no longer performs. "My middle period is over," she sighs. But she is still committed to keeping her body in shape to choreograph. "As long as I can learn lessons on myself, I will do that."

She now envisions her works being used in the same way that classical composers' pieces are practiced by music students. "Think where music would be if it didn't have a backlog of scores and pedagogical material that was developed by composers to produce better musicians." When I question whether young dancers can really understand the material without the physical presence of a Tharp dancer, she counters, "How many students play Chopin beautifully?"

She hopes to establish a central training ground, offering classes in ballet, modern, yoga, and repertoire. "One of the drives for me is unification, one of my big themes is unity, and the place to start with is the technique." She points out that now, many years after *Deuce Coupe*, ballet companies offer modern classes and modern rep.

Tharp and I were able to chuckle about our first run-in thirty years ago. In contemplating her own comment, she showed how much she's changed. "At that time, if you felt comfortable, it meant you'd done it before. That was no good; we couldn't have that. But we passed quickly from that phase. Each piece is about getting to the next piece. I have, over the course of thirty-five years—hello!—come to realize that there are times when you want dancers to feel very comfortable and very easy with the material, where it should be very natural and that there is a beauty in that, a great beauty in that."

But something grittier will always be part of Tharp's legacy. Sara Rudner, who was a star of the Tharp company for nearly twenty years, now directs the dance department at Sarah Lawrence College. When I recently asked her what she passes on to her students from her work with Tharp, she answered, "The experimental nature of it. Take a big bite, take the big challenge, and see what happens."

The Struggle of the Black Artist to Dance Freely

New York Times, June 17, 2001

In the late nineties I sometimes had lunch with Joe Nash, the revered historian of blacks in dance. We both worked at the "God Box," the Interchurch Center building at 120th Street and Riverside Drive. I was stationed at Physicians for Social Responsibility, he at the National Council of Churches. We would see each other in the basement cafeteria and talk about various black choreographers. He had danced with Pearl Primus (whose first dance teacher happened to have been my mother, at a modern dance club at Hunter College in the late thirties). Joe regaled me with stories of Primus, Katherine Dunham, Alvin Ailey, and the Harlem Renaissance. What I remember most was his saying, "We made a mistake to call it 'black dance.'" He felt that term too narrowly defined the huge range of what black dancers were doing and placed it in a racial rather than artistic realm. Thus, in this article, I was careful to avoid using that term.

Free to Dance, a richly resonant new documentary from PBS, shows how African American dance artists honor their heritage and transform their responses to society into glorious dancing. It also challenges the conventional wisdom that modern dance was a creation solely of white choreographers.

One of its revelations is the heartbreaking correspondence between Edna Guy and Ruth St. Denis. Guy, a black teenager ardently dedicated to dance, appeals to "Miss Ruth," icon of "aesthetic dancing," for advice on how she can become an artist. St. Denis, who begins her letters "Dear Girlie," at first denies Guy access to classes at the Denishawn school, but later, in 1924, opens the doors.

Instead of graduating into the company like the other girls, however, Guy is relegated to the job of seamstress. Discouraged, she creates dances with her friends to Negro spirituals and gets ousted from the Denishawn company altogether. On the rebound, Guy immerses herself in the Harlem Renaissance and eventually invites Katherine Dunham to perform in New York in 1936, becoming a key link in the history of dance in the United States.

A sense of freedom gained through struggle permeates the dancing on the screen as well as the words of the performers interviewed in "Free to Dance," which will be shown as part of WNET's "Dance in America" series next Sunday. From Dunham, the ground-breaking dancer and anthropologist, to the Cunningham-influenced Gus Solomons jr, we see the wide array of choices that black choreographers have made about how—or whether— to draw on their cultural heritage.

The connection of dance to daily life is kept in focus throughout the three-hour program. Dunham says of her research in the Caribbean, "I could not learn the dances without knowing the people." Just as Dunham participated in spirit-possession rituals in Haiti, Pearl Primus picked cotton in Alabama. Modern dance is not something remote and fantastical but connected to real lives, from the chain gangs of Donald McKayle's *Rainbow 'Round My Shoulder* (1959) to the domestic worker portrayed in Alvin Ailey's *Cry* (1971) to the young people dancing in clubs in Talley Beatty's *Stack Up* (1982).

Political awareness is inevitable. The dancer Jacqueline Goldman says, "I heard Alvin Ailey's dream before I heard Martin Luther King's dream." The issue of police brutality crops up as a child's rhyme in McKayle's *Games* (1951).

The communal spirit of the circle, as seen in the clapping and stomping ring-shouts of plantation dances and the black bottom of the 1920s, threads through the program. Juxtapositions between the old and the new affect us on a subliminal level. Bill T. Jones, dancing his 1987 solo *Etudes*, repeats a twisting movement, body low, arms swaying side to side in response to swiveling hips—a lyrical version of the twist.

Similar motions surface in the archival footage of ring-shouts of former slaves and the movements of the West African choreographer Asadata Dafora in the 1930s. Moments like these reinforce the idea of an "African cultural continuum" set forth by the art historian Richard Powell. For a pure dance high, there is Primus's forceful amalgam of African and modern dance accompanied by African drummers; Eleo Pomare's alarming portrayal of a junkie with the shakes in *Blues for the Jungle* (1966); Blondell Cummings's feisty gesturing in a television adaptation of her *Chicken Soup* (1988); and McKayle's and Ron K. Brown's individual versions of the rumba, seen in a rehearsal of their collaboration, *Children of the Passage* (1998). Other gems are clips of the young Alvin Ailey with Carmen de Lavallade in a duet by Lester Horton; Jones and Arnie Zane giddily bouncing off each other's energy; Gary Harris's spiraling arms and percussive chest in a reconstruction of Dafora's *Ostrich Dance* (1932); Tommy Gomez (unidentified in the film) coiling fiercely in Dunham's *Shango* (1945); and Maia Claire Garrison's tough pelvic moves in Jawole Willa Jo Zollar's *Batty Moves* (1995). The documentary also includes stirring excerpts from Talley Beatty, Garth Fagan, and Ulysses Dove.

Missing are black dancers who did not choreograph but who left their marks. Who could forget Mary Hinkson's etched lines and womanly power

Blondell Cummings in *Chicken Soup*, mid-'80s, bringing her
domestic traditions to dance. (© Lois Greenfield)

in Martha Graham's roles? Or Carolyn Adams, who infused Paul Taylor's
dances with a joyous buoyancy over a twenty-year period? What was their
influence on the white choreographers they danced for? And what about
Syvilla Fort (seen fleetingly in a *Stormy Weather* excerpt), the Dunham principal who led her thriving school? Also missing are many of the black choreographers who have emerged in the last ten or fifteen years. Another frustration for the curious: some of the footage is not identified.

But these are quibbles. The result of a ten-year project initiated by Gerald
Myers of American Dance Festival, *Free to Dance* is a gift to modern dance
and a moving addition to the field of cultural studies. By showing a glimpse
of the mighty contributions of black choreographers, the program, produced and directed by Madison Lacy, questions the accepted notion that

modern dance was launched by the four white "pioneers": Martha Graham, Doris Humphrey, Charles Weidman, and Hanya Holm. Certainly Katherine Dunham and perhaps Pearl Primus could be added to that list of elders. Anyone interested in dance as an art will savor every minute of this ambitious and illuminating program.

A Dance Turns Darker, Its Maker More American

New York Times, October 28, 2001

When I asked Patricia Hoffbauer to dance with me in 1991, I had no idea she would develop into such an outrageous performance artist. She managed to combine an almost slapstick humor with a scholar's erudition. Her duets with George Sanchez poked delicious fun at the budding fields of performance theory and cultural identity studies. In addition to the cultural aspects that came up, the value of this story is what Patricia says about the effect of 9/11. Although it's meant to be personal, she captures the magnitude of the terrorist attack for all New Yorkers. Patricia now dances with Yvonne Rainer.

If you cross Carmen Miranda with Lenny Bruce and Tina Turner, you might come up with Patricia Hoffbauer. A lusciously physical dancer with a theatrical face and a deep voice, she spices up performances with witty, sometimes raunchy rants. When she gets worked up, her body undulates for added emphasis.

She has collaborated with the choreographers Ron K. Brown, Cathy Weis, and Sara Rudner, among others. (In their student days at New York University, she worked with the playwright Tony Kushner.) In the mid-nineties she teamed up with the actor George Emilio Sanchez for *The Architecture of Seeing*, a hilarious example of deconstruction as entertainment.

In that piece Hoffbauer and Sanchez embodied the postmodern idea that performance "unpacks," or challenges, cultural assumptions. Sanchez wore a kind of tribal diaper and a warrior-like look on his face. Hoffbauer, as a wacky hostess/scholar, claimed him as "my work." He was the hunted, she the huntress. The performers exemplified artists as educators and presented cultural stereotypes as quarries to be excavated, creating a kind of *Saturday Night Live* for eggheads.

Hoffbauer, forty-one, is now preparing a new quartet for Dance Theater Workshop's "Around Town" series at the Duke Theater on Thursday through next Sunday. Departing from the performance art duets she created with Sanchez (who is also her companion), she seeks to mesh her interests in social issues with a commitment to dance experimentation. Her latest piece, *Over My Dead Body*, as seen in recent rehearsals, occasionally erupts into funny or brazen dialogue, but that is only one element in a fabric of sensual dancing (sometimes a samba sneaks in), inventive partnering, and Brazilian folk and pop music.

Growing up in Rio de Janeiro, Hoffbauer studied with Tatiana Leskova, a former principal of Colonel de Basil's Ballet Russe, and with Graciela Figueroa, who had danced with Twyla Tharp. Figueroa made an indelible impression on the young Hoffbauer, who headed to New York to discover the roots of the former Tharp dancer's magic.

"She was the epitome of freedom," Hoffbauer said recently of Figueroa. "She was completely abstract but incredibly powerful, like an Amazon. It wasn't muscle power; she was flight. We would perform in the streets, this band of women with a very intimate, wonderful feeling. One time, at a beach in Bahia, these men made a circle around us and stood there like they wanted to kill us. She was not political and yet she provoked so much"—she paused—"destabilization." Figueroa was her inspiration to do, as Hoffbauer put it, "just dancing" in a way that showed boldness of spirit.

That same sense of power through dancing together has surfaced again in the new work. About her current group of dancers—Peggy Gould, Mary Spring, and Francisco Rider da Silva—she said: "They are the people I'm connected with now. Dance is the place where that human connection can happen. You're holding everybody's sweat and you're smelling their feet. It's the most intimate you can be with somebody without being in a relationship."

She described coming to rehearsal the day after the World Trade Center attacks, feeling lost and devastated. But, she said, "When I went home after rehearsal, I had a little more room to withstand the tragedy."

The title, *Over My Dead Body*, was originally meant to be a tongue-in-cheek reflection on her own stubbornness. As Hoffbauer said, "I love making fun of myself, and making fun of everybody else, but starting with me."

Since September 11, however, the title has taken on a somber meaning. Hoffbauer continues to be affected by the terrorist attacks. "I have reached a level of sadness that I cannot digest anymore," she said. "I don't sleep, and I itch all the time like an old dog with fleas. I feel I have aged centuries, that I am back in 1492 with holy wars happening all around me."

But the attacks have had another effect too: she has become more at home in this country. Her previously critical stance toward U.S. policy in Latin America gave her a clear sense of herself as other. "But now, after the World Trade Center attack, I just felt like the U.S. is a big stupid giant who really didn't know that it was unprotected," she said. "Instead of being the predator, it was this big bear being victimized, being hurt." She suddenly identified with all the people working in offices whom she had disdainfully called "yuppies" before. And instead of separating the "us from the them," she said, "now I am part of the us."

"My skin crawls when my Brazilian friends call and say, 'This is not your war,'" she went on. "I cannot abandon ship; this is my home more than ever."

Explaining the difference between her experience of violence here and in her former life, she said: "I grew up in the dictatorship, and my dad was a lawyer who defended political prisoners, but I never saw anything. The torture and killing happened outside my viewing. The 9/11 attack happened a mile from my hands. From the Brooklyn promenade where I happened to be, I felt I could almost touch the flames. Whereas before, violence and destruction happened behind closed doors and in distant lands, and we were angered by it and were turned into activists, this time it made me stop in my tracks."

David White, the executive director of Dance Theater Workshop, has been watching Hoffbauer's work since the late eighties when she graduated from NYU Tisch School of the Arts. She was loosely associated with a group of artists from Central and South America, including Merián Soto and Carmelita Tropicana, who brought a Latino awareness to dance and performance. White says that issues of cultural identity deepened their work. "Patricia had a distinctive sense of humor and a lot of ideas," he said. "She tries to do work that engages the large questions."

She tackles not only gender and racial issues, but also the border between high art and popular art. She might wedge an *I Love Lucy* shtick into her performances.

Hoffbauer is nervous about the new work because it does not use her expert comic timing, her skill in goading the audience, or her physical daring as much as before. But *Over My Dead Body* is in tune with the reality of her current life. A year ago, shortly after giving birth to a daughter, her body changed.

"I ran from the moment I was born until I had the baby," she said. "I was pumping myself up constantly. Because of the work being political, of having to do a critique of the world, of feeling like I was against the world, my body was like a shield. I was forcing my legs and doing splits and wearing high heels and carrying men on my shoulders. That destroyed my sacrum. One day I was in the bathtub and I couldn't get out. I had to call a physical therapist. Then I learned to listen to the pain in my body and to work without pushing."

In a recent rehearsal, she concentrated on movement phrases as well as eye focus. She doesn't want to resort to "that far-into-the-diagonal gaze" that she says gives modern dance a studied, distanced quality, and yet she doesn't want to rely on the bravado that comes so naturally to her. So the dancers try alternative ways of focusing without getting too detached from one another. And they try a new section in which Rider da Silva, also from Rio, mournfully points out the parts of his body that are not beautiful in America—his ear, his hair, his hands—while the three women carry him tenderly.

It remains to be seen whether the spoken passages of *Over My Dead Body* have a clear relation to the "just dancing" passages. But what is clear is that this work is an intriguing blend of communal warmth, disconcerting intimacy, and full-out dancing.

Paying Heed to the Mysteries of Trisha Brown

New York Times, July 8, 2001

As I look this piece over, I think of the last time I performed Trisha's work, in January 2012. It wasn't on a stage, but in an art gallery for a benefit to raise money for the Trisha Brown Dance Company archives. As part of the event, which doubled as her seventy-fifth birthday party, five of us alumnae—all women in our sixties—lined up to do her "Spanish Dance." This is the iconic four-minute dance to Bob Dylan singing Gordon Lightfoot's "Early Mornin' Rain." Accumulating one at a time, we slowly tread across the space, loose in the hips, raising our arms in mock flamenco magnificence. Finally, as tight as packed sardines, there's a five-woman pile-up at the wall. But on that evening, as we passed by Trisha standing among the well-wishers gathered there, she was looking each one of us in the eyes, mouthing the words, "I love you" over and over. Knowing that Trisha had already had a series of debilitating mini-strokes, I lost my composure during the bows and burst into quiet tears.

Twenty-five years ago I was rehearsing with Trisha Brown and three other dancers in a former sheep fold in a wooded area near Aix-en-Provence, in the south of France. We were creating *Line Up*, which we made by improvising for maybe twenty seconds at a time, and then trying to recall, edit, and set our improvisation. (This was way before anyone used video to record the rehearsal process.) The instructions were to create lines in space while relating to one another and the environment, so there was lots of interaction among the five of us.

At one point during the recalling stage of the process, Trisha seemed to space out. I knew she was supposed to be standing next to me, so I beckoned to her, saying, "C'mon, Trisha, you're over here." But she just stared at me without moving. Again, I curled my hand invitingly: "C'mon, Trisha, c'mon."

Keeping her eyes on me, she backed away, then blurted out, "That's what I want!" What she wanted, I finally realized, was to put my coaxing gesture into the piece. Or, more generically, she wanted to capture the informal activity of creating the piece, and put that into a performance.

Trisha is in love with the process of making and performing dances. The behind-the-scenes aspects fascinate her. In 1983, for *Set and Reset* (which became a masterpiece of the postmodern era), Robert Rauschenberg designed a partly transparent set that let the dancers remain visible after exiting the stage. For viewers, the separation of onstage and offstage was blurred. In the "Sticks" section of *Line Up*, we talked to one another in performance not only to get our sticks connected up in one long line but also to let the audience in on the game.

In a recent conversation in her SoHo loft, Trisha said, "On long tours I look at my choreography from backstage. I get a lot of ideas from seeing the sides of my work. It's a skewed view. I spend hundreds of hours back there." She likes seeing the dancers throw on ratty sweat pants over gleaming costumes to warm up for a performance.

For the New York premiere of her jazz-saturated *El Trilogy*, July 18 to 21 as part of Lincoln Center Festival 2001, Trisha has made two interludes for a solo dancer that are performed while stage-crew work proceeds in full view. During the first one, which has uncharacteristically fierce, almost desperate moves, like clawing the floor, scenery changes are made and musicians rotate in and out of the pit. A crew member changes the color gels in the lights, unfazed by the gripping solo.

During the second interlude, the same dancer enters with her head poking through the rungs of a ladder—Trisha calls it a ladder necklace—and explores movement using that essential piece of backstage equipment while other dancers stretch out and warm up in a corner. As in Asian forms of theater like Noh and Kabuki, the labor of preparation is deemed worthy of aesthetic delight.

The paradox is that while Trisha reveals what is usually hidden, she conceals what is usually visible. It's almost impossible to see where a chain of movement begins. We see whipping, staggering, and folding motions seamlessly interwoven. We see movements travel through the body like a wave. But we never see where in the body the movement is initiated. Trisha is a master at deflecting the eye. Before you realize it, you've missed it, and something else grabs your attention. This is what makes the lifts look like floats. We don't see one dancer lift another; we see several bodies coming at one another, and suddenly a dancer is sailing.

Not every highly trained dancer can accomplish these tasks. When I asked Trisha what she looks for in dancers these days, she said, "I look for lust, for a deep pleasure in a certain kind of off-kilter, wind-in-your-face dancing."

Trisha started the trilogy in 1999 as *Five-Part Weather Invention*, a collaboration with the jazz composer Dave Douglas, the painter Terry Winters, and the lighting designer Jennifer Tipton. But it grew the following year to encompass two subsequent commissions from the American Dance Festival in Durham, North Carolina, so she kept the creative team together. "I keep going back into the earlier part of the piece and finding material that I have an idea about altering," she said. "It's like yeast; I make another loaf of bread. It grew like—magic."

An homage to two indigenous American art forms, jazz and modern dance, *El Trilogy* is Trisha's first foray into jazz music. She researched jazz and its relationship to dance, digging into the past of black culture. For inspiration, she and her group watched rare footage of dancers at the Savoy Ballroom in Harlem shot by Mura Dehn in the 1930s.

The second section of the trilogy, "Rapture to Leon James," takes its title from the dancer whose lindy hopping earned him the name King of the Savoy. King James often appeared as the caller for line dances in Dehn's films.

The role of the caller was something Trisha had already experimented with. In *Line Up* one dancer called out instructions to us in the super complicated "Solo Olos" section.

Trisha recently told me that her caller fantasies started even earlier. "It was a dream I had when I was with the Grand Union," the legendary improvisation group of the early seventies, "that I would take a mike out into the audience and tell the dancers what to do. I tried it once, but no one would mind me."

In the line dances in "Rapture," Keith Thompson, who has danced in the Trisha Brown Dance Company for nine years, is the caller. His finger snapping, jaunty hips, and fast footwork come across with sensuous verve and authority. In another section, he improvises arm movements over choreographed leg movements—nothing is simple in Trisha's dancescape—with the rest of the cast following behind him. Something of a trickster, he sends ripples of glee into the group.

About his role in *El Trilogy*, Thompson, who is African American, says, "There is a sense of coming back to something that has been buried in my soul and my bones." Remembering his childhood, he continued: "Down in the South, people could be standing in a grocery line, and any time the music comes on, someone could break out into a dance. It's a way of life, and that's how I think of the Savoy. People came together to pour out how they felt. It all came through the music and the movement. Everything else was left outside. And that's how I feel onstage when I'm doing the *Trilogy*. I have no other worries in the world."

The line dances Trisha saw in the Savoy films dovetailed with her own preoccupation with lines. Lines form and dissolve not only in *Line Up* but also in *Set and Reset*, *Astral Convertible* (1989), and in Monteverdi's *Orfeo* (1998), the first opera she directed. In *El Trilogy*, we see lines that loosen into ribbons, break up into partnering, or become contracting and expanding circles.

Trisha is aware that the roots of the lindy hop and jitterbug go further back than the Savoy. With an air of wonderment, she notes that Master Juba himself—the black jig dancer who won unparalleled fame in the 1840s—probably danced in the building where she lives when it was the Barnum & Bailey Museum.

But when she was in high school, like most white teenagers in the fifties, she didn't know that the popular lindy hop had come out of black culture. "I thought the seniors made it up," she said. At Mills College in Oakland, California, she had a black roommate, and they teamed up to dance for other students. "Someone would put on rhythm and blues in the dorm, and we would dance. We were a hot ticket after lunch."

She also took African dance classes in Berkeley, California, with Ruth Beckford, a former Katherine Dunham dancer, before studying with Anna Halprin and Merce Cunningham. She feels a kinship with movement that stems from the African diaspora. "I like isolated gestures, undulating backs, and pelvis-initiated movement," she said.

Douglas's music for the complete trilogy has a relation to jazz similar to that of Trisha's choreography to modern dance. It experiments not only with tone and rhythm but also with decidedly unmelodic sounds, like musicians coughing and moving their chairs and, as Trisha says, "generally creating havoc on their instruments."

She often goes "against" the music: for example, when the tempo slows to a funereal pace, the dancers may spring into the air. But in the last five minutes of the third section, "Groove and Countermove," the storm of dance joins the storm of music, culminating in a rousing finale, breathtaking in its spatial and rhythmic architecture.

Trisha Brown does not have the dramatic intensity of Martha Graham or the muscular force of Alvin Ailey. Her stage is not as orderly as Balanchine's or as deliberately random as Cunningham's. But she has a magnificence all her own. As some dancers lilt or sway, others streak through the space, creating a radical version of counterpoint. The limbs are used as calligraphy, but also to trigger momentum.

The stream of motion can be exhilarating kinetically—and philosophically. It seems to speak of universal motion, of an inevitability that is not about fate but an embrace of the ongoingness of life. Her ceaseless inventiveness is legend in both the United States and Europe. Many young choreographers consider Trisha Brown the gold standard for intelligent, impassioned movement invention.

As I watched a recent rehearsal at Trisha's studio, I realized all over again how elusive her work is. Just as she backed away from me twenty-five years ago when I thought I knew where she was, her choreography slips through my fingers—or my eyes. One must be alert to sight and sound. At a talk given recently at the Kitchen in Chelsea, she advised listeners how to approach her work: "I want you to drink it up with your eyes and your mind."

East (Coast) Meets West (Coast): Eiko & Koma Collaborate with Anna Halprin

Dance Magazine, October 2001

This October issue of Dance Magazine *came out just before September 11. That morning I was supposed to go to a meeting at the New School. Although both World Trade towers had already been hit and I had seen the footage on television, I stupidly thought the meeting might still go on. So I packed three copies of the issue to give to colleagues and took the subway downtown. I got out at the 14th Street stop to head toward the New School. Instead I joined the crowd at 12th Street and Seventh Avenue that had a good view of the towers a couple miles to the south. As I approached, a man leaving the crowd passed me, saying, "It just fell." I had no idea what could have fallen. I saw the North Tower, with flames where windows should have been, making its sides bulge and buckle—more terrifying with the naked eye than on television. I took some steps to look around it, where the South Tower should have been, and suddenly realized what fell. Then I knew that everyone else on that corner had seen the South Tower go down. People were stunned into silence; I was hyperventilating. I wanted to stay on that corner but I felt a strong pull to be with my son, Nick, who was at the Bank Street School, up in the Columbia University neighborhood. I started running uptown, only to hear a rumor that the Empire State Building would be the next target, so I ran farther west. (The subways had either stopped or were too risky by then.) To lighten my load, I took the three magazines out of my bag and left them on a ledge somewhere and kept running. Finally a crowded cab picked me up, and then another took me to Bank Street School.*

Many parents had rushed to the school. We were all shaken to our roots. In the lobby I saw Eiko, whose son Shin was in Nick's class. She had already read my article and reminded me that I had likened her and Koma to disaster victims. I had forgotten that part, but at this point, disaster was everywhere, and Eiko & Koma's work had a new relevance.

The collaboration between Eiko & Koma and Anna Halprin gave me an opportunity to write about both artistic entities and also to hint at some of the cultural convergences and collisions.

A revolving portable cave with stringy stalactites is lit from below as though from bubbling lava. The dancers Eiko and Koma fade into view, each in a separate hollow of this dreamlike environment. They are survivors, victims of a natural or unnatural disaster. Wearing a swath of rag or maybe nothing, ashen faced, bereft, they seem to have no particular gender. Existentially alone in this fire-and-ice, end-of-the-world scenario, they inch toward each other. The audience waits, with schooled patience, for the next small thing to happen. Depending on your inner resources, the wait can seem like mere forbearance, or it can be an opportunity to meditate on life and death, living and dying. Eons later, they finally make contact, skin touching skin. Without changing their demeanor, they suddenly seem ecstatic. Their relationship turns romantic, erotic. They seem to be in pre- or post-lovemaking embrace, damn the world outside. During the hour-long *When Nights Were Dark* (2000), audience members undergo the most extreme emotions while watching the most minimal action. Welcome to the mystery of Eiko & Koma, masters of their unique form of dance.

Into this mystery steps another mystery: the phenomenon that is Anna Halprin. At the age of eighty-one, Halprin joins Eiko & Koma in a world premiere at the Kennedy Center for the Performing Arts October 16 to 18. Halprin, widely acknowledged as a visionary in dance, community ritual, and the healing arts, has been helping plan this collaboration, entitled *Be With* because of its merging of generations and styles, for the past year. The fourth collaborator is experimental composer/cellist Joan Jeanrenaud, formerly of the Kronos Quartet.

In their apartment in Manhattan Plaza, a midtown housing complex mostly for artists, Eiko and Koma spoke about the development of their work. They met in Japan in a workshop given by Tatsumi Hijikata, founder of the Japanese contemporary form butoh, which means "dance of darkness." Each time Koma named a dancer they studied with—Hijikata, Kazuo Ohno, Manja Chmiel (a disciple of Mary Wigman), and Lucas Hoving—Eiko chirped, "very briefly, very briefly." They wanted only to taste, not to submit to, a master. They claim they were ready to quit dance, but Hoving told them, "You can stop any time. But before you do, go see New York."

They arrived in the United States in 1976. Within a few years, they earned a name for themselves as two of the most riveting postmodern, post-Hiroshima performers and image-makers. They've won numerous commissions and awards, including a MacArthur "genius award" in 1996. Halprin first saw Eiko and Koma dance in San Francisco in 1977. A mutual friend, the choreographer Kei Takei, had urged them to meet. Halprin was so struck with their artistry that she went backstage and gave them the key to her studio on Divisadero Street. "You can come any time," she told them. Since then, she has seen many of Eiko & Koma's thirty-some works, has kept up an e-mail relationship with them, and sends them videos of her work. The Japanese-born couple regards her as a friend and mentor, and more—as part of the family. She is pen pals with their two teenage sons (who performed in *Wind*), and keeps photos of the boys next to her computer in her study.

Last year Eiko and Koma flew to San Francisco to see Halprin's eightieth-year retrospective. During her talking solo, *Memories from My Closet*, she says the line, "And now that I am eighty, I am just beginning to understand the plants and animals, the ocean, the creepy-crawlies, the stars and the moon." Koma immediately felt the connection to their work, which strives for the elemental, the most basic unit of life. As Eiko says, "We always have the notion of dancing like plants and animals, because part of our desire to dance is to free from what is being human. We never wanted to express . . ." Koma finishes her thought: ". . . human emotions." He continues, "We are same: plants, animals, mountains. We are same." Adds Eiko, "The image I often use with my students is an amoeba. It's not about studying the outside look of it, but to allow yourself to say, 'I'm related.'"

The idea for the collaboration was ignited by Charles and Stephanie Reinhart, who have commissioned fifteen works from Eiko & Koma and had presented Halprin with the 1996 Samuel Scripps Award at the American Dance Festival, which they codirect. The Reinharts, also the artistic directors for dance at the Kennedy Center, posed the question to the creating couple: "How about dreaming of something that you would like to do above and beyond what you've already been doing? In terms of outside influences, working with someone else, what would attract you; what would entice you?" The answer was working with Halprin. Charles Reinhart's immediate reaction, he recalled recently, was, "This rings the bell! It couldn't be better!" He knew how much both parties respect each other, and he sensed the possibility for an exciting collaboration.

But Halprin resisted. She was daunted by the coast-to-coast distance, the difference in ages, the difference in cultures, and the pressure to produce on cue. She is more comfortable creating in relative isolation, deciding when the time is right to perform. Recalling her reaction to Eiko and Koma's proposal, she said, "It all seemed out of the question. At my age I am never sure about committing myself to anything over time." But she was attracted by their differences. Halprin, who has often worked with people of other cultures, said, "I like the idea of being shaken out of my old habitual ways."

In entering into this collaboration, Halprin asked for a "crash course" in how the other two work. Koma described this two-week course: "We have sleeping dance, dreaming dance, resting dance." Although Halprin passed with flying colors, she felt intimidated by the bond between the married couple in the studio. Even later in the process, during a five-day work period, she confessed, "I haven't yet found the way to dance when the two of them are dancing. It's like a closed circuit. They're so familiar with each other." But, she said with enthusiasm, "The working process is illuminating, challenging, and generous. We are stretching each other. We are working morning, afternoon, and evening. We're so busy working that I've just burned my food!"

The four collaborating artists have been sharing their life stories, but when it comes to rehearsals, they start with movement. Says Halprin, "We tried to follow the movement language, and let that evoke emotion and images." About the final piece, she said, "Whatever we come up with is going to be something that I would never do if I were on my own and they would not do on their own. We are always asking each other, 'Why are you doing that; why are you doing it this way?' There is constant negotiation."

Eiko and Koma, like Halprin or any highly unorthodox artist, have their share of detractors. As Eiko relates, wherever they perform, "Some people love it; some people hate it." Occasionally at post-performance talks, someone accuses them of not doing real dance. I ask Eiko how they convince people that what they do qualifies as dance. She answers, "We don't. We just change our words and say, 'This is art.'"

When asked why they often appear nude, Eiko counters, "A fish in water isn't wearing anything." The environments they dance in are as close to their skin as clothing. They performed *River* (1995) in creeks and rivers across the country and in Japan. For *When Nights Were Dark*, they hand-painted over five thousand strips of cheesecloth, cut them and hot-glued them onto the net hammock, which they then wove into a structure of lumber and driftwood. Working with several assistants, it took them a year to complete.

Likewise, participants in their "delicious movement" workshops may take a long time to find the deep pleasure in it. Even with the encouragement to enjoy the "juiciness" of the movement, many students find it difficult to move the limbs ultra slowly without shaking. "Young dancers may have to wait until they get sick and slow down," says Eiko. "They may have to wait until they get pregnant, or have some disappointment. I say, 'You don't have to get it today; you have the rest of your life to get it.'" Koma adds that it is really about lifelong pleasure. "When we die, the body stops moving," he says. "But until that moment, the body loves movement."

Their involvement in the creative process is constant. "We talk about the piece twenty-five hours," says Eiko. "It's terrible. One is asleep and the other is up, and then you wake up and talk about it." Do they agree on everything? "After fighting," she quips. "But, bottom line, our aesthetics are pretty close." What is the first thing they do after a performance? "We do laundry; it piles up."

Although the age difference is part of the "score," or general plan of *Be With*, Eiko realized that she does not have to treat Halprin as delicately as she feared. Her father died recently at age seventy-nine. "My body can't help remembering my own parents," she said. "But Anna is not weak. I swear she will live another twenty-five years." Fresh from a work session, she e-mailed me: "Anna's willingness is amazing; Koma and I feel challenged and inspired. Even when the communication gets a little tough, or nerve-wracking, I adore her. She is genuinely beautiful and vivid."

But folding Halprin in to their partnership will take some work. Eiko and Koma perform like two bodies with one state of mind. Says Eiko, "Sometimes I don't even have to look at Koma. I just feel how the audience starts to look at Koma, and then I don't compete. I just become more of the element." This kind of subtle sensing between dancers takes years to develop. Early in the rehearsal period, Eiko confided, "With Anna, we are not yet all tuned in. Our kinetic sense is not tuned in, but our wishing sense is. Sometimes we can talk about it. Sometimes we can't talk about it: we just have to do it."

Halprin has not danced "for" another choreographer since the early forties, when she appeared in a musical choreographed by Charles Weidman. So her new partners have taken care to make her feel artistically at home. For the set design, they will create a wall similar to the one in her Mountain Home Studio in Kentfield. And one of her favorite CDs—the Paul Winter Consort featuring an Armenian singer—is being used by Jeanrenaud as a point of departure for one section.

Last spring, during a break from a work period, Halprin said, "We have a lot of differences. The age difference: physically I'm not able to do what they do—not by a long shot. Pacing: they are slow and I tend to be frenetic. Cultural differences: Asian and Jewish are miles apart. And yet what's beautiful is to get to the bottom line and find our commonalities."

Bill T. Jones Searches for Beauty, and a New Home

New York Times, January 27, 2002

Well, he found a new home, but it's not in Harlem as he had envisioned. In 2011 Bill T. Jones merged his company with the venerable presenter of contemporary dance in Chelsea, Dance Theater Workshop, to form New York Live Arts. One of the factors that made this possible is that Jones had pulled in a pile of money from two Broadway shows: Spring Awakening, *which he choreographed, and* Fela!, *which he co-conceived and directed as well as choreographed.*

What struck me during the open rehearsal is that Bill T. had acquired a majestic patina that was vaguely familiar to me. Who was it who spoke like that—so sonorous, so sure of his own grandeur and wisdom? It was José Limón, with whom I had studied at the American Dance Festival at Connecticut College in the mid-sixties. Both had serious charisma, the history of modern dance emanating from their pores, only they were a generation or two apart. Both had young dancers at their feet, hanging on every word.

During an open rehearsal at Aaron Davis Hall in Harlem last month, Bill T. Jones spoke glowingly of the Beethoven quartet he had chosen to accompany a new work—its range, its expansiveness, its spiritual transcendence. But, after the run-through, while answering a question from the audience, he swiveled his pelvis (subtly) and said, "There are things this body knows from dancing in front of the juke box."

Jones relishes rubbing the loftiest of ideals against the down and dirty. He is devoted to both religious and physical ecstasy and can juxtapose them, or equate them, in his performances. He has been known for the beguiling physicality of his solos, the complexity of his group works, and his confrontational gestures and words. The Muhammad Ali of the dance world, he possesses an audacity, eloquence, and insolence that have elicited both awe and irritation.

He might, in an improvised monologue, say something startling about a critic in the audience. Or he might, as he did in the summer of 2000, refuse to perform at the Spoleto Festival because South Carolina flew the Confederate flag over its statehouse.

Now, as he nears fifty, Jones has shed a degree of his political vehemence and is searching, quite simply, for beauty—and for a new home for the Bill T. Jones/Arnie Zane Dance Company. The quest for beauty has produced three new works in collaboration with the Chamber Music Society of Lincoln Center to be performed at Alice Tully Hall beginning on Thursday and running through next Sunday.

The first, *Worldwithout/In*, to music by the contemporary Hungarian composer Gyorgy Kurtag, creates a fantasyland with animal masks, long blue veils, and fake money. The second, *Verbum*, set to Beethoven's String Quartet in F (Op. 135), has a range of movement from delicate to forceful, with dancers passing through large metal structures that look like wiggly frames or portals. The third, *Black Suzanne*, features daredevil tumbling and an ominous Japanese-inspired stage set in red and black, accompanied by Shostakovich's Octet (Op. 11).

While the pitch of experimentation remains high ("How crazy can the picture be and still be legible?" he asks), Jones takes care to incorporate the visual element, designed by his partner, Bjorn Amelan, into the choreography from the outset to form a fully integrated whole. A recent example of this kind of artistic endeavor is *The Table Project*, which was performed last year at Aaron Davis Hall. For this work, originally commissioned by the Walker Art Center in Minneapolis, Amelan built a huge table topped with hurdles. The performers—six middle-aged men in the first round and then six young girls, all nondancers from Harlem—clambered over it, under it and around it to the strains of Schubert's Notturno Trio for Piano in E flat. The effect was charming, breathtaking in its simplicity, and deeply moving.

The Chamber Music Society will serve as host for the current season of Jones's company. David Shifrin, the society's artistic director, is impressed with the range of textures and moods in the music selected by Jones. "When you're talking about music with him, you feel like you're talking to a musician because he listens to so much music and understands the historical perspective and style," Shifrin said.

Jones's career as a searcher started early on. His first experience of being moved by beauty was seeing his mother in church, tears streaming down her face: "My mother said, 'Child, you've got to get out of self to know the Lord!' She was talking about ecstasy. Then I went in search of it. The sixties was when I was coming to consciousness, so I had to find social rebellion. Drugs could help me have an ecstatic feeling. Sex could. Then there was this thing called art that could."

His path took him from being a track star at the State University of New York at Binghamton to discovering the literary and film avant-garde and then to dance. Through Contact Improvisation taught by Lois Welk, and African dance lessons with Percival Borde, he entered an arena where he— along with his former partner, Arnie Zane—could experiment freely. Their early work, with an electric energy and fearlessness, blended physical and intellectual exhilaration. (Zane died of complications from AIDS in 1988.)

When they started performing as an interracial couple in the seventies, they were immediately embraced by the predominantly white downtown scene. "We didn't want to be in any ghetto—gay ghetto, art ghetto, and definitely not a racial ghetto," Jones said. He considered himself to be "a world artist, an artist before I was a black person."

Being influenced by white postmodern choreographers like Trisha Brown and David Gordon, Jones had an ambivalent relationship to the black dance community. "I was saying to black folks: 'Don't make assumptions about who I am, but love me,'" he said. "My performances were like being in the black church: I was calling out and expecting to hear the response back, 'Amen.' But it was the wrong audience. I wanted that audience, but I didn't know if the audience wanted me, and I didn't know how to be generous enough to go in search of it."

Since that period, he has choreographed *Fever Swamp* for the Alvin Ailey American Dance Theater and recently completed a four-year residency at Aaron Davis Hall on the campus of City College. In fact, he has begun a capital campaign to find a new home for his company in Harlem. For Jones, Harlem is "a place where I can find a spiritual platform."

"Being in that community reminds me of what it means to be an American, and how complicated that's been in my life," he said. "Harlem is an environment which is asking deep questions about what color it is, what class it is. It's one of the most promising areas of the city, and I want to be part of it."

Jones's current group of ten dancers forms a picture of diversity. One dancer is austere while another is playful; one may be versed in the technique of Merce Cunningham while another has classical Russian training. But they all have bounding energy and versatility. "Bill's style ranges from release to athleticism to Contact Improvisation to formal classical lines to the street dance he knew as a kid to African movement," said Janet Wong, the company's rehearsal director. "He goes from wiggling on the floor to a suspended attitude turn. He switches all the time, and he'll sometimes break into song to illustrate."

In creating movement sequences, Jones uses mathematical concepts. He may borrow Trisha Brown's "accumulation structure" (adding movements one at a time while also returning to the beginning after each addition) or he may say to his dancers, "Make a phrase in which you move for five counts and hold still for three." The miracle of his work is that, despite the cool postmodern approach, an emotional heat emanates from the dancing. The new works are so rich, so interactive and so playful in their relation to the music that one does not miss the charismatic Bill T. Jones presence.

Jones's role as a lightning rod in the culture wars of the nineties is well known. In 1994 the critic Arlene Croce attacked him in the *New Yorker* for producing dance outside the borders of fine art. Without attending a performance of his work *Still/Here*, she called it "victim art" because of its inclusion of video footage of participants in his "survival workshops." At that time Jones, who had been HIV positive since 1985, was leading workshops for people with terminal diseases to fulfill his own psychological and artistic needs. The article prompted a debate within critical circles. Ultimately, it crystallized a question about the nature of art: Is art a haven, an escape from everyday life, or is it part of the messy social reality we live in?

When asked about the controversy during a recent interview, Jones bristled, saying, "The perpetrators of that attack owe me an apology, and I will go to my grave feeling that way." After a moment, he added, "I don't want to put more gasoline on that fire anyway. But that fire never went out. I just put it in an asbestos-lined room."

Two weeks short of turning fifty, Jones says he did not think he would live this long. "The unprotected have to die young," he wrote in his 1995 memoir, *Last Night on Earth* (Pantheon Books). But he said recently, "I'm in pretty fantastic shape." Aside from lower back problems and a bruised toe, he has never been hospitalized or had a serious injury, an amazing record for a dancer of his age.

Today, he says, he feels a greater sense of responsibility, largely out of respect for his dancers. "I have more at stake now," he said. "I have this company, this possibility for a home in Harlem."

"What does it mean to institutionalize?" he asked and then went on to answer his own question. "The dancers look to me for their paycheck; they look to me to know what we're dancing to next. It's my job to make my vision clear."

His search is for more than a new building; it is to ensure the future of his choreography and his company. Last year, the dancers started receiving health and retirement benefits, a rarity for a small modern dance company.

Where has his former rebelliousness gone? Perhaps it has gone into his creative fervor. "As an irate person who is a descendant of slaves and who has marching freedom rhythms in his blood, I say: 'Make something beautiful, Bill, really beautiful. Make something that comes honestly from you. Dare to fail.'"

Jones's striving and determination have set a standard of postmodern edginess for younger artists. Sean Curran, one of the many alumni of the company who have gone on to choreograph, said, "Bill and Arnie were the best composition teachers you could have."

"Bill was never precious about anything," he added. "He made so much great material that he didn't care about letting go. He was really all about getting to the essence."

The essence that preoccupies Jones these days is beauty. "I want to know what is beauty that is not conditioned by one's perception of gender or race," he said. The search itself is part of his art.

Snip, Snip: Dance, Too, Needs Editing

New York Times, June 30, 2002

After years of anxiety when starting to choreograph, I learned to just doodle or noodle
to get any kind of movement going, and then I'd have something to play around with
and reshape. It's in the editing stage when the piece tells me where it wants to go. From
the other side, as an audience member, it's sometimes frustrating to see where or how a
piece could have been edited to save itself. Choreographers neglect editing at their peril.

"All dances are too long," Doris Humphrey wrote forty-some years ago. Her pronouncement was surely exaggerated, but her admonition is as apt today as it was then. Novelists submit to editors, and directors and playwrights have dramaturges to help them maximize theatrical impact. Filmmakers trust editors to make the final cut of movies. But choreographers get no such formal assistance while making work. Often it is not until a piece is performed for an audience that its flaws are revealed.

When dances feel too long to audiences, it has little to do with how long they actually run. Rather, they tend to suffer from too much repetition or too little structure.

Trisha Brown tells a story about the time she was working on *Set and Reset* in 1983 with the artist Robert Rauschenberg, who designed the set and costumes. During a rehearsal, Brown showed Rauschenberg a section of the piece in which she suddenly dived into the arms of another dancer, seemingly catching him by surprise. This daredevil maneuver originally appeared three times. Rauschenberg told Brown, "You're only allowed to do that once." She took his advice. As a result of this kind of restraint, *Set and Reset* possesses an exciting momentum that makes you want to see the dance again and again.

Rauschenberg was acting as a colleague rather than as an editor. But such informal feedback isn't heeded often enough. Choreographers must have tunnel vision to a certain extent, but it's easy for them to become too stubborn about their own ideas.

Dancemakers who repeat indiscriminately may be overly attached to favorite motifs or may be looking for a way to achieve cohesiveness. But when the choreography doesn't progress beyond its opening themes, it gets bogged down. Repetition lends dance resonance, but only if each time the gesture or phrase is repeated it is given a new context by the surrounding movements or a change in scene. If not, a seasoned dancegoer may ask:

"For whom is this movement or sequence being repeated? Where are the surprises?"

The problem of nonessential repetition crops up across the board: choreographers creating lavish ballet productions sometimes struggle to fill out the music, modern dance choreographers may feel obliged to fulfill a theme-and-variations format, and experimental dance makers may wade through a period of aimlessness on the way to clarity or spontaneity. (An extraordinary performer, of course, can often overcome the shortcomings of a piece of choreography.)

Whether or not a dance has a narrative element, the order in which the sections are presented is crucial. Audiences want to feel that some form of logic—even if it's dream logic—is operating. And we want to feel that each section, no matter how ample or lean, is essential to the expressive thrust of the work. Sections that do not shed light on the whole should be tossed, even if the dancers have worked long hours on them.

Have our shorter attention spans made us less tolerant of longer works? Is this an American phenomenon, or are there cultural biases involved?

Makhar Vaziev, the director of the Kirov (Mariinsky) Ballet in St. Petersburg, Russia, acknowledged in a radio interview a few years ago that the company shortened its full-length ballets for American audiences. "In Russia," he said, "our public is ready to watch ballet for four, five, six hours."

Are Russians more patient than Americans? Perhaps they don't have to worry about paying babysitters or catching up on their e-mail.

In the seventies, we seemed to possess endless stores of patience. Sitting through Robert Wilson's five-hour performance piece *Einstein on the Beach* was no strain at all. Even today some artists make compelling work that operates outside a conventional theatrical time frame. Merce Cunningham's "events," as he calls his choreographic collages, unfurl with no overarching theme but demand that viewers pay close attention to each action. When Kei Takei or Eiko & Koma extend their minimal movement over time, they don't repeat moves so much as linger in a single mood, transporting us to a meditative state.

Dancemakers are often eager to put all they know into one piece. George Balanchine said that working with the composer Igor Stravinsky taught him to limit each ballet to the vocabulary that's relevant. During their collaboration on *Apollo* in 1928, he realized that he could "dare to not use all my ideas."

The tendency to give too much can backfire. The vaudeville maxim "leave 'em wanting more" is sound advice for choreographers. A painter friend of mine, after watching a wonderfully inventive performance that became re-dundant, sometimes said, "It killed itself."

Humphrey's admonition has endured. Dance presenting organizations like the Field, the Kitchen, and Joyce SoHo have adopted a process in which an experienced artist or critic is brought in to help shape or streamline a work in progress. While these attempts are just a beginning, they nonethe-less encourage the choreographers to ask themselves, What is the essence, the heart of a work? The choreographer's job is to cut away the fat and to clear the pathways around that heart.

Batsheva Dance Company: *Naharin's Virus*

Brooklyn Academy of Music

April 30–May 4, 2002

Review, *Dance Magazine*, August 2002

For the first Batsheva appearance in New York since Ohad Naharin took over twelve years before, they brought a piece that showed all the strangeness and emotional power he's capable of. Although I had loved his Sinking of the Titanic *(which he made in 1990 when he was still in New York) for its beautifully sad vision, the production of* Naharin's Virus *seemed to renounce the beautiful and replace it with an almost twisted vision. Naharin's wife, Mari Kajiwara, who had been a force of nature in* Titanic *(not to mention her longtime presence in Alvin Ailey American Dance Theater), had died of cancer in 2001. I do not know if that tragic loss had any impact on this turn toward the odd and aggressive. But* Naharin's Virus *was bracing in the same way that any good art is bracing.*

Sixteen dancers line the front of the stage and stare at the audience. Each possesses a different torque, an asymmetry in the torso that gives them a slightly damaged look. One person dances in place with a fast, wrenching fury, as though trying to rid herself of a clinging nightmare. She stops, then another dancer enters into a similar fury while all the rest are still. Then the whole row, in unison to music by Arab-Israeli Habib Alla Jamal, pound with fists on invisible walls with high-powered African-style chest contractions, and the cycle begins again. There is energy, there is unity, there is rhythm, and there is rage.

Naharin's Virus is not the most beautiful or imaginative dance that Ohad Naharin has choreographed. But its visceral force is unforgettable. We cannot turn away from these young people of the Tel Aviv–based Batsheva Dance Company, most of whom have probably been soldiers, fighting for their survival.

One performer wearing a man's suit, perched atop a stage-wide wall that doubles as a blackboard, recites the script of the absurdist play *Offending the Audience* by Peter Handke. The words wedge an insidious distrust between the performance and audience (Handke's virus?). "No mirror is held up to you. Because we are speaking to you, your awareness increases. You become aware of the impulse to scratch yourself." But what saves the evening from verbal overload is that, quietly, this man slips out of his suit and emerges wearing the same strange unitard the other dancers wear. The suit remains standing exactly where it was, without the hands and face of the dancer. This moment, repeated later, perfectly separates the dance with text from the dance with music. It provides the irony necessary to put Handke's rebellious declarations—by turns sophomoric, contradictory and merely clever—into perspective: the speaker is just trying something on. So, toward the end of the play, when Handke hurls insults at "us," we are more delighted by the word play ("you bubbleheads, you atheists, you butchers, you deadbeats") than hurt or shocked.

The costumes make the dancers look uncomfortable, paralleling how the text makes us feel. Naharin may be hinting at the discomfort of living in a country where hostilities are so out of control. The unitards extend to cover the hands, giving the dancers unnaturally long arms, and the thigh-high black leg warmers give them short legs. In the first section, the dancers drift toward each other in small groups as though to sniff each other. Their arms hang long and they curl their hands like simian creatures, ready to scratch themselves or to grub for food. Some of the couplings are also animal-like, lizards mating perhaps.

But the message on the blackboard is very human. The word *you* gets scrawled on one side, and *atem*, the Hebrew for the plural form of *you* on the other. Kristin Francke, who begins the piece by drawing on the blackboard, drags the chalk behind her, around her elbow, echoing her tracings with her body parts, all while her body is distorted with tension. Throughout the evening, dancers go upstage to draw on the blackboard, sometimes adding a soothing sound element. Toward the end two dancers madly etch a blood-red asterisk shape that takes on a glow. Is this the source of the virus, an angry nucleus of hate? Or is it a burst of the heart's emotion?

Occasionally a single person dances to a taped voice, presumably about that person's life. During Inbar Nemirovsky's solo, we hear a young woman's voice telling us that, as a child, "I would get naked, and my mother would beat me. I found I liked it." (Her mother also beat her because she questioned the existence of God.) This and other moments of dark humor contribute to the compelling strangeness of this U.S. premiere.

There are occasional leavening moments, as when a microphone is dropped down to a dancer who squeals, barks, sighs, and meets her own sounds with similarly unpredictable movements.

What seems to have carried over from Naharin's work with Graham is that the motivation comes from a deep core in the center of the body. But his style, he has said, owes more to Pina Bausch and American experimentalists like Gina Buntz. Therefore, the Batsheva, which was formed by Martha Graham and Batsheva de Rothschild in 1964, went through an overhaul in both choreography and dancers when Naharin took over as artistic director in 1990. His repertoire for the company includes funny, joyous works as well as difficult ones.

Naharin's Virus is infectious, but not everyone will respond to it. The experience is comparable to reading Dostoyevsky's *Notes from the Underground*, with its fevered self-questioning, or seeing the work of German painter Anselm Keifer, which leads one into a depth and complexity rare for an American artist. If you have gone to that well of darkness, seeing it reflected on the stage is familiar and even satisfying. If not, it can be frightening—or offending. But there is something vital and bracing about artists who delve into difficult areas, into the darkness of our souls. Artists like these possess an undeniable courage, and this is the virus of the title, for the Batsheva dancers have caught Naharin's courage.

Kirov Classics Hit and Miss

Review, *Village Voice*, July 23, 2002

Although it was the Bolshoi's fierce abandon that made me fall in love with Russian bal-let, the Kirov captured my imagination with its ethereal port de bras. Perhaps because of my high expectations, I came down hard on the company in this review. On the other hand, ballet critics respect Marius Petipa so much that I kind of enjoyed pointing out the boring aspects of this supposedly authentic Bayadère. Note: This was at the height of Svetlana Zakharova's international career, but just at the beginning of Diana Vish-neva's.

The first two productions of The Kirov (Mariinsky) Ballet at the Lincoln Cen-ter Festival elicited opposite responses. They are both more than a century old, have lavish sets and costumes, and feature spectacularly limpid danc-ing from the female lead. But *Swan Lake* hit the spot, while *La Bayadère*, claiming to replicate the 1900 version, misfired.

On Thursday night, Svetlana Zakharova played the dual role of Odette/ Odile in *Swan Lake*, leaving both the audience and her prince, Danila Kor-suntsev, breathless. For all the times he placed his hand on his heart as one stricken with love, he was actually convincing, partly because she was so dazzling. Arms flailing delicately behind her, legs shimmering in the bour-rées, her Odette personified a fugitive bird with human qualities (or is it vice versa?). Every arabesque, every split leap seemed a cry for freedom from a creature trapped in an evil spell. In the central adagio with Prince Siegfried, her leg lifted into passé and unfolded to the back like a time-lapse sequence of a flower blooming. An enthralled quiet blanketed the audience.

Odette's poignance was balanced by the manic Jester, danced with gusto by Dmitri Zavalishin, who presided over the first and third acts. Without his revelry those acts would have been merely grandiose. But he added wit, non-stop mischief, and astounding gyroscopic turns.

In this Soviet version of *Swan Lake*, staged by Konstantin Sergeyev (after Petipa) in the sixties, a small flock of eight black swans infiltrates the corps of twenty-four white swans in the fourth act—a nice touch. And the Soviets insured a happy ending: the Prince, in a battle with the vulture-like sorcerer Rothbart (Andrei Ivanov), rips off a wing, leaving him to writhe on the floor. The moment Rothbart collapses, Odette rises up to be united with her true love. The Tchaikovsky music, conducted by Boris Gruzin and played by the Kirov Ballet Orchestra, seemed heaven-sent throughout.

La Bayadère was strong on pageantry and weak on choreography. The heart of the performance on Tuesday was Diana Vishneva's Nikiya, a temple dancer, or bayadère. Her expansive rib cage and pinched lower back gave her a vulnerability and almost unbearable sensitivity to her surroundings. With her high-strung expressivity, she embodied the idea that a loved one can continue to haunt after death.

The Indian warrior Solor, played by Adrian Fadeyev, pursues Nikiya in the first act, but turns away when Nikiya is dying of the asp's bite. His dancing is marked by an elegant lengthening of the back and arms, but there is a sense of restriction in his legs. He does well in a ridiculous trio in which he juggles his partnering of Nikiya's shade (ghost) and Gamzatti (her rival) in the middle of an irrelevant celebration.

During this almost four-hour ballet, women wore veils of every color attached to the ankle, hip, or back of the head. Men carried long peacock feathers or parrots. The backdrops were magnificent, from a valley bounded by storybook boulders to a Taj Mahal–type palace with lovely foliage, all in muted colors with ornate designs. The lushness of the environment contrasted with the repression of Solor's being forced to marry someone he doesn't love.

An occasional gesture reveals the power of movement to tell a story. When the jealous High Brahmin informs the Rajah (father of Gamzatti) of the love between Solor and Nikiya, his whole body tilts as though his head is too heavy with the knowledge. Later, when Gamzatti orders the death of Nikiya, she slowly presses her palm down with a lethal force, leaving no doubt as to her effectiveness.

But static staging and endless rows of people dancing standard ballet vocabulary, often returning for more when we thought they had finished, rob the production of momentum. (Whether the choreography, reconstructed from Stepanov notation by Sergei Vikharev, is truly authentic is anyone's guess.) One accepts that the Russians love to immerse themselves in the aura of the theater, doting on their favorite ballerinas. But for non-insiders, large portions of pantomime and lackluster variations eclipse brief moments of full-out dancing. (The action comes to a dead halt during ten hey-is-anything-happening-onstage seconds preceding Solor's third-act variation.) It makes one realize why Michel Fokine and George Balanchine left Petipa behind for more fertile approaches to choreography.

But these classics celebrate three things: the fantasy that all personal dramas can be played out in public, the belief that no infidelity goes unpunished, and the reality that exquisite dancing can touch one's core.

Way Up High, Soaring, Floating, Diving, Dancing

Feature, *New York Times*, August 18, 2002

I had found Joanna Haigood's Invisible Wings *at Jacob's Pillow in 1998 absolutely haunting. Her own performance as a runaway slave, her transformation of the Pillow landscape, and her aerial work to represent both folklore and freedom transported the audience back to another time. The piece was epic in its embodiment of how black culture turned suffering into hope. In her ability to integrate art, history, and social conscience, Haigood was and is an under-recognized major figure. The project discussed in this feature was epic too, in its treatment of place, history, community, and physical risk.*

An abandoned grain elevator rises high above the docks of Red Hook, Brooklyn. With fifty-four joined silos, it looks like a pack of gigantic cement ladyfingers. During its heyday, from the twenties through the fifties, bulk grain was weighed, cleaned, and dried there by laborers who lived in the neighborhood.

From Thursday through Saturday, in *Picture Red Hook*, Joanna Haigood will be scaling the heights of this massive twelve-story grain terminal with

Joanna Haigood, tethered to a grain silo in Red Hook.
(© Suzanne DeChillo / *New York Times* / Redux)

her San Francisco company, Zaccho Dance Theater. Produced by the adventurous arts presenter Dancing in the Streets, the show is a result of several years' preparation to create a performance work involving the community. The area, which includes the Red Hook Houses, a large public housing unit, is a blue-collar neighborhood in transition. Troubled by drug-related violence in the past, it is now attracting businesses as well as artists in search of low-cost housing.

Last month in San Francisco, Haigood rehearsed in her studio, a former mattress factory that is rigged for aerial dancing. One woman, a few feet off the ground, was swinging like a pendulum, while another advised from the floor, "There's a little moment of weightlessness, and that's a good place to turn yourself around."

In *Picture Red Hook* members of Zaccho Dance Theater (the name comes from the segment of a Greek column that anchors it to the ground) will expand that "little moment of weightlessness" into an extended foray of soaring a hundred sixty feet in the air. Seven dancers will strap themselves into climber harnesses that are clipped to cables. The cables will be secured to the structural steel at the top of the building. Two more lines will be anchored to the ground on either side of the audience, so the dancers can fly directly overhead, hundreds of feet in front of the silos. (Note to the audience: bring lawn chairs or blankets.)

Asked if aerial dancing is risky, Haigood replied, "We all work very, very hard to take the risk out of the work." Still, though the dancers are intensely watchful during what mountain climbers call "the approach," there are risks. "You have to watch that you don't knock your head when you come into contact with any surface," said Suzanne Gallo, a dancer/choreographer who is a member of Zaccho.

In a practice session, one dancer momentarily lost control and looked like a fish out of water, flopping against a wall. Another got an instant skin abrasion and had to wrap a layer of neoprene around his hips before reharnessing. But aerial dancing, done correctly, gives the dancer a powerful sense of freedom that translates into a kinetic and psychic thrill for the audience.

In *Picture Red Hook* the dancers will glide through space using airborne versions of familiar actions like running, jumping, and diving. A theme of harvesting, with movements reminiscent of cutting grain, becomes transformed as the cutting gesture lifts the dancers further into space. Behind them, projected onto the facade of the silos, will be a video that includes larger-than-life faces of local residents talking about their hopes and dreams for the neighborhood. They were interviewed by Mary Ellen Strom, a video artist who is collaborating on the project.

Haigood, forty-five, is a graduate of Bard College, where she was influenced by the choreographer Aileen Passloff. She later attended the London School of Contemporary Dance, which has a curriculum based on Martha Graham's teachings. "It wasn't suiting me very well," Haigood said of the conservatory-like program. (She had also studied dance improvisation with Lorn MacDougal, a disciple of Daniel Nagrin.) "I went on some wonderful escapes with a neighbor who had been an aerialist with Barnum & Bailey. She took me to circuses, where I got to see the Flying Wallendas."

Haigood incorporated what she learned into her choreography. "It was interesting to get off the flat, two-dimensional plane and explore movement that was lateral, diagonal, and vertical," she said.

Haigood creates site-specific works, delving deeply into the history of each place. She has brought her flying techniques to a variety of settings, including a clock tower in San Francisco and the wooded area surrounding Jacob's Pillow. She has created works on subjects like the Underground Railroad, the paintings of Marc Chagall, and the first African American labor union, the Brotherhood of Sleeping Car Porters. (Haigood is of mixed race. Her father, a retired Army officer, is black and her mother, a retired school administrator who was born in Germany, is white.)

Called a "poet of memory" by the *San Francisco Bay Guardian*, she blends research and fantasy to evoke a world that draws the viewer in. Witnessing a work of hers can be both edifying and disturbing.

Haigood, whose choreography is in the repertories of the Joffrey Ballet of Chicago and Alonzo King's LINES Ballet in San Francisco, relates aerial dancing to a personal dream world. Dancing off the ground requires a disorientation that may be a clue to the magical quality that marks her work.

Gallo observed: "You need a sense of ease being inverted. For Joanna, she does it all the time. When you're inverted, you look at the world differently; you respond differently; you have a heightened awareness."

For the last few years, Haigood and Strom have given creative workshops in Red Hook schools. One project sent middle-school children to social events to observe dances, culminating in a swap in which different generations taught one another the popular dances of their day. (Scenes from the swap appear in the video.) Another project trained teenagers to assist in interviewing residents. The final interviews from the neighborhood—a mix of Italians, Irish, Latinos, and African Americans—reveal a common desire to work together to address issues like toxic dumping, youth violence, and gentrification.

As Haigood prepared for the performances, she tried to picture the grain terminal as it looked decades ago. Built in 1922, the Port of New York Authority Grain Terminal was a stop along the Erie Canal shipping system until 1965, when the increasing use of container ships drove the waterfront activity to more open ports in New Jersey and Staten Island. According to John Quadrozzi Jr., president of the Gowanus Industrial Park, in the ensuing period of economic decline, the granary was infiltrated by crack users and prostitutes. Since 1997, when the industrial park bought the facility and surrounding lots and waterways, it has become part of Red Hook's renewal.

Haigood regards the granary as a symbol of abundance, loss, and revitalization. In that context, she said, "The flying represents the will to transcend social challenges." But there are formal factors as well. "For me, choreographically," she said, "working with the human body and the human scale next to something so colossal is an artistic challenge."

Picture Red Hook will include live video close-ups of the dancers aloft, a sound collage by Lauren Weinger (grain pouring—think ocean waves) and a stilt walker from the community.

Strom has shot footage of the granary as well as scores of interviews for the video, which will be projected from scaffolding twenty-five feet high, at times giving the illusion that some of the silos are revolving. About the building, Strom said: "It's extremely beautiful in its purity of form. It looks like a seventies minimalist sculpture, like a Donald Judd upended."

Quadrozzi said that the site had been used for scenes in the films *Vanilla Sky* and *Shaft*, as well as for fashion spreads in *Vogue* and *Elle*. But nothing seems to have elicited the sense of wonder that Haigood's aerial dancing has. After watching her rehearse, he said: "She appeared to be flying in slow motion. She looked like a seagull up there. It's beautiful, and it's scary."

Seeing the economic polarization in the community between longtime residents and the new arrivals, Haigood decided to organize a group photograph of the people of Red Hook. Dancing in the Streets enlisted the help of churches, community centers, and other civic groups. In the spring of 2001, residents from every sector gathered in a nearby baseball field. During *Picture Red Hook*, this celebratory image, in which hundreds of people posed for the camera, will appear on the face of the historic grain elevator, radiating hope.

Russia Makes Room for Contemporary Dance:
Cross-Cultural Festival in Yaroslavl Breaks the Ballet Barrier

Feature, *Dance Magazine*, February 2003

*As I mentioned in my review of Sasha Pepelyaev ("The New Russia" in "The Nineties"),
I was interested in the new dance scene in Russia. I heard about Lisa First, the mover
and shaker from Minneapolis who organized exchanges with Russia, and got myself invited to her festival. There I saw that Pepelyaev was the tip of the iceberg. Modern and
postmodern dance had taken root all over Russia. This was exciting not only because
modern dance in Russia had been denied for so long, but also because it meant that the
land of supreme ballet was opening up to Western influences—and to the challenge of
artistic originality.*

Cabbage soup, quaint streetcars, and magnificent, green-domed basilicas
might be what most Americans would remember about Yaroslavl, an ancient city northeast of Moscow. But those of us who participated in the Fifth
International Festival of Movement and Dance on the Volga last August
were struck by the rich diversity of contemporary dance drawn from Russia and Eastern Europe. Americans from Minnesota, California, Tennessee,
and New York performed, led workshops, and engaged in cross-cultural collaborations. Although the tram ride was not guaranteed to deliver us from
the hotel to the theater any faster than walking, the three-ruble (ten-cent)
ride over corroding pavement reminded us that we were in an entirely different time and place.

But the dancing put us all on common ground. Modern dance, jazz dance,
and Contact Improvisation abounded. Companies from Russia, the United
States, the Czech Republic, and Poland gave performances and workshops.
The Russian students—about two hundred—plunged into sessions led by
Americans in jazz, hip-hop, and modern. A band of at least ten translators
facilitated the flow of communication. Participants and audiences filled the
750-seat theater and a smaller one for seven evenings.

Lisa First, the American organizer, came to Russia and fell in love with it
in 1989. A dancer and practitioner of Alexander Technique, she had read an
article in *Dance Magazine* about the American Dance Festival's program in
Moscow. By then, she says, she had met soul mates in Yaroslavl and started
to plan for an exchange: "We already had the idea for a festival. It happened
simultaneously. The doors were opening." Her partners in Yaroslavl have

been Alexander Girshon, a dancer and improviser influenced by experimental theater, and Nadia Proshutinskaya, a folk dancer turned economist. They inaugurated the festival in 1993 and continued to hold it every two years. Last summer, it was overflowing with twenty-one companies and fifty workshops.

The Provincial Dances Theatre from Yekaterinburg led off the festival with *Maple Garden*, a surreal evocation of romantic relationships by artistic director Tatiana Baganova. Six dancers gave masterful performances, supporting strange or striking images: A man wiggled toward a woman's face and, with his mouth, pulled a long string out of her mouth. Another woman approached with a pair of scissors and snipped the thread that bound them. A bare-branched tree, artificial fog, and eccentric costumes helped create a bleak, mysterious landscape.

In contrast, a group of spunky girls from Siberia called Second Parallel Dance Workshop skipped and jumped and played pranks on each other in *Six Milk Drops*. For example, one girl sat on a chair; another sneaked up behind her and grabbed the chair, leaving the first girl sitting strong in midair—a possible metaphor for self-reliance.

Local dance star Anton Kosov, a gamin-like creature of astounding versatility, contributed a solo that strung together jazz, ballet, and break dancing.

Slinky dancing came from the three men of Contemporary Dance Theatre, from Chelyabinsk, in Olga Pona's *Expectation*. Loose-limbed in black suits, they slithered and sliced in choreography that looked like a cross between Stephen Petronio and Bob Fosse.

Far, Far Away, by PO.V.S. TANZE from Moscow, combined the brainy energy of current European dancemakers like Anne Teresa De Keersmaeker with the grounded martial arts of *capoeira*. The piece sparkled with witty and inventive choreography.

From St. Petersburg came Kannon Dance Company with *Songs of Komitas*, choreographed by artistic director Natalia Kasparova, a powerhouse of a dancer. (Komitas Vardapet was an Armenian composer who went crazy after witnessing the Armenian massacre in 1915.) The cast moved through ingenious partnering with exceptional fluidity.

Saira Blanche Theatre, the Moscow-based group that started the first Contact Improvisation club in Russia, presented a duet consisting of two tall, gangly men: Oleg Soulimenko and Andrej Andrianov. As though in a talk show, they sat comfortably in armchairs. But instead of alternating talking, they alternated moving. They would each get up from the chair to do something—and that something became increasingly odd or funny. They gnarled themselves into knots, and got stuck in bumpy subversions of Contact Improvisation. Truly, hilariously eccentric.

The Americans contributed smooth fifties-style jazz dance (Cathy Young Dance from Minneapolis); wry and methodical duets (Hijack, also from Minneapolis); a languid, catlike exploration of a table and chair (Ray Chung of San Francisco); and an exuberant site-specific work on the banks of the Volga River (by Julia Ritter, who teaches at Rutgers University's Mason Gross School of the Arts). Scott Heron (from New York and Tennessee) made a gloriously ridiculous solo wearing pointe shoes and a leotard with underwear sticking out. In *Sweet Willie Mae*, contributed by Andrea Woods's Souloworks (from New York), the dancers oozed, sassed, and bounded to the blues music of Big Mama Thornton—and brought down the house.

Capping off the week was a giddy evening of collaborations. Soulimenko paired with Chung in a nutty but entirely logical improvised duet, and the joining of Hijack with Heron resulted in a wonderfully madcap exploration of the theater environment.

Three companies collaborated on a piece inspired by the paintings of Marc Chagall. While members of Poland's Lublin Dance Theater and duWa Dance from Slovakia slashed through space, Alexander Girshon and Anna Garafeeva of Performance Trio moved together as if in a dream. The men hoisted Garafeeva onto a high ledge, where she, resembling one of Chagall's floating women, pulled petals from a flower and watched them drift to the ground.

The last piece, masterminded by Irina Dolgolenko, turned everything on its head. Dolgolenko, a strong dancer from Moscow who had given classes combining jazz and something close to Limón technique, invited local dancers and critics to re-create moments from the week. The result was a wacky lampoon involving dolls, newspapers, and rolls of tape. The physical humor transcended linguistic and cultural differences.

Festival goers could bear witness to the flourishing of contemporary dance in ballet-rich Russia. All this activity sprouted in the last ten or fifteen years, a reflection of the political and artistic thaw since the breakdown of Soviet rule. Before, Russians had little access to contemporary Western influences. But in the last few years, Russians have been exposed to Western dance on TV, in theaters, and through visits by American dancers such as Rick Odums (now based in Paris), Christine Dakin, Iréne Hultman, Jeanne Ruddy, and Bill Young.

"Russian contemporary dance now is in the moment of transition from teenage enthusiasm to mature, confident acting," observed Girshon.

During this transition, approximately ten annual or biannual festivals have sprung up in the former Soviet republics. Vadim Kasparov, executive director of Kannon Dance Company and School, enthused, "This is my favorite festival because of the spirit of collaboration."

Postscript: The experimental dance scene in Russia has been virtually ignored by the two giants of classical ballet— the Bolshoi and the Mariinsky (Kirov) companies. But in February 2013, the Bolshoi commissioned Tatiana Baganova, the first choreographer mentioned in this story, to create a new *Rite of Spring* for its "Age of Modernism" festival. Following the chain of events triggered by the horrific acid attack on artistic director Sergei Filin the month before, the company had to find a quick replacement for British choreographer Wayne McGregor, who had withdrawn. Kudos to the Bolshoi for venturing into the land of the avant-garde within their own land. Now it's even more true that Russia is making room for contemporary dance.

Wendy Whelan: The Edgy Ballerina

Dance Magazine, March 2003

Wendy Whelan transformed ballet into something new for me, something utterly contem-
porary (see "Seeing Balanchine, Watching Whelan," in Section V). I felt charged up to try
to describe her dancing for this cover story. The other editors at Dance Magazine—*they*
were in the California office and probably had never seen Whelan dance—deemed my
descriptions too effusive, so they scaled back my praise. I resented it, but what could I
do? Well, I've reinstated it here.

Shortly after this period, Whelan became known as a muse for Christopher Wheeldon,
and her partnership with Jock Soto became equally celebrated. You can see glimmers of
both these developments in this story.

The boyfriend she speaks of is David Michalek, who later made a name for himself
with his monumental Slow Dancing *film series. They were married in 2005.*

As the curtain opens on Christopher Wheeldon's *Polyphonia*, four women
and four men line up in a row upstage. Even in stillness, one dancer stands
out. With hollows in her upper arms and hips, she looks more like a fascinating sculpture than a lovely ballerina. But for anyone who has seen
Wendy Whelan dance, the heart quickens. We are about to see some exciting dancing.

In roles that range from the lethal Novice of *The Cage* to the regal Titania
of *A Midsummer Night's Dream*, from the modernist duet in *Agon* to the poignant Odette in *Swan Lake*, Whelan dances with an energy and daring that
take your breath away. Your eye watches her and clings to her. You feel you've
never seen port de bras with such clarity and amplitude. A simple passé can
bring revelations. In the famously angular pas de deux of Balanchine's *Agon*,
she charges the space around her with electricity. And her Odette can make
you weep.

Her dancing with New York City Ballet was declared "a miracle" by dance
historian Lynn Garafola in a 2001 review in this magazine. And last summer
her performances in London with an offshoot company garnered praise like
"astounding," "seductive," and "awesome." One critic called her the "Sarah
Jessica Parker of the company."

For those who like their ballerinas soft and feminine, however, Whelan
is not a favorite. She is rail-thin, with wiry arms and jutting ribs that strike
some as unhealthy. But she is undeniably a world-class ballerina at the top

of her form. And more: she brings a sharp contemporary edge to classical ballet. Wendy Whelan is the ballerina modern dancers love.

Growing up in Louisville, Kentucky, Whelan had a surplus of energy. When she was two and a half, a sister was born. "Apparently I used to jump on the baby," she said. "My mom said, 'Get this middle child out of the house!' and she took me to the same ballet teacher she had." While studying with Virginia Wooton, "I saw the *Nutcracker*, got the record, and just went bananas! I performed it every day for everybody. By then my little sister was my backup dancer." At eight, she was chosen by Alun Jones to appear as a mouse in the Louisville Ballet's *Nutcracker* and started studying at the Louisville Ballet Academy. By ten, she was taking class every weekday.

It wasn't all smooth sailing at ballet class. Whelan was frustrated by her lack of coordination. "I was a little slower then the other girls," she recalled. "Pas de bourrée was very hard for me. I remember Alun telling one of the girls, 'Take her into the corner and teach her how to do that.'"

At thirteen she was given a scholarship to the summer course at the School of American Ballet in New York. Two years later she left home and enrolled at SAB full-time. At first she resisted the direction to "be pretty," but eventually absorbed the school's formidable training. After a while, she said, "I could do anything they asked me to do."

She became an apprentice in 1984 and was asked to join NYCB two years later. As a corps member she still had trouble learning steps, so she would go home and write out pages of notes. But her dancing was already an example to her peers. Margaret Tracy, whose career paralleled Whelan's, said, "From the moment I met her she had an amazing facility. She's incredibly grounded in her dancing, but never heavy. I tried to learn from her groundedness. When she steps out onstage, you're never nervous."

Whelan also caught the attention of ballet master in chief Peter Martins, who chose her to dance in a small new ballet, *Les Petits Riens* (1987). "I was surprised," said Whelan, "but I knew Peter trusted me technically."

Sixteen years and countless lead roles later, Martins still trusts her. "She has a fantastic work ethic," said Martins, "and that's a huge part of a successful career." She takes company class or goes to Wilhelm Burmann, a popular teacher at Steps on Broadway. "I can't do without class," she said. "I'm not good when I'm on my own. I have to have that whip." But she's clear about how class and stage are different: "In class you're trying to control what's going to happen, and onstage you're allowing things to happen."

When asked what makes a good partner, she answered, "I like any guy who will look into my eyes. Then I can relax and let go." She often dances with Jock Soto, known for his excellent partnering. "Jock makes most of my lines for me. It looks like I am, but I couldn't do it without him."

Although some observers feel she embodies George Balanchine's neo-classical ideals, she came to the company after his death in 1983. "I'm usually in awe," she said about his ballets. "It's like a perfect puzzle every time between movement and music. And I'm always discovering new things in his choreography."

But it is the current director of NYCB to whom she is devoted. It was Peter Martins who plucked her from the corps. It was Martins who cast her in one lead role after another. "Very few people can do everything," he said. "She comes pretty damn close."

Martins's support did not prevent her from getting stage fright. "Before my first Dewdrop and my first White Swan, my body turned to rubber and I couldn't even make it through class." As she gained confidence, she lost her nervousness in new roles.

One of those roles was the Novice, the female insect programmed to destroy males, in *The Cage* by Jerome Robbins. With jabbing elbows and a spine that moves with the force of a lobster's tail, she is unforgettable. At the ballet's end, when the Novice kneels and turns her head to the audience, Whelan conveys a glimmer of sorrow and loneliness that puts the concept of instinctual aggression into question. When asked about the role, she said, "That was home for me. I could be ugly; there was no lipstick involved in *The Cage*. I could use my weird assets. Jerry let me go with that ballet."

And what are those weird assets? "Long spindly arms and flared out hands. Crooked back," she answered. Whelan has scoliosis, which skews the spine and rib cage. (As a young teen she had to wear a back brace constantly, unless she was in dance class—which was an incentive to take more classes.) Another interesting asset is her face. Seen from the front, she is conventionally beautiful, but her profile reveals a line from her forehead to her nose that makes her look as though she is carved from stone.

Her presence brings a modernist aspect to ballet. Her explanation? "I've always had a bit of tomboy in me. I'm not naturally dreamy or caught up in a fantasy world. I'm a Taurus, very grounded and earthy, and that gives me the modern quality." Whether a role calls for modern edge or romantic fullness, she knows what her non-weird assets are: "What I can do is to give movement a different dimension, to show it with more detail. The way I work, the detail becomes evident in my body."

Hearing about negative reactions to her body over the years, she has learned how to handle it. "At first I would cry about it; I took it very personally; I didn't understand it. That was the whole ugly-hideous-I'm-not-attractive thing. I now know that I don't have to please everybody, and I trust that whatever I am doing is okay for me."

At thirty-five, Whelan is feeling centered, sensing that her body, mind, and spirit are in line. Contributing to this new maturity is her boyfriend, a photographer from Los Angeles. "He's got an artist's soul, and he's taught me where to look for mine. He's opened up my eyes to a gazillion things in the four years we've been together."

Whelan is interested in choreographers like Wheeldon who approach their work collaboratively: "I like being part of a process and not feeling like I'm just a lump of clay." And Wheeldon is thrilled to work with her. "She's such a creature unto her own," he enthused. "Working with her is constantly surprising. I create a sketch and she fills in the color. She's rather unsure of her beauty, so the sexual tension she creates onstage is unique—more intense. She changed my idea of the way dance could be romantic. There's no one like her."

Whelan recently learned that Alun Jones is retiring from the Louisville Ballet. To honor him, she will bring three other principals from NYCB to dance the leads in a Louisville Ballet production of *Stravinsky Violin Concerto*, Jones's favorite Balanchine ballet.

What advice will she have for young Louisville dancers? "I think fate takes you where you're supposed to go," said Whelan, "and you have to just trust your gut."

Last year was the first time she incurred an injury, a strain in the lower leg, which led her to start envisioning her post-dance future. As a child she had enjoyed drawing, so she thinks she may get involved in visual arts. But for now, she relishes every danceable moment. In describing a recent performance when everything clicked—the music, the partnering, the audience response—she said, "It was bliss."

VI From 2004 to 2007

The moment I was appointed editor in chief of *Dance Magazine* in February 2004, my workload increased exponentially. I was editing, assigning, writing connective bits, interviewing, and meeting constantly. It took at least a year to figure out how to delegate among my small staff— which is why there is nothing here from 2004 and only one review from 2005. Once the workflow eased a bit, I had my pick of what to review. I wanted to challenge myself to cover major ballet seasons like New York City Ballet and American Ballet Theatre along with a range of other performances.

As editor of *Dance Magazine* I tread the line between critic and advocate. I tend to sympathize with the dance artists showing work; I trust that they are creating the best art they can at that moment. I never feel that a performer is trying to dupe me. I also have a critical streak, but I try to slow down before unleashing it. Whenever I type out words that cast even the slightest negativity on dancers or choreographers, I get a twinge of the heart. But I was always critical of myself as a dancer and choreographer (it goes with the territory), so I'm used to those pangs. In this batch of reviews, I got used to being judgmental. Actually, I sometimes got the sensation that I was *practicing* being judgmental, practicing being a critic unambivalently.

For the next two sections, I've written fewer introductions. My previous entries consist of pieces that were so far in the past that I felt they needed some telescoping back to make sense of them in the present. But as I looked at the more recent forays, it was as though I were still working on each one. I could improve the word choice here, lop off a sentence there, but in only a few cases did I feel the need to put them in a context.

All the entries in Sections VI and VII are from *Dance Magazine*; some originally appeared in the print edition, others on the website. The sequence follows the dates I wrote them rather than the publication dates, which, in the case of the print magazine, are usually about three months after the actual writing.

Tere O'Connor Dance

Dance Theater Workshop, New York City

July 13–16, 2005

Web review, dancemagazine.com

Tere O'Connor's work ricochets between chaotic and geometric, absurd and natural, robotic and raunchy. *Frozen Mommy*, premiered at the Kitchen last year and brought back by popular demand, crystallized the rhythms of ambivalence.

In a bare performance space, the five dancers engage in a stylized version of familiar—or familial—interactions. Accompanied by silence interrupted occasionally by scary, machine-like sucking noises (music by James F. Baker and O'Connor), each one has a different persona. Heather Olson is doll-like, bewildered; Matthew Rogers is a gangly teenager; Christopher Williams moves with outrageous sinuousness; the stout Hilary Clark exhausts herself with a rage that is funny and finite; the small Erin Gerken has a quiet sensuality. They do simple things like little step-together-steps that go nowhere, saying crisply, "Enter. Enter. Enter." Are they trying to enter each other's lives or are they obsessing about the Internet? The emotional tone has something akin to that of *Petrouchka*, with arms thrust out as though asking for love, as though trying to burst out of the wooden bodies that encase them.

Slivers of affection and/or aggression are dispensed and then forgotten. As Williams languishes against the back wall, Rogers rushes toward him and lifts him, pinning him to the wall—a sudden but relaxed crucifixion. Olson thrusts her pelvis into Gerken's, then Gerken takes her by the hand to lead her forward and says, "Thank you, Heather."

Some things may seem like shtick: the sudden laughs, the abrupt return to nonchalance. But the choreography, splicing together tantrums, apathy, affection, and play, is always surprising and deeply felt. It all seems to say that no matter how much we brush against someone else's private world, we land in a world of our own.

At the end, a long stillness takes hold. Halfway through it, Rogers, upstage, drops to the floor and sobs quietly. The other four are left standing, frozen, as the lights dim.

Lori Belilove and the Isadora Duncan Dance Company

Isadora Duncan Dance Foundation, New York City

January 12–14, 2006

Review, *Dance Magazine*, April 2006

When my mother taught "interpretive" dance in our basement (from 1952 to '55), she would sometimes give us the "Isadora skip" across the floor. You skip on the left leg with the right knee coming forward while you round your back, and then you skip on the right leg as you arch your back and the left leg swings behind you. The closing and opening of the chest propels you across the floor with a certain power. I felt like I was flying. So I always had a soft spot for Duncan dancing, not knowing much about it except that sense of freedom in my body.

Lori Belilove is arguably the most authentic Duncan interpreter in the United States. When she performs Duncan's dances, you see the glorious sweep through space, the oppositional skips, the swooping torso. You see the emotional range from breathy joy to seductiveness to earthbound despair.

The setting was an intimate salon, the kind that Isadora might have held in her early days. On display were seventeen short dances performed by women in billowy tunics. Many of the piano pieces were played wonderfully by Matthew Ward, the only male performer. Of the company members, Beth Disharoon seemed to best embody the qualities associated with Duncan: womanly lyricism, full-bodied buoyancy, and arms moving with the fluency of a river.

Four of the dances, made between 1921 and '24, commemorated Duncan's association with the Soviet Union. In *Varshovianka*, a young woman in red galloped across the space brandishing a flag, then mimicked being shot. As she lay dying, she passed the flag to a newcomer, who galloped and brandished just as fervently. This happened five times, making the fervor of revolution and the futility of war equally clear.

Other dances were not narrative, but projected a strong mood. In *Bacchanal* (ca. 1908), three women in garlands skipped and swirled giddily until they toppled onto one another in exhaustion. In *Death and the Maiden* (ca. 1916), another garlanded young woman concluded her dance by hurling her headpiece to the floor.

The juiciest and most edifying dances were those that Belilove performed herself. Her slightly severe face is totally believable theatrically. Her body is probably more disciplined than Duncan's ever was, which gives her a contemporary look. And yet, one can glimpse in her face, hands, and upper chest flashes of Arnold Genthe's famous photographs and Abraham Walkowitz's drawings of Duncan, lending the illusion that one can for a moment touch that time.

Perhaps the most moving work was *Hope* (ca. 1915), in which Belilove stood strong above a prone, despondent child, then coaxed her into life. When the child (Hayley Rose Brasher) raised her head, Belilove was looking upward, not at her. But the woman got the child to rise by making gathering motions, after which the two created parallel Grecian-urn shapes with their arms above their heads. The triumph of womanhood? The renewal of hope? The merging of art and culture? In any case, the dance's restraint generated an emotional power.

Susan Marshall & Company

Dance Theater Workshop, New York City

March 8–18, 2006

Review, *Dance Magazine*, June 2006

Enchanting. Whimsical. Magical. It's hard to say why Susan Marshall's latest work is so satisfying. A string of gently surreal vignettes, *Cloudless* reveals a sexy imagination and a bemusement about human connection. Stripped of the elaborate costume and set elements Marshall has used in recent years, *Cloudless* makes clever use of the occasional chair, table, and ladder, as well as fragments of recorded music and video. The episodic format seems to free Marshall to follow her imagination to wherever it leads her, whether in full-blown hilarity or in quietly poetic observation of life.

Marshall's penchant for repeating gestures unduly is tempered here by her assured use of props, theatrical clarity, and the commitment of her five dancers. In fact, the repetition helps you see how she mines a simple image and allows it to grow and change until it imprints on your mind's eye.

In one scene, Joseph Poulson and Luke Miller sit at a table with a heavy

Susan Marshall's *Cloudless*. An eerily beautiful moment with Darrin M. Wright, Joseph Poulson, Kristen Hollinsworth, and Luke Miller. (© Jeffrey Ladd)

tome before them. They reach over each other's hands to turn its feather-light pages. When someone switches on a standing electric fan, the pages turn over by themselves in the breeze. Kristen Hollinsworth and Darrin M. Wright, sitting behind Poulson and Miller, rise to softly whisper in their ears. It's an eerily beautiful moment that seems to say knowledge is fleeting, whether you get it from a book or from people.

In another scene Hollinsworth is rigged by a rope and hoisted up so that she floats horizontally, her feet reaching back toward a ladder. Three people are helping her, or perhaps hindering her—it's hard to tell which. Poulson, who has been the active rigger off to the side in the dark, ends up climbing the rope and dangling before her as she sits atop the ladder. It's a little like Chagall's upside-down men and women in the sky, and a little like the racy duet on a swing in Stroman's *Contact*. But mostly, it is like itself: one of Marshall's haiku-like gems.

Stan Won't Dance

Performance Space 122, New York City

March 15–19, 2006

Web review, dancemagazine.com

Like the movie *Brokeback Mountain*, the British group Stan Won't Dance brings the danger of gay love to center stage. The place is a smoky gay pub in London, and the movement idiom is rough-edged Contact Improvisation with sinister overtones. Choreographed by Rob Tannion and Liam Steel (both are former dancers with DV8 Physical Theatre who got together and co-founded Stan Won't Dance in 2003), the dance-theater duet *Sinner* traces a nervous flirtation between two men. Ben Payne's script is a fantasy of what happened in the hours before the real-life David Copeland planted a bomb in a gay bar in 1999, killing three people and wounding many others.

This is a powerful performance, filled with a sly kind of precision: the men's limbs and heads seem to just miss each other, fitting into a revved-up kinetic puzzle. What makes it engaging is not just the nifty lifts and throws but also the physical wit, sweaty humor, and the uncertainty of how far to trust someone you've just met. The dancers, Steel and Ben Wright, didn't seem to be acting; they had an almost alarming curiosity and intensity. "Robert" (Steel) is small, insecure, ambivalent. "Martin" (Wright), tall and oozing self-confidence, moves with a kind of offhand gusto and sharpness.

The story leads down a psychological path from frightened to frightful, suggesting that hate crimes are, deep down, fueled by fear. The refrain of a cell-phone ring precedes an ominous, one-sided conversation: "Who is this? Leave me alone." It culminates in an aria of self-hate from Robert: "You're my brother. . . . You're my disease. . . . Whoever you are, that's what I am." The two men seem to switch identities, becoming two sides to one coin: confidence/fear, aggressiveness/insecurity, bigotry/empathy.

The religious overtones sink in bit by bit: first the title; then T-shirts emblazoned with kitschy images of Christ; and then . . . the crucifixion. Small, sweet Robert takes a hammer and nails Martin's jacket—with Martin inside it—to the table, then knocks the whole pile over and tosses chairs on top of the mess. His sudden violence was all because of the fear and confusion and wanting to "be somebody." Possibly not too far off from the real David Copeland's psyche and others like him.

Urban Bush Women

Dance New Amsterdam, New York City

April 5–9, 2006

Web review, dancemagazine.com

Jawole Willa Jo Zollar goes to extremes of emotion that most choreographers never get near. This concert (one of two programs) brought on a sharp, spicy joy as well as overwhelming feelings of grief and rage.

Investigating the life and work of Pearl Primus has been fertile territory for Zollar and Urban Bush Women. The first half of the program, *Walking with Pearl . . . Africa Diaries* (2004) represented Primus's exploration of Africa. Wearing loose, earth-colored clothing, the dancers enacted various tasks. Zollar set the tone by slowly walking along a diagonal (Primus walking through history?) before she took a seat in the corner to read the revered choreographer/anthropologist's diaries, which speak of her trust in dance and her feelings of connection to Africa.

But it was the second half, devoted to Primus's investigations of the American South that shook the rafters. In one section of *Walking with Pearl . . . Southern Diaries* (2005), four women shuffled in a circle. (Zollar had explained before the show how the shuffle and the "shout" originated.) One at a time, each laughed from her center—from the center of the Earth, it seemed. Each had a different rhythm of mirth—one guttural, one giddy, one drumlike—until we all wanted to laugh. But afterward, to the words of "Strange Fruit," sung by Nina Simone (to which Primus had made a solo in 1943), the dancers stood around simply reacting, in their faces and bodies, to the subject of that song—lynching. The words ("Black bodies swinging in the southern breeze . . . The bulging eyes and the twisted mouth") needed no choreography, and Zollar offered none. Some might say that the performers were overacting, but simply dwelling on this song and what it meant was so powerful that I got choked up. When the song ended, the women held one among them who was so affected that she could barely stand up, as though it was *her* brother or son who'd been lynched.

With African dance steps and a communal resolve, the Urban Bush Women gradually worked their way back toward affirming life in glorious gratitude—the shout. Masterfully, Zollar had brought us from cackling joy to despair to celebration. Response was raw: The audience rose to its feet, and Zollar and some of the dancers were in tears.

Miguel Gutierrez and the Powerful People

Dance Theater Workshop, New York City

June 6–10, 2006

Web review, dancemagazine.com

Nietzsche called that very rare person who can handle uncertainty an "über-mensch." In the same vein, or so its seems, Gutierrez is calling his group the "powerful people." They are the ones, in Nietzsche's words, who "dance on the edge of the abyss," who do not depend on what's known or familiar. This could be seen in both pieces on this program.

In *Retrospective Exhibitionist*, Gutierrez strips the layers of artifice to reveal a raw state of mind/body. He slowly drops to all fours and vibrates his entire being, letting out a guttural noise that's a cross between a howl and a wail. On the next exhale, the sound emerges from his throat with a slightly different blend of yearning, hurt, puzzlement, and terror.

He aims a tiny video camera at a stash of snapshots of his younger self. On the screen his fingers draw across these pictures, simultaneously loving and dismissing his earlier self.

As searing as these moments are, the movement sections are equally compelling. Like Yvonne Rainer's *Trio A*, but triple the speed, there is no visible connectedness between the movements, so each transition instantly empties the body of what came before. In this way Gutierrez shifts from a wiggle to a grand stubbing leap to a happy sashay.

The abruptly changing impulses of this hour-plus solo project a sense of anarchy, but the sections are well ordered and nothing rambles. Gutierrez uses deliberate devices—like doing the opening section in the nude except for sneakers and baseball cap—to psyche himself into a state that goes way deeper than mere exhibitionism. He plumbs a rigorous, self-questioning state of catharsis.

The following dance, *Difficult Bodies*, begins with three women in glittering black dresses. They roll languidly toward us, shedding their dresses, so by the time they get downstage they are wearing only black bras and briefs. Anna Azrieli, the dancer in the center, was pregnant but unfurled her clothing as smoothly as Michelle Boulé and Abby Crain. Julie Alexander, in T-shirt and briefs, then replaced Azrieli, and, now standing, began lip-synching a song, fiercely exaggerating the movements of the mouth. The women danced till exhausted, yet somehow retained their sexiness and defiance.

The lights were hot white on the audience for a good portion of the evening. Toward the end, Gutierrez and the women chanted robotically, "I am perfect and / You will love me and / Everyone in this room is in this f——— dance." We couldn't and wouldn't try to escape.

American Ballet Theatre

Metropolitan Opera House, Lincoln Center

May 22–July 15, 2006

Season review, *Dance Magazine*, October 2006

The night that Julio Bocca gave his farewell performance, the Metropolitan Opera House turned into a stadium of yelling, cheering fans who threw things at the stage—oranges and flags—even from the highest side balconies. Each principal dancer who had partnered him, from Cynthia Gregory to Julie Kent, showered him with kisses and flowers. Confetti glittered, and Bocca guzzled a bottle of beer—in profile. The unruly audience (which included clusters of Argentineans) held on to each opportunity to say goodbye. Alessandra Ferri, who had just given a gloriously reckless performance of MacMillan's *Manon* with Bocca, joined him on a few of the curtain calls. Each time he reappeared the crowd roared yet again.

Another big moment in the spring season was the company premiere of James Kudelka's *Cinderella*, a strange and satisfying ballet. It's not easy to find a new full-length that can hold its own amid the beloved chestnuts of *Swan Lake*, *Giselle*, and *Romeo and Juliet*. ABT has been trying out a new one every spring, often with lackluster results. This time it finally hit the mark, and in doing so, brought the spring season into the current century. Kudelka's *Cinderella*, which premiered for National Ballet of Canada two years ago and was later taken by Boston Ballet, is not shy about being either funny or romantic, and the choreography holds the attention throughout.

Visually it's very contemporary, with a ballroom that looks like it's made of origami paper (design by David Boechler). The duet between Cinderella and Her Prince Charming at the ball is delicate, wistful, complex, and totally convincing. Before they actually get together, they dance in parallel worlds across the front of the stage, building up suspense. He reaches for her hand and then pulls back. They invite each other to dance with a little swaying balancé. Kudelka knows the value of simple moves. Once they decide to dance together, Prince Charming lifts Cinderella and moves her three inches to the side. It's just a little lift, but it shifts everything. She has surrendered without surrendering. When they finally kiss, you really feel it. Julie Kent made a luminous Cinderella and Marcelo Gomes was gallant as the prince who travels the world to find her.

During Prokofiev's passage of deep, thundering tympani and French horn, twelve men sitting in a circle, all wearing big pumpkin heads, jump up one at a time. The action itself is ridiculously simple, but because of the turbulent music, complete with glock, it's a strangely stirring way to represent the clock striking midnight. It's also a potent warning to Cinderella to not turn into a pumpkin—to not miss life's moment of opportunity.

There were other treats too. Erica Cornejo as a myopic stepsister recklessly threw herself into ridiculous lifts and straddles, eliciting belly laughs. Martine van Hamel as a drunken stepmother tottering over to the cabinet for the bottle, even climbing on the drawers to reach for the high shelf, was priceless.

The other company premiere, Cranko's *Jeu de Cartes (A Poker Game in Three Deals)*, is a silly ballet. It's mildly amusing to see dancers emerge from behind giant cards. It's hard to follow the lead role of the Joker—is he a tyrant, a wild card, or a scapegoat?—but Carlos Lopez fulfilled his many moods with aplomb. Irina Dvorovenko as the Queen of Hearts went at it like a vaudeville trouper. Sarah Lane (a dancer I'd love to see more of) was charming and impetuous as the Two of Diamonds.

Ashton's *Sylvia*, a lavish ballet with choreography stretched thin over a long plot, opened its run with Gillian Murphy as Sylvia and Maxim Beloserkovsky as Aminta. Murphy radiated strength as the huntress but was not particularly expressive in the head and upper chest. Beloserkovsky made a princely shepherd, with bursts of energy that showed his ardor. Carmen Corella, onstage only a few minutes near the end, made a powerful Diana, trying to break up the lovers. The lifts in the final pas de deux are remarkable: Aminta looks like he's taking hold of a statue—Sylvia's body is all in one piece—rather than a woman.

As for ABT's chestnuts, the performances I saw were top-notch. Diana Vishneva's Giselle was divine. In the first act, she dipped her head in a way that showed her shyness and vulnerability. Vladimir Malakhov was magnificent in line and leaps but didn't look at his sweet peasant girl much, even when she melted into his body. Her mad scene, though less aggressive than some, was quietly affecting. She seemed already to have a ghostlike cast, as though she were becoming a Wili before our eyes—not waiting for intermission. Malakhov was more convincing when he got to be tragic in the second act. His brisés sped toward Myrta as though pushed by fate. Stella Abrera shone in the peasant pas de deux. (Oh, how much longer do we have to wait to see her do Giselle?)

Dvorovenko and Beloserkovsky delivered a superb *Swan Lake*. His aristocratic bearing and caring gestures helped you believe in the story. Her Odette was a real creature, head pressing forward in anguish, arms reaching back like wounded wings. His Siegfried was a seeker even before he met

Odette, looking for something loftier than the material wealth he was to inherit. The pas de deux was exquisite.

As Odile, Dvorovenko was as sure as a venom-dipped arrow that knows its path, as glittering as a knife blade. Throwing us conniving glances, she colluded with the audience in duping the duplicitous prince. When she lured him and suddenly turned away, you couldn't help but feel sorry for him. Gomes, meanwhile, relished his own allure as the evil von Rothbart, almost outrageously so. Back at the lakeside, Dvorovenko's Odette was even more limpid than before. Her very slowness signaled her forgiveness; a sadness hung in the air.

Le Corsaire, with its explosions of spectacular jumps and turns, is always a crowd pleaser. Dvorovenko as Medora commanded the stage with her silken yet crisp dancing, but Angel Corella as the Slave stole the show. His bounding power startled and his pirouettes seemed endless. As Gulnare, Abrera gave an extra breath to her port de bras; she was a pleasure to behold. Roman Zhurbin wiggled like Jell-O as the clueless pasha.

The most powerful performance came from Vishneva in MacMillan's *Romeo and Juliet*. Although she did not make the transformation from young girl to woman—she seemed already too grown up to be playing hide-the-doll with her nurse—she later brought an emotional despair that was deeply affecting. In the balcony scene, her body opened up to Romeo in beautiful ways. Corella was a fine Romeo, but his greatest scene was the swordfight with Tybalt. He tore into the duel, and you knew he wouldn't let up until he had destroyed Tybalt. Veronika Part as Lady Capulet and Susan Jones as the Nurse had their moments of high grief. David Hallberg, the newest principal, made an interesting debut as Paris; he was clearly drawn to Juliet, but ultimately slightly sinister.

Let me say that I think Herman Cornejo is one of the great dancers of our time. He infuses classical roles with a lightness and joy that is natural, subtle, and immediate. His double cabrioles open and close languorously as if he's floating in the air, and his landings are soft and quiet. His dancing is never forced, but flows form the core of his being. In the pas de trois of *Swan Lake*, his soaring leaps show his open-heartedness. As Lescaut in *Manon*, he is hilarious in the drunk scene when he staggers around while managing to partner his mistress. As Mercutio he is so full of life that his death heightens *Romeo and Juliet*'s overall sense of tragedy. His presence deepens the pleasure of watching any production.

Feelings Are Facts: A Life, by Yvonne Rainer, MIT Press, 2006

Book Review, *Dance Magazine,* July 2006

For generations of dancers, Yvonne Rainer is an avant-garde icon. In the sixties she was a moving force behind Judson Dance Theater, the incubator of postmodern dance. With an Olympian stubbornness, she was hell-bent on making her rough-hewn, "difficult" dances. She was a feminist and antiwar activist who spoke her mind. Even now, thirty years after she turned to filmmaking, her name holds a mystique for young choreographers and budding dance historians.

Her autobiography, *Feelings Are Facts,* is a gripping account of her life up until the seventies. The book is also a window on the sixties, the decade that exploded the existing methods for making art—and the decade that questioned both authority and chastity.

Rainer grew up an outsider. Feeling beleaguered, her immigrant parents placed her and her brother in foster care. Rainer's tendency toward moroseness later blossomed into a debilitating depression that she called her "engine of self-destruction." She points out that even as a child she supplied ammunition to her enemies (and later to her critics). As an adult, her medical enemy was an intestinal problem that would strike with such force that she would be hospitalized for weeks.

An anarchist almost by birth, she was horrified by banality and complacency. She refused to "bedeck" herself for social occasions—the first refusal of many. Her letters and diary entries as a seventeen-year-old are as exquisitely conscious, as intellectually nimble, and as full of moral fiber as Susan Sontag's famous postgraduate essay, "Against Interpretation." As an adult, her distrust of expressivity was shared by the minimalists of her time—of whom her lover Robert Morris was a key figure. Other influences ranged from Cocteau's *Orpheus* and theater director Richard Foreman to dance artists Erick Hawkins, Simone Forti, Steve Paxton, Anna Halprin, Trisha Brown, and Merce Cunningham.

A charismatic performer, Rainer's strong, quiet face thinly veiled the passion underneath. No one who saw her solo *Inner Appearances* (1972) can forget the charged reverie in which she vacuumed the floor while sentences about her innermost thoughts were projected on the back wall. This was a pivotal piece because she realized she could express more about her feelings on a screen than in a performance space. The irony is that, in her rejection

of the heroism of Martha Graham and in her embrace of "the human scale," she sort of barred herself from making dances on the larger themes of relationships, love, and suffering—thus her turning to film.

Perhaps the happiest time in her life was when she first started dancing. "All I knew was that I loved running and jumping," she writes. She embraced Merce Cunningham's edict, "You must love the daily work." Another highpoint was an idyllic camping trip with Morris. Later she found out that his previous lover had given birth to his baby during their two weeks of harmony. After she and Morris broke up and she later learned he had married yet another woman, she took a killer amount of pills. Luckily (to say the least) a dance buddy found her in time to have her stomach pumped.

Rainer's prose is alarmingly frank, touched with mordant humor and a blunt brand of brilliance. She makes no attempt to sound sophisticated or "original" (so different from Isadora Duncan's highly theatrical autobiography, *My Life*). Her modesty is almost disturbing. She doesn't consider her childhood unusual until she sees the reaction in her friend Nancy Meehan's face after she tells her about it. During Judson's heyday (1962 to 1964), when she should be reveling in her success, she is so envious of Rauschenberg's mega-success that she calls the whole Judson group "the tail to his comet." Likewise, when she makes the landmark work *Trio A*, she doesn't think much of it until, while describing her process to Morris, she sees the "light in his eyes." Like many women, she lived for that light, no matter how independent she was as an artist.

As director of Yvonne Rainer and Group, she famously abdicated her authority when she realized that the contributions she had invited from the dancers created a freer environment. But it was her device of framing wild moments with rigorous structure that helped make the Grand Union a legendary improvisation collective. In her letters to her dancers at the time—an all-star group that included Steve Paxton, Barbara (Lloyd) Dilley, Douglas Dunn, and David Gordon—she carefully deconstructs the idea of authority, especially her own.

When Rainer was recovering from her suicide attempt, Pat Catterson brought Rainer's students to the hospital and performed *Trio A* with them on the sidewalk below. Beautiful gestures like this pass by without comment, without framing. As in her dances and her films, Rainer leaves us to make our own sense of it.

The most recent thirty years are crunched into an epilogue. This includes several films plus her choreography for Mikhail Baryshnikov's "Past Forward" tour in 2000. It also includes a frustratingly quick mention of her shift from straight to gay, from turmoil to stability—frustrating, given the forthrightness with which she describes her earlier affairs.

Much as the minimalists would deny it, Rainer's life is a testament to that old cliché about artists having to suffer. The darkness she lived contributed to the power of her work. Her feelings, more than her achievements, were the facts of her life. She struggled to find a way to express those overwhelming facts. She found it in her groundbreaking dances and films, but also in rare moments of utter abandon in performance.

New York City Ballet: Winter Season 2007

January 12–February 25

New York State Theater, Lincoln Center

Season review, *Dance Magazine*, May 2007

My original first sentence of this review was "American Ballet Theatre has the men, but New York City Ballet has the women." At that time ABT famously had the most spectacular contingent of male dancers on the planet—Herman Cornejo, Ethan Stiefel, Angel Corella, Jose Manuel Carreño, and on and on. (All but Cornejo have retired from ABT.) I wanted to make the case for NYCB's women being that good. But my fellow editors talked me down from making a comparison with another company in a review.

In a season of thirty-eight ballets, the dancing of NYCB's female principals blossomed into their full ballerina glory. Janie Taylor gave Robbins's *Afternoon of a Faun* an outsized sensuality that was mesmerizing. . . . Ashley Bouder, every inch a creature of flight, put the fire back in *Firebird*. She's impulsive, she's powerful, she shimmers and shatters the demons. . . . Jenifer Ringer burst into joy as an innocent Aurora and oozed glamour as the woman in black in *Vienna Waltzes*. . . . Wendy Whelan, slow as a floating cloud, light as air, imbued *Mozartiana* with a celestial tranquility. . . . Jennie Somogyi, jazzy and juicy, had a thrilling physicality in *Symphony in Three Movements*. Her Lilac Fairy ruled *The Sleeping Beauty* with such expansive benevolence that I wished she could come and bless my household too. . . . And there was something inexorable about the swooping and soaring of Sofiane Sylve, as dazzling as her bejeweled crown in *Tschaikovsky Piano Concerto No. 2*.

Among the men, Damian Woetzel was superb in *A Suite of Dances*, the solo Robbins made for Baryshnikov in 1994. He graciously communed with Ann Kim, the onstage cellist playing Bach's *Suites for Solo Cello*. Mischievous and nonchalant, he slipped from earthy folk steps into whizzing multiple turns. He was the welcoming host, virtuoso technician, and wise-guy adolescent all at once.

The soloists, who danced lead roles as often as the principals, were less dependable. We saw a lot of Teresa Reichlen, Sterling Hyltin, Abi Stafford, Tiler Peck, and Daniel Ulbricht. Hyltin tends to overdo and is weak in her center, but was fun and flirty in Martins's *Jeu de Cartes* and elegant in Feld's *Intermezzo*. Stafford tends to have more determination than flow; however she loosened up in *Walpurgisnacht Ballet*. In Mauro Bigonzetti's *Il Vento*,

Janie Taylor in Jerome Robbins's *Afternoon of a Faun*: mesmerizing sensuality.
(© Matthew Karas for *Dance Magazine*)

Peck was gutsy in a brazen broken-limb solo and duet, but in Martins's *Friandises* she was merely a showgirl and trickster. Reichlen's lovely gentleness and fluidity graced many roles, but she could have used more crispness in the *Agon* castanet solo and more authority as the Lilac Fairy.

The sprightly Daniel Ulbricht and the full-bodied Sara Mearns were the most consistent soloists. One of the best technicians in the company, Ulbricht bounded with unforced eagerness in all his roles. Mearns projected warmth and allure in all of hers.

And some corps members stood out. Wide-eyed Tyler Angle breathed fresh air into classical roles with his ease, smoothness, and classical line. Stephanie Zungre teased and snapped her paws with expert comic timing as the White Cat in *Beauty*. Sean Suozzi boldly extended into space, exemplifying the drama of black and white in *Agon*. And Kathryn Morgan was achingly lovely as the ingenue in Wheeldon's *Carousel (A Dance)*.

Choreographically, the highpoint of the season was Jorma Elo's *Slice to Sharp*. One of four ballets repeated from last spring's Diamond Project, it takes NYCB's nonnarrative tradition and rockets it into the future. With its sheer momentum, veneer of anarchy, and a semaphoric code language that lends a touch of mystery, it blows away the orderly lines of both Petipa and Balanchine. Using centrifugal force, it sends the dancers spinning and hurtling through space off-kilter. There are daredevil slides along the floor, windmilling arms, jutting pelvises, big wheeling lifts, and a lot of "open sesame" hand moves. The whole piece is a magic carpet ride. The motif of touch-reaction—or rather near-touch-guess-the-reaction—makes it seem like invisible strings tie one dancer to another. A man touches a woman's waist and her knees knock inward. A woman whips her leg and just misses the chest of a man in a backbend. Facing upstage with her hand behind her neck, Maria Kowroski slithers her head sideways and back into place behind her hand. It's a bit of fun voguing, one of many small surprises that spill out and make you keep your eyes peeled. The men dance to the hilt, especially Edwaard Liang and Joaquin De Luz, who dive into their crazy pirouettes and partnering with relish.

The one premiere, Christopher d'Amboise's *Tribute*, in honor of Lincoln Kirstein, has clear structures, a gentle humor, and old-time chivalry (lots of bowing and curtsying). Embedded in it are quotes from famed Balanchine ballets, like the sudden opening into first position of *Serenade*. *Tribute* is topped off with a beautifully spooling pas de deux for Bouder and Tyler Angle. She dances with authoritative delicacy, and he really seems to care about her. Twice, he assists her mid-leap before taking her for a big lift. You can hear a collective sigh from the audience when they go whirling off.

The major revival was Robbins's *Dybbuk* (1974), which seems to be about a wronged couple facing society—or at least a posse of rabbis. (A dybbuk, in Jewish folklore, is a lost soul, a spirit of the dead, whose voice enters the body of a living person.) Seven men in black with caps could be cousins of the bottle dancers in *Fiddler on the Roof.* However, the hieroglyph-like backdrop by Rouben Ter-Arutunian gives it a mystical tinge. Leonard Bernstein's score, with its vocal sections à la Stravinsky's *Les Noces*, emphasizes community and ritual. The high point is an entwining duet for Ringer and Benjamin Millepied, as though to get under each other's skin. But never does the ballet have the power of the original play, *The Dybbuk*, by S. Ansky, in which the voice of Leah's dead lover possesses her—two tormented souls in one body.

Another popular holdover from the Diamond Project was Alexei Ratmansky's *Russian Seasons.* With long, bright-colored dresses, it has a folksy charm. There is a wonderful twisty solo for Albert Evans (it's good to see him *move*), and a fine solo with sudden jumps for Suozzi. There are funny touches, as when two crouching men, their shirts riding up in back, pull their shirts down in unison. Ringer has a nice playful solo and a poignant scene where she walks on a path in the air made by the men's hands. But some moments are hokey, like a line-up that looks like a bunny hop. It had the quaint feel of a work from long ago, like, say, Sophie Maslow's *The Village I Knew* (1949). More intriguing was Ratmansky's *Middle Duet*, performed only once, on opening night. In that brief sketch, with haunting music by Yuri Khanon, Kowroski's elegant attention to simple tendus was somehow transporting.

Mostly, the Balanchine ballets provided the perfect setting for the dancers to shine. But a few of them, for example, *Monumentum pro Gesualdo*, *Duo Concertant*, and *Stravinsky Violin Concerto*, may be losing a bit of their appeal. Some people argue that these ballets are no longer performed well by NYCB. However I feel that choreographically they represent a time gone by, a time of orderliness and politeness. Ballets that slice through that remoteness (other than *Slice to Sharp*) are the atmospheric ones: Robbins's *Afternoon of a Faun*, Martins's staging of *Sleeping Beauty*, Wheeldon's darkly glamorous *Klavier*, the Balanchine/Robbins *Firebird*, Bigonzetti's *Il Vento*, and Balanchine's lush *Vienna Waltzes.* These ballets pull you into a different world and make you care about the characters. When they are over, you feel nourished by the art, sated with the fullness of people dancing.

Enchanted by Cuba

Feature, *Dance Magazine*, March 2007

Havana is a city where, when you tell a taxi driver to take you to the theater to see a ballet, he (or she) asks, "Who is dancing tonight?" Tickets for the biannual International Ballet Festival of Havana are sold out weeks in advance. The audience, a mix of all economic classes, bursts into applause when their favorites appear. There's yelling and clapping even before the dancers enter the stage—just the first notes of familiar recorded music can drive the crowd into a frenzy.

In this country where buildings are made of ancient stone and the cars hark back to the American fifties, ballet is king. Or rather queen. When Alicia Alonso, the former Ballet Theatre superstar who founded the Ballet Nacional de Cuba, arrives to take her seat in the house, she is greeted with applause befitting a people's heroine. There's even a popular ice cream called Coppelia, so named in her honor.

During the twentieth edition of the festival last fall, stars from around the world—except, of course, the United States—came to share in this feast of dancing. Carlos Acosta, Julio Bocca, Carla Fracci, Jose Manuel Carreño, and the latest young partners from the Bolshoi, Natalia Osipova and Ivan Vasiliev, added luster to the festival, which spread out over several venues.

THE COMPANY

Ballet Nacional de Cuba, the world-famous company that produces the festival, occupies a building of light-filled studios in the lively Vedado district. The doors and windows of the rehearsal rooms are wide open in this tropical climate. Sunlight streams through the stained-glass transoms, projecting aqua and red patches on the floor. In the second-floor studio, dancers can step outside onto a narrow terrace and take in even more sun.

American Ballet Theatre's Jose Manuel Carreño, who comes from a ballet family here, takes class from ballet mistress Carmen Hechavarria, a former classmate. Fresh from class, he told this visitor, "I love the energy here. I always recharge my batteries when I come."

What is that energy? How does the Cuban training produce so many exciting dancers? There's Acosta, Carreño, Lorena and Lorna Feijoo, and younger ones like Rolando Sarabia, now at Houston Ballet, and many more in other companies. The short answer, I would say, is the combination of a culture that loves to dance and the ironclad discipline of Alicia Alonso.

Jose Manuel Carreño taking class at the studios of Ballet Nacional de Cuba, in Havana, 2006: "I always recharge my batteries when I come." (© Nan Melville for *Dance Magazine*)

Clean lines and fast footwork lie at the heart of Alonso's approach, says Hechavarria, who has written a book on the technique. For example in passé, the toe must point to the knee and never cross it. But she also teaches dancers to interact onstage in a way that makes the characters as real as everyday life.

What is the secret of the super-long balances of the women (most spectacularly of reigning star Viengsay Valdés) and the endless pirouettes of the men? "Alicia taught us to concentrate with our eyes closed," Hechavarria said through a translator. (Alonso started losing her eyesight at a young age.) She also pointed out, with charming candor, that the body type of the Cuban women necessitates lots of pulling up.

Undoubtedly, this training accounts for the exquisite effect of BNC in Fokine's *Les Sylphides* during the festival. With feather-light arms, the corps de ballet breathed as one. They were constantly, subtly, in motion—a rapturous vision of femininity in a forest.

The company also gave a strong performance of *Don Quixote* in an outdoor plaza with an eighteenth-century cathedral as backdrop. Although the choreography did not take advantage of the potential humor of the ballet, Anette Delgado's saucy Kitri and Romel Frometa's Basilio showed stunning virtuosity. The biggest surprise was the last three seconds: Frometa tossed Delgado high in the air, where she did a lightning-fast split before falling into the final fish dive.

A dramatic situation unfolded when Viengsay Valdés danced *Diana and*

Acteon with Carlos Acosta even though she was sick with allergies. She managed the turns and lifts in the first half, but only marked the coda. After a long delay, the two finally came out for their curtain calls. Her audience cheered her on as she took a humble—and prolonged—bow alongside the fantastic Acosta. Apparently she had collapsed backstage. But she made a quick recovery. On the last night of the festival, she danced *Swan Lake* and then rushed across town to appear in *Pas de Quatre* for the gala.

The company showed several new works, including Alonso's own rather quaint fantasy ballet, *A Trip to the Moon.* In a more contemporary vein, Spain's Goyo Montero created the starkly dramatic *El dia de la creacion* (Creation Day). While some dancers sat on the edge of the stage, others performed Kylián-inspired duets in which you could feel the electricity pass between each couple through touch. In conversation later, Montero enthused about the dancers. "They have the will to learn new things," he said. "There's an excitement about new choreography. They were there one hundred percent."

THE FESTIVAL

Since 1960, when this biennial festival started, it has attracted top ballet stars including Kevin McKenzie and Martine van Hamel, Cynthia Gregory, Sylvie Guillem, Nina Ananiashvili, and Alina Cojocaru. This year, Acosta and Leanne Benjamin, both of the Royal Ballet, bowled us over with an excerpt from *Mayerling*, Kenneth MacMillan's ballet about a drug addict. With slicked-back hair and a mustache, Acosta looked like—and had the easy charisma of—Clark Gable. The partnering was wildly precise and more than suggestive. Audiences cheered the most graphic, thrusting moves boisterously. (Acosta, like Carreño, enjoys the rare privilege, bestowed by Alonso, to come and go as he likes.)

The choreographer Mats Ek and his wife, Ana Laguna, both of Cullberg yore, gave us two witty and poignant duets: *Memory* and *Potato.* These vibrant, no-longer-young dancers partnered each other with wistful and wise humor. I wanted each five-minute duet to stretch to fifty.

Other fare included Cisne Negro from Brazil, Nafas from Spain, and the fiery flamenca Maria Juncal. Julio Bocca brought his company from Argentina, Bocca Tango, and he danced his last Siegfried on earth, only slightly upstaged by a cat that sauntered across the stage in the third act.

THE SCHOOL

The National Ballet School, training ground for the BNC, is newly housed in a high-ceilinged, pre-Castro commerce building with twenty studios.

Through annual auditions, it accepts children at the age of fourteen from elementary schools around the country, and the competition is stiff. The school has only 292 students, most of them ballet majors, and of those, half are boys. All tuition is paid for by the government.

Fernando Alonso, who started the school in the sixties along with Azari Plissetski (brother of Bolshoi superstar Maya Plisetskaya), greeted our small group of journalists. An elegantly serene man, he exuded a love for ballet with every word. When asked why the training in Cuba has produced so many stellar male dancers, he chose to ignore the gender reference and answered, "Behind all good dancers are good teachers."

As we were filing in to observe a men's class, one seventeen-year-old boy instantly caught our eyes. Yonah Acosta looked heaven-sent, with a lithe body and beautiful feet. He is Carlos Acosta's nephew, and he radiates the same extraordinary grace his uncle has. [Update: Yonah Acosta is now a junior soloist in English National Ballet.]

LAST THOUGHTS

Cuba is a poor country but is rich in dance—on the streets and in the theaters and plazas. It's not surprising that some Cuban dancers leave home for more prosperous shores. (There have been about twenty defections in just the last two years.) Whether you agree with the u.s. embargo on Cuba or not, once you get here, you see an oasis where spirit transcends ideology. It's amazing how much talent is cultivated with so little financial resources. Perhaps, without the distractions of a consumerist culture—instead of billboards outdoors you see miles of clothes on laundry lines—dancers can more single-mindedly strive toward excellence. And the passion of the public matches the passion of the performers. In any case, the Ballet Nacional de Cuba is as busy as ever. The day after the festival ended, the company left for a tour to South America.

SIDEBAR: MODERN DANCE IN HAVANA

The modern dance in Havana is only tangentially connected to the festival. The government-funded Danza Contemporánea de Cuba, housed near Revolution Square, was given a master class by Ana Laguna, who taught a terrific excerpt of Mats Ek's powerful version of *Swan Lake*. These swans travel in aggressive herds, bringing out the rhythmic vigor of Tchaikovsky's score. The movement requires vigorous use of backs and hips as much as legs. The thirty-seven young dancers of Danza Contemporánea, which is directed by Miguel Iglesias, were up to the task.

On another occasion, Iglesias's son Julio showed an out-there multimedia piece with group work influenced by Contact Improvisation (father and son had both worked with Steve Paxton).

Danza Contemporánea draws some of its dancers from Instituto Superior de Arte, just outside the city. This is an arts school and conservatory for the performing arts similar to Juilliard. A few of us trekked out there to watch a modern class taught by Lourdes Ulacia, who has danced internationally with Sasha Waltz and David Zambrano. Her exercises include curving or undulating the back during every combination—even tendus. Rotating the hips inward and outward in difficult positions, for instance, while on the floor in a wide second, showed unusual core strength and flexibility. In the last diagonal the students spurted across the floor, tumbled into a *capoeira* handstand, and scooted back up to a leap. Clearly Ulacia is willing to demand the most intense work.

VII From 2007 to 2012

The Internet explosion affected everything about magazine publishing. In the blogosphere I found a more immediate outlet for my (at times swoony) enthusiasms and (at times cantankerous) observations. It also became a way to engage in the online conversations that were heating up in the dance world. If I had an argument to make, I wanted to just blurt it out—or at least start with the blurt energy. This could get me into trouble, and the Internet loves controversy, so a few of my posts "went viral." Of the hundreds of postings in the last seven years, I include here only fifteen—the ones I feel went beyond the flicker of the moment.

While learning how to connect through blogging, I continued to write reviews for print and the web. Some of these reflect the opportunities I had to travel, for instance to festivals in Spoleto, Tel Aviv, and Lyon.

The only feature story in this section is on diversity in dance, still a fraught subject. In "The Times They Are A-Changin'" my first interviewee, Eduardo Vilaro of Ballet Hispanico, set a tone of curiosity and playfulness, so this became a more upbeat story than I expected. Artistic directors like Vilaro and Benoit-Swan Pouffer of Cedar Lake Contemporary Ballet are finding that diversity today goes beyond black and white—many dancers are of mixed race—and goes beyond political or ethical convictions. Diversity, they feel, is artistically necessary.

A Brave, Illuminating, Terrific New Book

Blog post, August 2, 2007, dancemagazine.com

For anyone who has devoted herself to a choreographer and still wonders
    what that person thinks of her,
For anyone who has been puzzled by Merce Cunningham and John Cage's
    work,
For anyone who loves the Cage/Cunningham work,
For anyone who has ever seen Carolyn Brown dance,
For anyone who separates modern from ballet, Cunningham from
    Denishawn,
For anyone who sees a continuum between all forms of dance,
For anyone who wants to understand how modern dance morphed into
    postmodern dance,
Chance and Circumstance: Twenty Years with Cage and Cunningham (Knopf,
2007), by sublime dancer Carolyn Brown, will give you hours of pleasure, de-
mystification, and insight.

This book is one dancer's account of working with one choreographer.
I learned so much about Cunningham's early work that it made me want
to re-see his choreography right away and apply the new knowledge. Not
theoretical knowledge, but something more real: knowing what a struggle it
was to become accepted . . . how many years and tours their audiences were
either indifferent or battling each other . . . how many years Cunningham,
with his unstoppable appetite for making dances, met with scant success
. . . how many years John Cage's love for Merce and his work kept the company going—in finding performance dates, organizing the tours, keeping
the dancers cheerful, and of course, providing music ideas and *the* idea that
was the conceptual foundation for everything Cunningham did. (Which was
basically that separating the choreography, music, and visual decor in the
creative process produces an entity in the eyes of the viewer that is different
for each person but valid for everyone. Oh, and another idea—that art and
life are not so different.)

If you want to know about Cunningham, Cage, Rauschenberg—the
people as well as the theories—gorge yourself on this book. Each of its six
hundred pages has insights and realizations, small and huge, that help us
understand the evolution of dance and art in the twentieth century. Every
page carries Brown's absolute honesty—about herself, her insecurities, her
interactions, her observations about Merce. About John. About Merce and

John. About Merce and John and Bob (Rauschenberg). You start to realize that though there were many obstacles and few triumphs during those years (1953–73), those three were a charmed circle that collectively exploded the previous rules of choreography. Their collaboration (though there were other major players, like composer David Tudor and painter Jasper Johns) formed the crucible in which all of Cunningham's work is made.

One of the surprises is that Brown, for years, flirted with the possibility of dancing with the Metropolitan Opera and with Antony Tudor. (She did occasionally take gigs as an extra.) She adored Margaret Craske's ballet class and would nearly go broke to pay up her debt on classes. Another surprise (or rather non-surprise considering her unforgettable writing about Merce in James Klosty's 1975 book of photographs titled *Merce Cunningham*) is that the book is written beautifully.

Though Brown's dancing was famously serene, she herself was not. Her life was filled with ups and downs and doubts galore. Like any dancer who strives, falters, gets frustrated, gets tunnel-minded, opens up, loses her footing as a performer, and has exhilarating moments onstage, she sometimes gets depressed.

And like any other genius choreographer, Cunningham has his moments of bad behavior, i.e., noncommunicativeness, depending on others to do damage control.

But this is also a book about love. The love between a choreographer and dancer of longstanding partnership, however unspoken, demonstrated solely in the gifts they gave each other. He gave her many challenging roles to dance, and she gave him her beautifully fluid and alert dancing, which nudged his ideas of pure movement onto a heavenly plane of existence.

New York City Ballet: Winter Season 2008

January 2 to February 24

New York State Theater, Lincoln Center

Season review, *Dance Magazine*, May 2008

The big news this season was Mauro Bigonzetti's world premiere *Oltremare* (Beyond the sea). It transformed the stage at New York State Theater into a dark place, full of uncertainty yet rich with emotion. Gone were the upright, clean, pure bodies with sparkling tutus or sleek leotards. In their place was a band of fourteen immigrants wearing muted, Fellini-esque layers of clothing.

They troop in single file, each with an old-world suitcase. Suddenly they all duck at the exact same moment. It seems too orderly, too unison for this rag-tag group, but it signifies the alertness to danger these characters must have.

The partnering is tempestuous—almost violent. Andrew Veyette has more energy than I've seen him have in years. It's as though the character and the clothes loosen him up, so you don't see the stiffness in the shoulders that mars his classic line. You see a passionate, troubled, almost desperate working-class man. Georgina Pazcoguin, in ocher dress with black hair flying, matches his wildness. He pulls her off the floor so forcefully that she seems to fly up toward him. The duet with Maria Kowroski and Tyler Angle has an S&M edge; she places her foot on his chest in what seems like a power play. These characters are not shy. They seem to be fighting for their lives.

What's missing in this picture are children and old people, but you sense that they are nearby. Also missing are stable partnerships. Once you see a really strong duet, where the two people are clearly sharing their lives, the narrative weakens when one of them acts just as fierce with a different partner (and this story is not about wife-swapping).

Bruno Moretti's original music is a warm blend of Italian and Jewish tonalities. The dancing is weighted, evocative. Not least of *Oltremare*'s accomplishments is that the dancers are individuals—which does not always happen in City Ballet's repertoire.

Rococo Variations, a quartet to Tchaikovsky, is Christopher Wheeldon's last premiere as resident choreographer. It's choreographically thin in some parts, but contains a duet as gorgeously interesting as *After the Rain* or *Liturgy* (and that is saying *a lot*). Sara Mearns, wearing a brown knee-length tutu, begins the dance by placing a hand on her pelvis and deeply rounding her back. (Wheeldon is the only ballet choreographer I know who asks for a real contraction.) Then Adrian Danchig-Waring folds himself around her. It's a compelling beginning that returns as a motif, but it's just a beginning. The choreography only takes off in that central duet, where Mearns's dancing is full and luscious—as it was in everything this season.

Wheeldon's *The Nightingale and the Rose* (based on a story by Oscar Wilde), new last season, brought a burst of inventiveness. As the Nightingale, Wendy Whelan is a sliver of a bird, with bent wrists and elbows. During her tangled duet with the Student, she dives into his arms horizontally like a glider. When the sixteen men of the Red Rose Tree surround her, she is lifted straight up, then falls through them. Her arm shoots up in a last dying breath, à la the Dying Swan.

Two ballets that were pleasantly new to me were Balanchine's *Divertimento from "Le Baiser de la Fée"* (1972) and Robbins's *Ives, Songs* (1988). In the first, Benjamin Millepied and Megan Fairchild lead a corps of women wearing tutus with richly colored bodices. The man's variation is devilishly difficult, with outside turns followed right away by inside turns. The choreography for the corps is unremarkable except that they occasionally walked on their heels. The mysterious oboe of Stravinsky's music hints at a lost romance as the man looks for his lady through a line of dancers. When they are left alone, Millipied goes to touch Fairchild's hand, and she turns her head away. From that moment on, drama is in the air, where before there were just patterns, colors, and steps. On separate planes, he and she open their arms, giving up on each other but seeking guidance in a parallel universe.

Ives, Songs is beautiful, thoughtful, sad. Children play on a bench while an older gent (Robert La Fosse) wanders around, lost in memories and perhaps regret. Later a group of villagers follows him with their eyes, then part and flow around him in feathered lifts and weaving lines. The ballet is a pastel frontier: *Seven Brides for Seven Brothers* meets *Dances at a Gathering*.

Two of Balanchine's ballets this season struck me as quaint: *The Steadfast Tin Soldier* (1975) and *Raymonda Variations* (1961). They have their charms, but they probably shouldn't be on the same program. In *Tin Soldier* Megan Fairchild is half doll, half nervous girl; Daniel Ulbricht is a bit Petrouchka, pained at being unable to show his love.

Raymonda Variations starts with group patterns for a corps of women in pink and progresses to solo variations. If it weren't for Ashley Bouder's dazzling mastery, it would be just a difficult exercise in pointe work. Savannah Lowery is very strong in her many hops on pointe although ungainly in her upper body. Tiler Peck, fast and crisp, has an assemblé that lands on pointe with a twisted torso. And Teresa Reichlen turns on pointe with bended knee.

All admirable, but it's Bouder's dancing—swift, clean, powerful—that gives the ballet its sense of purpose. Her final dive, straight downstage, is spectacular. Veyette was replacing someone, so there was a moment when both she and he had a look on their faces like "Are we ready for this?" And indeed she seemed to almost dive past his arms toward the audience.

I was lucky to catch my personal dream cast of Robbins's *Fancy Free*: Damian Woetzel as the rumba sailor, Tyler Angle as the wide-eyed one, and Daniel Ulbricht as the energetic "first" one. Pure pleasure.

Like *Fancy Free*, *Ives, Songs* was a harbinger of the coming Robbins festival this spring. So was *West Side Story Suite*, in which Amar Ramasar was menacing as Bernardo, Robert Fairchild bloomed as Tony in "Something's Coming," and Pazcoguin sizzled as Anita. Although this suite is only a series of excerpts, it packs an emotional punch.

A high point of the season was Wheeldon's *Liturgy*. Wendy Whelan shows how exhilarating nonnarrative dance can be, through detail, through love of movement, through her individual brand of spirituality.

I hope to see many more of Wheeldon's works return to the repertoire. While other ballet companies still favor twentieth-century works, Wheeldon's oeuvre as resident choreographer has established NYCB as utterly contemporary in the twenty-first century.

New Works Festival: San Francisco Ballet

War Memorial Opera House, San Francisco

April 22–27, 2008

Festival review, *Dance Magazine*, July 2008

This festival of ten world premieres, celebrating SFB's seventy-fifth anniversary, put its faith in contemporary ballet. Almost all the works had live music (hallelujah!) and elegant sets. I would wager that six of them will have long lives.

The three pieces that were about sheer movement and music also happened to be the three that I would travel great distances to see again: Jorma Elo's *Double Evil*, Christopher Wheeldon's *Within the Golden Hour*, and Stanton Welch's *Naked*.

The combination of tutus and drums thrust *Double Evil* into a mode that could be called tribal/classical. The snaking heads; undulating bodies; and big wheeling, slicing lifts that have become Elo's signature moves were put to propulsive use here. Inventiveness flowed, momentum mounted, and the dancers reveled in the music by Philip Glass and Vladimir Martynov. In the oeuvre of Elo's dances here in the United States, *Double Evil* (someone please help this man with his titles) is among his exhilarating best.

Wheeldon's *Golden Hour* was calmer and more intense. Five couples in shimmery blues, ochers, and greens (costumes by Martin Pakledinaz) performed Wheeldon's typical bent-knee lifts and legs-like-scissors lifts to Glass-influenced music by Ezio Bosso. But I've never seen Wheeldon slow down as radically as he did in the central duet for the mesmerizing Sarah Van Patten and her partner Pierre-François Vilanoba. In this exquisite pas de deux, she makes a developpé seem like an alchemical reaction.

For piquant use of music, Stanton Welch's *Naked* was a winner. The accents in the choreography beautifully intersected with those of the Poulenc score. A single girl in salmon-colored (naked?) tutu seemed to collapse part of her body just at the moment one hears a kind of raindrop in the music. The synergy between the partners and the single dancer helped crystallize certain moments, like when four women were in arabesque in the four corners, one woman held aloft also suddenly struck an arabesque. Clarity of shape, musicality, and choreographic surprise came together in this sparkling ballet.

Standout pieces for their vividness of mood were James Kudelka's *The Ruins Proclaim the Building Was Beautiful*, Yuri Possokhov's *Fusion*, and Val

Caniparoli's *Ibsen's House*. Kudelka's *Ruins* was nostalgic, sad, noir. A small group of women in feathered, tutu-y skirts drifted in from downstage right. Their tutus were dripping with torn shreds of something—perhaps the women were swans from somebody's attic. Their dreamy bourrées allowed them to shift and glide among themselves, changing places against a velvet darkness (lighting by James F. Ingalls). This impressionistic dream turned dangerous when three Victorian-suited men started to partner these creatures. Toward the end Yuan Yuan Tan entered in a sequined red and black dress. Vilanoba, the count with the longest waistcoat, danced with her in a way that felt like he was trapping her—just a shade Dracula-esque. But it was that first image of swans in an attic that lingered through the whole ballet.

To the sounds of tabla music by Graham Fitkin and Rahul Dev Burman, Possokhov's *Fusion* finds four men in white dervish-like outfits sitting on the floor doing chest and shoulder isolations like you would do in a jazz class. Four women, and then additionally four men, emerged from the upstage darkness wearing sleek blues and grays. A shape of elbows up and palms down lent an Eastern flavor. There was a breathtaking scene where Yuan Yuan Tan seemed to get sucked toward Damian Smith past a flank of the four dervishes, and the two got caught up in a beautiful pas de deux. In the end, the four men in blue performed the same chest isolations the dervishes had opened with, signaling a complete transfer of style—with many stories along the way.

Caniparoli's gloss on Ibsen's female characters (based loosely on five of his plays) was a bit Tudor-like in its portrayal of angst-ridden women, but less spare, more lush in the body. Each of the five women was assigned her own signature gesture. The five men seemed to suffer as much as the women, but with less individuality. They were all given the same gestures: fingertips meeting and swiveling around the palm, making a diamond shape of the arms, bringing a palm to cover one eye. The huge, high window with a swooping black drape (designed by Sandra Woodall) and Dvoràk's Piano Quintet in A Major, Op. 81 added dramatic tension. In some ways, this austere psychodrama was the biggest surprise, as Caniparoli's ballets tend to be blithe and fun.

Two choreographic masters seemed to toss off their pieces: Paul Taylor and Mark Morris. Taylor's *Changes* depicted a cartoon version of the sixties, complete with social dances like the pony, the hitchhike, and the shimmy. During the Mamas and Papas' song "I Call Your Name," a blond sexpot flaunted herself for four randy guys. Another low point was "Dancing Bear," with a young man cavorting in pajamas. This was Taylor's silly side minus the ballast of his dark side. All could almost be forgiven when "California Dreamin'" regaled us for a finale.

In Morris's *Joyride* the dancers wore shiny unitards and numbers on their chests. Was this an audition? Were they human speedometers? They walked, pranced, skipped, and jogged, occasionally launching into more virtuosic solo forays. John Adams's original music, conducted by the composer, lent the piece some momentum. But there was no joy on this ride.

Disappointing too were the two works by women—for an opposite reason. Both Julia Adam's *A rose by any other name* and Margaret Jenkins's *Thread* were belabored. *A rose* was a spoof of *Sleeping Beauty*, though I didn't get it until the roses showed up. Her choreography seemed to be for the outer limbs only, and the attempt at humor went flat. *Thread* was a sprawling semi-narrative, ostensibly about the myth of Ariadne. The group hoists felt heroic, but the choreography took a back seat to the other effects: a set like a geometric cave, a film that showed trees changing into a woman's eyes (scenic and projection design by Alexander Nichols), and an intrusive poem. There were too many threads to follow.

No matter the highs and the lows choreographically, the dancing was wall-to-wall excellent—often exciting. In addition to the dancers mentioned, sustained bursts of energy came from Garen Scribner and Pascal Molat, lovely fluidity from Frances Chung and Vanessa Zahorian, crystal clarity from Katita Waldo, and a touching tristesse from Nicole Grand. Lorena Feijoo projected a diva-like glamour and rooted strength, and Yuan Yuan Tan was astonishing in her etched lines, daring, and electric stillnesses.

Akram Khan's *Bahok*

Blog post, April 24, 2008, dancemagazine.com

Akram Khan embodies a contemporary global perspective that has changed the dance landscape in England and beyond. Bahok, like his previous pieces, transformed culture clashes into art. His work is very physical, not at all theoretical. In Bahok, it was the light moments, the humorous miscommunications, that revealed how deeply we are all connected. I've done three public interviews with Khan (the one after this performance, at City Center, was the second), and he's always responded to curiosity with curiosity. He never pontificates; he speaks with discovery in his voice.

Bahok, a collaboration between the Akram Khan Company and dancers from the National Ballet of China, exerts a certain spell, and by the end I felt overwhelmed by its beauty and vulnerability. Parallel streams of consciousness, one of talking and the other of dancing, gave us a view into the eight dancers' lives. The very real situation of a bunch of people from different countries waiting in an airport (or is it a train station?) with frustration, built up aggressions, wanderings, and problems with customs gives rise to both combustion and humor. The dancing followed its own inner rhythm; the talking was mundane or fanciful and led us into delightful cultural confusions.

At the "talkback" afterward, which I moderated, Khan said that he likes the word confusion better than fusion because it allows different stories to overlap or intersect. In his work one sees a lightness and a heaviness at the same time, a Western-ness and an Eastern-ness at the same time.

One scene in *Bahok*: a man starts contracting repeatedly in the upper body, like a violent hiccup that won't stop. Others, in their different languages, try to find out what's wrong. Finally he utters his first discernible word, "Stuck!" A woman embraces him until his convulsions subside. Another dancer comes to embrace them, and another and another. The last one comes—to dive madly through them.

Another scene: a short South Indian man tries to partner a tall Chinese ballet dancer, just managing to dodge her slicing limbs—with hilarious results.

During the talkback, Khan spoke about the walls we make in our heads, for instance defining classical ballet or classical Kathak (the form he trained in) while keeping out other influences. He told us that when, as a child, he asked why Kathak dancers wear bells on their ankles, the answer he got was: because your teacher does, and *his* teacher did, and so on. Khan asks questions—of himself, of the theater, of the cultural attitudes we all carry in our bodies. The word *bahok* is Bengali for "carrier." He also talked about the terrorist bombing in London in 2005, and how he wasn't really aware of the brown color of his skin until that moment. He had many stories, and the dancers onstage had many stories that made you want to know them better. I don't think I have ever seen a dance-and-talking piece that was so full of humanity, wit, and vulnerability.

Flamenco Master in Silence:
Was Israel Galván Improvising?

Blog post, June 18, 2008, dancemagazine.com

On a terrace in front of the Hispanic Society of America up in Washington Heights, Israel Galván walked out to dance on a small platform. Dressed in black, he started by clapping his hands in that special flamenco way (*palmas*), feeling the rhythm well up inside him. This usually happens when the dancer and musicians are setting up their rhythms together. But Galván was alone. It was quiet.

According to the woman from Dia Art Foundation who introduced him, he chose silence so that he could listen to his own body. And he did listen, by pausing every few phrases, but also by making various sounds: foot scraping, heel tapping, *palmas*, grunts. He even spiraled his ringed fingers in his mouth, playing his teeth like castanets. Every sound was crystal clear.

He would freeze in a position, either arched way back or in a perfect Egyptian profile. But then he would come flat front and pierce us with his gaze. He often thrust his pelvis forward, in a wide second, scooping his hands at pelvis level. It looked pretty sexy, but only lasted a few seconds.

His flattened hands, when raised, looked like cobra heads, or a periscope. One time a single hand lilted in front of him like a falling leaf. Sometimes his hips pushed forward into an extreme hinge that erupted into a barrage of heel tapping. Twice he stepped off the platform, faced the stone wall behind it, and stuttered his heels so that his knees seemed to vibrate against the wall.

Toward the end, he sat down, took off his shoes and socks, and then walked to a square sandbox in front of the black platform. He scooped his feet through it and flicked sand behind him, making a softer version of the scraping sound from before. Then it was over. We all cheered.

He had captured our complete attention without music, lights, the magic of a theater, or people around yelling "Olé!" And the thing I most want to know is, Was he improvising, or was it set? The steps and stops looked so definite. And yet he seemed to be following his thoughts of the moment. Maybe "listening to his own body" is just another term for improvising.

Trey McIntyre Project

Jacob's Pillow Dance Festival, Becket, Massachusetts

August 20–24, 2008

Review, *Dance Magazine*, November 2008

Trey McIntyre is doing something right. Anchored in strong craft, his dances invite the audience to enjoy his mix of classical ballet, playful movement invention, and down-home humor. His music choices are full of pleasure and we walk out smiling. A great start for his newly full-time company, based in Boise, Idaho.

Surrender, a world premiere, shows a slightly lost girl (Chanel DaSilva) put upon by a goofy-looking guy in headphones and muscleman outfit. When one reaches for the other's hand, that hand pulls away. Attraction, resistance, ambush . . . and finally surrender. The first music is funky Grand Funk Railroad; the second is a surprise use of the "Mirlitons" divertissement from Tchaikovsky's *Nutcracker*. The last section (to Regina Spektor singing "Real Love" by John Lennon) releases the two from the yes-no-maybe phase and yields a simple frolic toward each other. This time when one reaches out, they join hands. Jason Hartley, who was such a strong presence in the Washington Ballet, gives the piece both its urgency and its humor. With his deadpan look and compact, forceful body, he dances as though he's got a joke up his sleeve.

But this delightful duet was just a warm-up act. The second, more substantial world premiere, *Leatherwing Bat*, opens and closes with one lone figure: John Michael Schert, who beautifully embodies McIntyre's blend of twitchy hips and velvet extensions. Peter, Paul, and Mary's fanciful songs turn childhood fears into something quizzical ("I'm being swollered by a boa constrictor and I don't like it very much"). People are attracted to each other in a slippery, polymorphous way. The piece shifts to family fun (a zoo song) and then to something a little more caustic, but never loses its sense of play. At one point, a paper airplane sails onto the stage from the wings. Nothing fancy, but it reminds you of how a small object can release the imagination. *Leatherwing Bat* combines a child's sense of wonder with adult inventiveness. The familiar song "Puff (The Magic Dragon)" takes us through to the end. Although Schert does not do any dragon-y moves, the song casts a spell. As he backs away from us, he takes on the aura of a magical figure. (Note: "Leatherwing Bat" is the title of a Peter, Paul, and Mary song that is not part of this score).

In *The Reassuring Effects (of Form and Poetry)* from 2003, to Dvorak, McIntyre's sense of form, shape, and musicality blend into a glowing group piece. Liz Prince's delicious blues and purples, with flouncey little bustles for the women, add a bit of whimsy. The dancers alternate between orderly shapes and an impulse to burst out. Schert and Lia Cirio (a wonderful dancer on leave from Boston Ballet) give this beautiful, sweeping duet an undercurrent of danger. A recurring motif has Schert extending an arm across Cirio's neck as though to strangle her, but it leads into something entirely benign. McIntyre loves to throw naughty and nice up against each other.

Pacific Northwest Ballet: All Tharp

September 25–October 5, 2008

McCaw Hall, Seattle

Review, *Dance Magazine*, December 2008

Not every brilliant choreographer can be tapped for three ballets that, when put together, yield a varied, satisfying evening. Upping the ante in PNB's "All Tharp" program was the fact that two of the three ballets were world premieres.

The two new works are radically different from each other: *Opus 111* is supremely musical, whereas *Afternoon Ball* is character driven. The first opens on two people already dancing to a Brahms quintet. They are soon joined by four other couples, all elucidating Tharp's seamless blend of high virtuosity and playful moves like running backward and heel-first strides. The ballet is even more successful than the beautiful *Mozart Clarinet Quintet K. 581*, her classical foray of 2000 (mentioned in Section V), because here she slows down to feel the quiet parts of the music. Thus the ballet dips into the valleys as well as rises with the hills. At one point, lead dancers Carla Körbes and Batkhurel Bold simply walk in circles; at another, all twelve dancers step side to side while slowly lowering one arm. Moments like these give the eye a rest before filling up again, so that by the rousing folk dance that wraps it up, we are totally with them. All the dancers handled Tharp's challenges well, with Körbes being particularly fluid, gorgeously riding the waves of Brahms's music, which was played live by the PNB Orchestra.

The three main characters in *Afternoon Ball* give off the whiff of a circus. Guest artist Charlie Neshyba-Hodges, who is fabulous as a crazed Vaudevillian with a compulsion to perform, stuffs every measure with shudders, shakes, and flirty posing. Wearing a glittery vest and torn fatigues, he is perhaps a troubled cousin to the jazzy women in Tharp's *Eight Jelly Rolls* (1971) or the slippery, sly Baryshnikov in *Push Comes to Shove* (1976). Mercurial and manic, he shows his muscles one moment and hits his head against a wall the next. Kaori Nakamura, wearing fishnets, shorts, and doll makeup, fulfills her role as a waifish coquette with precision and charm. Olivier Wevers, as an interloper, a possible drifter type, appears menacing at times, but has the most expansive choreography.

After much manipulation and crossing of paths, these three never really connect with each other. The minimalist score by Vladimir Martynov doesn't support Neshyba-Hodges's shenanigans, and the characters do not illuminate the music—until a ballet couple (Ariana Lallone and Stanko Milov) enters and the music turns classical. Neshyba-Hodges's wannabe desire suddenly clarifies, and he dances harmoniously with them. When the ballet couple disappears, the original three return to their chaotic noninteractions.

Finally Lallone reenters alone, this time in angelic white. Neshyba-Hodges lays his head on her shoulder, and together they walk toward a bright white light. It's an overwhelmingly stunning moment. Neshyba-Hodges's hyper-kinetic heroic antihero seems spun right out of Tharp's own personality, and the purity of the ballet figure, like the purity of the sole ballet beacon in *Deuce Coupe* (1973), represents an ideal that seems to be a healing balm for her.

Considering the puzzlement of *Afternoon Ball*, *Nine Sinatra Songs* comes as a relief and a feast. Beautifully paced and at one with the music, it's a showcase for brilliant partnering with touches of glamour and humor. Jordan Pacitti was super spunky in "Something Stupid," and Sarah Ricard Orza had a velvet fluidity in "All the Way." Louise Nadeau, deliciously daring in the off-the-shoulder red dress for "That's Life," provided a glamorous defiance.

Boston Ballet: Diaghilev's Ballets Russes Centennial Celebration

Wang Theatre, Boston

May 14–17, 2009

Web review, dancemagazine.com

The year 2009 saw many ballet companies paying tribute to the Ballets Russes, which was launched by Serge Diaghilev in 1909. But it was only this program at Boston Ballet that led me to an epiphany about the mystique of the legendary company: It was all about forbidden desire. Yes, the period was famous for the interdisciplinary collaborations that Diaghilev masterminded. But what pulled the audience in was the sense that each narrative was based on some illicit passion. In Prodigal Son, *it's the young man's desire for something far from home. In* Spectre de la rose, *a girl fantasizes about a flower—or a man she may have danced with at a ball. In* Afternoon of a Faun, *it is a nymph who leaves a scarf behind—and we know what the faun does with that scarf.*

How can a living choreographer match the visual splendor of three works from Diaghilev's Ballets Russes? In this case, Georges Rouault's boldly primitive backdrop for Balanchine's *Prodigal Son*; the elegant, dreamlike interior of Fokine's *Le Spectre de la rose*; and Leon Bakst's massive, drenched forest for Nijinsky's *Afternoon of a Faun.*

For his *Sacre du Printemps,* Jorma Elo decided to fight fire with fire. Literally. He put a line of actual flames upstage (supervised by two fire wardens) that immediately showed the audience that he wasn't backing away from the passion and extravagance of the Ballets Russes. At times when the flames were concealed, their reflection shimmered on the floor. Diaghilev would have loved it! (More about this world premiere later.)

In *Prodigal Son* (1929)—one of the best narrative ballets ever made—Jared Redick was an energetic, rebellious son, if at times clipped in his movement. When, exhausted and broken, he looked up at his two kindly sisters, his face was filled with humility. Kathleen Breen Combes's Siren commanded the stage with an alluring strength.

Larissa Ponomarenko was a true ballerina in *Spectre.* As the dreaming girl nudged by her fantasy Rose, her arms floated up, lifting her off her chair. It was the first *Spectre* I'd seen in which I felt it was *her* dream rather than a showcase for the Rose. I had an eerie sensation that I was seeing Karsavina, who created the role in 1911. Perhaps it was that white Bakst bonnet with puffy ears, but more likely it was the wholeness of Ponomarenko's dancing that was transporting. Although James Whiteside could handle the turns and jumps of the Rose technically, he had no real presence—in a role that requires not only presence but also flamboyance. A man playing a rose has to have some sense of androgyny, or at least perfume. You have to be able to smell the rose. Ponomarenko could, but we couldn't.

In the role of the Faun, the dancer has to be precise in the highly designed, Greek vase–type movements but also have an animal sensuality. Altankhuyag Dugaraa was fairly natural as the Faun—an achievement in itself—though he could have infused his first arm movements with more consciousness. However, the twelve-minute reverie, with seven beautifully draped nymphs, and the Boston Ballet Orchestra playing Debussy, was mesmerizing.

Jorma Elo's new *Sacre du Printemps* might have been titled *The Revenge of the Chosen One*. Instead of a whole community choosing one young woman (Ponomarenko) to sacrifice her life, a single perpetrator, wearing a satin Satan outfit (Yury Yanowsky in the cast I saw), kept trying to snuff her out. The whole atmosphere seemed to be building toward a crime of passion. All sixteen dancers wore red, as though they were part of the fire.

The piece started with girly-girl primping, but it was the spinning, whipping phalanx of men that took on Stravinsky's cataclysmic music. When Yanowsky touched Ponomarenko and she shuddered violently beneath his touch, you knew that something sinister was going on. She kept escaping his aggressions until finally, in a surprise reversal, she struck out at him. He melted to the ground. As she bourréed off like a wili without her veil, he was left burning in hell—or at least crouching in front of a small segment of flames.

Spoleto Festival (Festival dei 2Mondi)

Teatro Nuovo and Teatro Romano, Spoleto, Italy

July 3–6, 2009

Web review, dancemagazine.com

Alessandra Ferri, new director of dance at Spoleto's interdisciplinary Festival of Two Worlds, organized three programs of international significance. One program, Choreography Today, gathered works by three of the hottest ballet choreographers alive: Alexei Ratmansky, Christopher Wheeldon, and Wayne McGregor. Another presented Pina Bausch's company, Tanztheater Wuppertal, newly stunned by the news of her death five days before, in the joyous *Bamboo Blues*. The third paid tribute to Jerome Robbins, who had loved Spoleto—both the festival and the ancient town. (As an invited guest of the festival, I moderated a preperformance talk.)

The program of Ratmansky to Wheeldon to McGregor, held in the outdoor arena of Teatro Romano, traveled from innocent to sophisticated to jaded. Ratmansky's *Russian Seasons* for New York City Ballet gives off the flavor of an old-world village, depicting various incidents, romances, and rituals. Rebecca Krohn seems to have a snitfit, Jenifer Ringer emerges from a group of three men in wonder, and Wendy Whelan stoops to pick flowers. Several dancers take a bow in the middle of the piece. It doesn't quite add up (maybe if you know the lyrics to the Russian songs by Desyatnikov, it does), and the unflattering color-block dresses don't help. But the men tear through their sections, giving the piece a thrust, and the moods change in a nicely shifting rhythm.

The rarely seen first half of Wheeldon's sextet *After the Rain* (also for City Ballet) is more dramatic than I remember. At times the three women bourrée in parallel as they drag the men along the floor to the ominous sounds of Arvo Pärt. In a brilliant transition from the heavy first half to the elegiac second, Wendy Whelan and Craig Hall, now wearing nearly nude leotards, return to the stage with a big loping circle while the other four exit. They settle into stillness before performing the celebrated duet that is the second half of *After the Rain*. Whelan, long hair flowing, is glorious in the celestial lifts and tender gestures, like when she slips her fingertips over Hall's shoulders from behind. On the second night, when they weren't worried about slipping on a wet stage, Hall made a secure and attentive partner in the Jock Soto role. This duet is a small miracle that always sends me into raptures.

Wendy Whelan and Craig Hall in Christopher Wheeldon's heavenly *After the Rain*. (© Erin Baiano)

The hyper-aggressive *Erazor*, from Wayne McGregor|Random Dance, had the advantage in this big open space of being framed by fluorescent lights on the ground. Driven by adolescent rage, the work had some pretty nasty moments. One person might plant a kiss on another's face and then shove that person or just walk away. Without the infusion of elegance that the Royal Ballet brings to McGregor's work (judging from their breathtaking recent performance of *Chroma* at the Kennedy Center), *Erazor* seemed locked into a kind of mean-spiritedness. I report dutifully that the audience loved it.

Bausch's *Bamboo Blues*, held in the smaller Teatro Nuovo, overflows with a magical exuberance—at least the first part. Each solo is both sumptuous and urgent; each interchange brims with flirtation and inventiveness. The one dark moment, though, is powerful: A man runs in a circle at top speed with a woman jostling on his back. It's impossible to tell from her screams whether she is thrilled or terrified. In another daredevil section, a woman dashes over a chair and flings herself at a guy halfway across the stage; he catches her and they topple to the floor. This, like other episodes, happens over and over. There is the sense that they can't get enough of something— sex, dance, daring the person who is there for you?

At the end, when the sixteen dancers joined hands for a bow and walked forward, you could see their mind-set shift to the terrible reality at hand: Pina Bausch was no longer with them. Their faces were suddenly drained of pleasure, and they drew even closer together in their grief during the standing ovations.

The Robbins tribute was rained out of the Teatro Romano and got squeezed into the much smaller Teatro Nuovo—with a raked stage and no tech time. In fact the City Ballet dancers were still rehearsing onstage with ballet mistress Christine Redpath when the audience filed in—dress rehearsal, Italian style, I guess. After the performance officially started, Tiler Peck and Gonzalo Garcia gave a spirited rendition of Robbins's charming *Other Dances*. Light and playful with a mischievous sense of timing, Peck seamlessly glided from wandering and wondering to a balancé—very Robbins. Garcia relished the twist-stomps and other folksy steps.

In the Night was a bit rougher, but all six dancers rose to the occasion. Jenifer Ringer softly yielded to Amar Ramasar; even the way she simply leaned toward him was ravishing. Maria Kowroski and Jonathan Stafford were proud in the second, slightly military pas de deux. Wendy Whelan threw a good fit when Jared Angle carried her onstage in the third dramatic duet. At the end, after all six spent about five seconds switching partners, they each took a lovely breath of contentment before waltzing off with their chosen mate.

Luca Veggetti, who claims Robbins as an influence, makes intensely interior dances. In a neat programming choice, his new duet followed a showing of *Passage for Two*, a film in progress (produced by Sean Suozzi and Ellen Bar and starring Craig Hall and Rachel Rutherford, all from NYCB) based on the slow duet from Robbins's *NY Export: Opus Jazz*. Veggetti's premiere, *Upon a Ground*, echoed the alternation of attraction and ambivalence that marks that duet. His movement had some precarious, spidery crouches that were quite vivid. But the two dancers, Ramasar and Georgina Pazcoguin, looked at the ground a lot, which undermined any sense of relationship. Veggetti, too, had to direct his last run-through with audience looking on, which is hardly the ideal situation for showing a premiere. I look forward to seeing this duet under more civilized circumstances.

But all of the above contributed to the feeling that Alessandra Ferri had put Spoleto, Italy, back on the dance map.

Note: The complete film *NY Export: Opus Jazz* is now available on DVD at www.opusjazz.com.

The Forsythe Company: *Decreation*

Brooklyn Academy of Music

October 7–10, 2009

Review, *Dance Magazine*, January 2010

In *Decreation*, the performers each find a fertile center of madness within themselves. From the first moments, when Dana Caspersen yanks herself by the collar while reciting both sides of a conversation from poet Anne Carson's "Decreation," to the last, when one dancer sits atop a table while others lunge at her, the characters careen toward insanity or violence.

Forsythe's movement vocabulary is extraordinary. One dancer flops as though his body were part fish and part very precise spider. Another punches the air as though with a boxing glove while he undulates his back superfast. (These are not technically Forsythe's movements but come from the dancers themselves under Forsythe's direction.)

Several planes of reality coexist: wayward dancers, a live video camera, a screen, a table, several conversations echoing back and forth, people in drastically different states of mind. The preverbal sounds that escape from their mouths, sometimes amplified, veer between fascinating and alarming.

There is just enough convergence of shape for the eye to take it all in. Uncanny timing has a lot to do with it, so that somehow, you are just this side of being overloaded. Frustrated, yes, but you cannot turn away.

Anne Carson's text can deflate the intensity with humor, or it can goad the dancing into absurdity. The statement "There is no hurt where there is belief," repeated in different circumstances, can be uttered as a revelation or an accusation. Other lines have the ring of a real conversation: "It's hard to tell when you're joking, or when you're just being obnoxious." Some of the sardonic accusations are funny, as in "I love your drama," and "It's getting operatic." Other lines cross over into sadism: "This is the deal: You give me everything and I give you nothing." There are also mentions of "the soul," but in this dance, the soul gets cornered, triggering wild, obsessive behavior.

A remarkable sequence begins when Georg Reischl appears, claiming, "I'm just here; I like my spiel." Endearing in his freedom and innocence, yet hampered by another dancer wrapping himself around him, Reischl is different from the other, more jaded, characters. Eventually though, Reischl's joy is dimmed by constant, prolonged self-questioning, and he becomes more and more tortured and slithery. He is now saying, "I hate my own spiel." We've witnessed self-love turn and churn into self-hate, and our hearts go out to him.

At the end, the camera zooms way out on a screen figure, as if to give us perspective on everything, shrinking the sorrows and joys of being human.

Postscript: At the post-performance talk, I asked a question from the audience about how Forsythe got such intense performances from the dancers. "With this group," he said, "I couldn't stop them."

Twyla's New Musical Flies, But . . .

Blog post, October 6, 2009, dancemagazine.com

What a ride *Come Fly with Me* is! It's great to see Twyla Tharp return to Frank Sinatra; she gives his songs such zing. The women are luscious, totally in charge of their sexuality. This piece, which just opened at the Alliance Theatre in Atlanta, is midway between *Nine Sinatra Songs* and *Movin' Out* in terms of narrative. Instead of a series of duets as in the former, *Fly* keeps circling back to four couples, tracking the changes in each relationship. And instead of a full plot as in *Movin' Out*, it uses Sinatra's lyrics mostly for mood, not to create an arc.

What knocks me out more than the good fit between music and dance, more than the dazzling choreography, is how Twyla has created roles that celebrate the individuality of each dancer. Charlie Neshyba-Hodges, as a lowly busboy, ushers us all into this glamorous joint with a nearly-nothing shrug. Of course (some of us know) he will set off technical fireworks later on. But his character—a shy, self-effacing guy in love—is perfect for him. And Laura Mead makes a wonderful partner to his innocence.

Karine Plantadit's charisma almost blots out everything else when she's onstage. You get used to her being the life of the party, and the party goes on. She's sexy in an all-out, devil-may-care way—she'll dance with anyone—while paying attention to every leap and dive and twist. But she has always been larger than life onstage.

The big news is Holley Farmer, who has been transformed from a Cunningham dancer into an elegant femme fatale, just as sexy as Plantadit, but in an entirely different way—languid and classy and utterly beguiling. She's classy because she is so queenly, but she's also classy because she wants just one guy: John Selya. And Selya plays it hard-boiled, more like a gambler from *Guys and Dolls* (which was the last musical he was in) than like the sensitive Eddie from *Movin' Out* (a role he originated). In fact, he acts downright pimp-like at times. Only in his solo, to "The September of My Years," does he reveal more depth.

As terrific as the women are, part of me is wistful for that time in the early seventies when Twyla's women were strong, gutsy, and independent. Most of her female characters since *Movin' Out* have been more or less seductive, sometimes feisty, but always defined by men. Okay, I know it's a different time now, what with TV shows like *Sex in the City* declaring women's right to obsess about men, but was the feminist movement just a blip in the seventies? Do all great female dancers have to ooze and sass around men? Or is this just how you get to Broadway?

Even so, when/if *Come Fly with Me* comes to Broadway, I'll have a great time seeing it there like everybody else.

Postscript: When the musical came to Broadway the following March, the title was changed to *Come Fly Away*. After a year and half, it went on the road for another year and a half.

International Exposure

Suzanne Dellal Centre for Dance and Theatre, Tel Aviv, Israel

December 9–13, 2009

Web review, dancemagazine.com

This festival of bracing Israeli dance spanning twenty-seven choreographers (I caught only eleven) concluded with Israel's crowning glory, Batsheva Dance Company. Other exciting pieces included Barak Marshall's *Rooster* and Inbal Pinto's *Trout*. (It was a week for animals.) There were also an intense effort to unify Jews and Arabs through dance from Arkadi Zaides, a light-and-color extravaganza from Rami Be'er of Kibbutz Contemporary Dance Company, and a zany duet by Yasmeen Godder.

Loosely based on I. L. Peretz's short story "Bontsha the Silent," *Rooster* followed one hapless young man through a night of fitful dreams. The characters were as captivating as the ones in that more famous shtetl story, *Fiddler on the Roof.* The movement was terse, individual, urgent, as though this village were mysteriously compelled to go through certain rituals. Idan Porges, remarkable as the unremarkable Bontsha, led the group in rhythmic, almost mime-like gesture. He's a thin, rangy guy with purpose in his movements and an energetic innocence in his eyes.

Moments of lightness—as in Bontsha getting hoisted into the air and lying there comfortably with a pillow under his head, or a man huffing and puffing to produce an egg from his mouth—helped make this work enchanting. Another plus was the presence of the great Margalit Oved, who threaded through this dream like some archetypal figure, offering Bontsha a music box or emitting a shrill lullaby. (A dancer/singer known for her extraordinary performances with Israel's Inbal Dance Theater in the fifties and sixties, Oved is Marshall's mother.) The image of rooster combs appeared small, within the ensemble's rapid-fire string of gestures (fingers on top of head like a crown), and large, as big purple feather fans snaking after the dancers. The collage of music—some klezmer and some forties jazz—added to the vintage feel of this sad/funny/moving piece of dance theater.

Also dreamlike, but more formal and surreal, was Inbal Pinto and Avshalom Pollak's *Trout*. In a walled performing area with six inches of water on the floor, the performers waded or splashed vigorously. Again, the antihero was plagued by outside forces. Played by Ido Batash with a painfully rounded back, he trudged through the water, sometimes getting cornered by pairs of strange women. The live music from Norway's Kitchen Orches-

Hora by Ohad Naharin with Batsheva Dance Company:
their defiance got under your skin. (© Gadi Dagon)

tra, which began with the trumpet player fishing in the water, was bold and
haunting. Stray people popped in and out of the doors on both sides, with
our antihero desperately trying to keep them out. The only character who
stayed mostly dry was a formal, serene woman, upright in a proper Elizabe-
than dress. She mumbled without opening her mouth, the sound growing to
almost earthquake proportions. Although Batash wore a butcher's apron (do
butchers kill trout?), he embodied the terror of the hunted rather than the
hunter. The sharp, agitating contrasts of *Trout* still hung in the air when, at
the end, lily pads floated out toward the audience. A plea for harmony? An
offering of forgiveness?

Yasmeen Godder's *Love Fire*, a wacky duet about a relationship, seemed
to have neither love nor fire. Instead, a huge stuffed animal (a lion, a pig?)
lay on the stage and was eventually eviscerated (for our amusement?) by
Godder's partner, Eran Shanny. A series of waltzes on tape did nothing to
make this situation more romantic, and it lost its way to such an extent that
even the wacky parts didn't register as inventive by the end.

Yossi Berg and Oded Graf created a quartet called *4 Men, Alice, Bach and
the Deer*. Again, a stuffed animal lay on the stage, this time at least identifiable as a deer. The four men, wearing creepy masks, crawled, jumped,
and slithered, combining the sinister and the comic. The most startling mo-

ment came when one of them cut the invisible strings holding up the deer's antlers, letting its head suddenly droop as though it had been shot.

(An aside: It's interesting that both these pieces listed dramaturges in the credits, yet both were pretty opaque in terms of narrative clarity.)

Arkadi Zaides's work in progress *Quiet* was almost unbearably intense. Four men—two Israeli and two Arab—seemed locked in either combat or some kind of brotherly tough love. What looked like praying close to the ground turned into a self-hating rage that another man tried to calm. As disturbing as it was, this piece has potential to be an artistic component of a peace process. [See more on this performance in my blog below.]

On the other end of the emotional spectrum was *This Now Is*, a sweet duet from Tami and Ronen Izhaki. All about kissing, it was fun and romantic, but had enough rhythmic wit to keep you guessing when and where the next kiss would come.

Rami Be'er's *Infrared* juxtaposed military figures against creatures from a surreal imagination, like a man with a cushion-y humpback and a woman with a braid going past her ankles. The soldiers changed from blue to red to yellow skirted uniforms and engaged in luscious, full-body movement. The costume designs (by Maor Tzabar) were magnificent, but the relationship between the soldiers and the creatures was not clear, and the episodes seemed unconnected. Outstanding dancers were Shay Partush, who had a forceful, slightly wild quality, and Yuko Harada, who danced a happy solo on the red floor as though it were sunny yellow.

A rousing finale to the whole week, Ohad Naharin's new piece, *Hora*, jolted us with its apple green floor and walls—just the right color for this kinetically thrilling work. It had many of his signatures, like starting with all dancers facing front, crazed solos just this side of losing control, and hands held like paws. He built suspense so expertly that even when the dancers were absolutely still, you held your breath waiting to see what would come next. Isao Tomita's arrangements of theme music from movies like *Star Wars* and *2001, A Space Odyssey* (with a sliver of Debussy's *Afternoon of a Faun* thrown in) made it feel familiar and fun without detracting from the dancers' amazing energy.

Naharin's sense of theatrical timing is infallible. Just when you think it's too intense, he lightens up. Just when you think you've seen enough solos, he launches into unison—and that unison is broken in crafty ways. There are wayward actions, like a single dancer crashing into an ongoing duet, or a threesome stubbornly slowing down while the eight other dancers are playing a version of "follow the leader." Each dancer is a strong individual, and by the end of this hour, you appreciate Rachael Osborne's strength, Shachar

Binyamini's ferocity, Iyar Elezra's sensuality, and Ian Robinson's buoyancy. You grow attached to these people; their defiance gets under your skin.

The styles of Israeli dancemakers vary, but they all share a certain ground-edness—I saw lots of second-position pliés. The animal motif this year was indicative of how close to nature, and yet also how close to the realm of the ridiculous, many of them are. It seems to me that Israeli choreographers are not interested in the kind of technical virtuosity that many American choreographers are. You won't see gratuitous six-o'clock extensions or triple pirouettes, or even the rippling muscles of Ailey dancers here. What you do see is struggle, awkwardness, and a willingness to be raw.

Postscript (from a blog I posted during the festival): An uncanny thing happened in the middle of Arkadi Zaides's work in progress. Being a quartet for two Jewish men and two Arab men, it was very intense—the most intense, hard-to-watch thing I've seen here at International Exposure. One duet sequence had two men almost locked together in a kind of battle that was occasionally affectionate—but they kept their hands two inches from actually touching each other, so you felt a hard-earned restraint, but the intent to fight was there. In another section a guy was squatting with his head to the floor, like in Muslim prayer, but he was full of rage at himself, at the floor, at whatever, and trying to contain his rage all in the small space between himself and the floor. Then another guy, maybe the oldest of the four, put his hand on the nape of that guy's neck and comforted him, but instead of soothing talk, he was chuckling to himself. Gradually, the chuckler, after he calmed the first guy down, looked at his own hands and tried to keep laughing but then started thrusting his hands away from himself like he wanted to get rid of them. He was torn by two opposite and overwhelming impulses.

Suddenly a light bulb from the ceiling fell and shattered on the floor. The four men looked at each other, and one smiled like, "Of course, something violent had to happen." It took a few seconds for us in the audience to realize that this was not planned. Some staff people had to clear and mop the floor for about fifteen minutes to make sure it was safe for the barefoot dancers to continue.

This work in progress is called *Quiet* and it was in no way fully crafted or edited. I heard that it took eight months of long hours every day to get it to this point. Part of the difficulty, in addition to the obvious, was that Arab men traditionally have restrictions around touching. The courage of these four men makes me think, Wouldn't it be great if this could happen on a larger scale, and really bring people who are culturally and politically set against each other to some kind of understanding?

Lemi Ponifasio

Théâtre de la Ville, Paris

January 27–30, 2010

Review, *Dance Magazine*, April 2010

A mysterious, cataclysmic piece, *Tempest: Without Body* descended on the audience like an apocalypse. Starting in dimness with noise so loud that you felt your seat vibrate (sound composition by Russel Walder, Marc Chesterman, and Ponifasio), the piece features a huge, thick, textured wall that hangs in the upper reaches of the stage space. As the dimness and loudness slowly fade, a lone man inches forward, his gestures barely visible.

Later six or seven men of Ponifasio's New Zealand–based group MAU scurry across the space, signaling their arms steadily like a highly classified semaphoric code in unison. One gesture may be a salute or a slap while another looks like pulling a thread from one's heart. All in black, they could be doing a highly formal folk dance, or they could be a Greek chorus warning of impending doom. (Ponifasio is from Samoa and his dancers are from several Pacific Islands including Java, Tonga, and Samoa.)

The single woman, Ade Suharto, is a strange, disheveled angel who screams in long exhalations. When she raises her right hand, we see the palm is blood red. Perhaps this angel is a murderess. A matching red stain ominously appears on the huge, airborne wall; it spreads and seeps into the rest of the wall, creating seething splotches.

Upstage on a table, a man whose body is painted silver wriggles like a fish and pulls himself down into a hole—and gets stuck midway. Later, Tame Iti, an elder with a tattooed face, comes forward and addresses us in a foreign tongue, mounting his case forcefully, even spitting—an angry Buddha. Maybe this is part of some cultural ritual, or maybe he is giving some kind of warning.

The final episode is the most frightening. One man, alone onstage, lifts what looks like a plate of glass covered with dust. He throws it to the floor, shattering it, sending white powder everywhere. The music amplifies the shattering sound to an almost unbearable degree. The other dancers rush in one at a time, each one hurling an object to the floor, each object breaking into many dusty pieces. It seems like it happens a thousand times, and I can't help but think of the multiple earthquakes that have just demolished Haiti.

Necessary Weather (revival)

Baryshnikov Arts Center, New York City

May 13–15, 2010

Review, *Dance Magazine*, July 2010

An oasis of calm, light, and exquisite simplicity, *Necessary Weather* is an extraordinary 1994 collaboration between two dancers and a lighting master. Although Dana Reitz came up with the concept, Jennifer Tipton's lights and Sara Rudner's dancing contribute equally.

A beautiful restraint guided all decisions. As in a Japanese tea ceremony, each action is completed before the next action begins. You can lavish your attention on each movement as it happens — so different from other artistic and social stimuli these days.

Circles of light divide the space or sneak up on the dancers. The shadow of one dancer grows large and conceals the dancing of the other. Light/dark is a third character, so this really is a trio, not a duet. The light finds them in the space, tells them what to do, invites them to investigate. They look at their hands in the light as though for the first time. The quality of attention is sharpened by silence.

A narrow beam of light falls into the bottom of a straw hat, turning it into a pot of gold. Although the ray comes from above, the light seems to emanate from the inside of the hat, casting a glow on Reitz and Rudner's faces as they hold it. And just so the scene doesn't get too precious, too magical, the two dancers start talking low, as though surrounding a campfire, barely audible. We hear Rudner murmur in delight, "It feels warm now."

Sometimes they separate, free to explore on their own. Rudner plays havoc, gently flailing her limbs with great spirit. Reitz lounges on her side. A recurring phrase, beginning with pushing of the right hand, palm pressing the air, brings them back together.

The different qualities of their dancing are very much like they were sixteen years ago. Reitz is vertical, contained, precise in her gestures, sharp in her shifts. Rudner's movement is more rounded; she's dreamy and creamy and full of pleasure. Her physical, emotional, and spiritual selves merge into a single harmony. One's eyes and heart follow her, whether she is gesturing with a single hand or galloping about the space. Rudner is lit from within.

Why Don't Women Make Dances Like That Any More? Or, What Made Martha So Mad?

Blog post, June 10, 2010, dancemagazine.com

Like a bat out of hell, each woman bounded across the space with leap/runs, hands in fists, face set in determination. The all-female ensemble of *Sketches from "Chronicle"* (1936), led powerfully by Jennifer DePalo, worked up to a fever pitch, infusing the spare geometry of Graham's choreography with energy and resolve. I couldn't really glean the difference between what the program notes call the prewar states (Parts I and II) and the antiwar protest (Part III), but I was overwhelmed by the collective force of these women of the Martha Graham Dance Company. The driving rhythm of Wallingford Riegger's music pushed the dance along with unstoppable momentum.

At the opening of their Joyce season Tuesday night, artistic director Janet Eilber read a statement Graham wrote in response to Goebbels's invitation to perform at the Olympics in Berlin in 1936. She refused because of her abhorrence of the growing fascist German state. It was in this frame of mind that she made *Sketches from "Chronicle."*

In early Graham dances, elbows puncture the space around the dancers. They are an expressive element—spiky, strong, stubborn. And they are a shape element—angular, giving the choreography an almost Egyptian look. Those elbows helped define modernism in dance. In this piece they contribute to the feeling of an inexorably mounting purpose. By the end of this three-part work, you're cheering for these women—their strength, their unity, their indifference to prettiness. (Two years later, in 1938, Erick Hawkins joined the company, and that was the end of the all-female dances.)

The audience left the theater jabbering and speculating about Graham's divine anger. I ran into Carmen de Lavallade and Geoffrey Holder. "It's that Irish blood of Martha's!" Holder was saying. Carmen had a different opinion: "I think she was just so mad at Goebbels." And I said, "Or she was mad at Louis Horst." (Horst was her lover and musical director who forced her to put counts to the choreography.)

Any way you slice it, the source of Graham's theatrical fury is a source for contemplation . . . and for wondering, Where is that energy today? What female choreographer will bring us that kind of vehemence? In the meantime we can thank the Graham company for preserving this incredible work.

Postscript: A note about the music for "Steps in the Street," the second—and quite astounding—section of the dance. In an e-mail message to me, Charles Woodford, Doris Humphrey's son, said the music by Wallingford Riegger for Yuriko's re-creation of "Steps in the Street" was originally commissioned by Doris Humphrey for her *New Dance*, which premiered in 1935. Riegger had also composed the original music for Graham's "Steps in the Street," which premiered in 1936, but that score had been lost.

This explains why I had such a strong kinetic reaction to the Riegger music: I had learned Humphrey's *New Dance* in the sixties at American Dance Festival (then held at Connecticut College) in a repertory class supervised by José Limón. I felt the music as a powerful force back then, so, decades later, my body memory reacted to it without even knowing it was the same music.

Blogging about the Process of Choreography—Ugh!

Blog post, July 26, 2010, dancemagazine.com

I have to admit that when I wrote this, I wasn't remembering that I myself had written about my creative process ("Containing Differences in Time," in "The Eighties.") Now, of course, that irony is not lost on me. However, as I tried to make clear in the posting, which turned out to be inflammatory (see postscript), I was objecting not to the after-the-fact account, but to the on-the-ground, of-the-moment blogging that assumes people are interested in your every whim.

There's an annoying new trend of blogging about the process of making a dance. I am not talking about Tere O'Connor, who writes very considered contemplations about dance making, based on his decades of experience. I am talking about young choreographers, anxious to be in the public eye, who think that writing about what happened that day in the studio will somehow (1) bring them a wider audience and/or (2) make them a better choreographer.

I realize a blog is a good way to keep your website alive and to involve your potential audience. But *explaining* how you make a dance, the problems you encounter and how you solve them, is not going to help either you as the choreographer or your potential audience. To dig into your imagination enough to make a dance, you need to be embroiled in a place where there is no explanation. As Igor Stravinsky once said, you have to dig underground, in the dark, like a mole, groping for what comes next. You have to be willing to sink into that layer of not knowing in order to come up with something you've never seen or done before. During that beginning period, putting it into words denies the groping phase. You should be utterly at a loss for words, just feeling your way. After a while, you can start to justify your decisions to yourself, to your dancers, or to your audience if your presenter so wishes. But first, you have to be willing to be lost in that preverbal place.

Suppose you're in the studio working on a piece and you're thinking about what you're going to say about it in your blog. Wouldn't that compromise your process?

I think this rush to explain is part of a larger trend of people thinking a simple how-to set of instructions can make them into an artist. In the *Atlantic*'s Fiction 2010 annual issue, the novelist Richard Bausch points out, with dismay, that there are 4,470 titles under the rubric "How to Write a Book." He thinks they are pretty much useless. In his essay "How to Write in

700 Easy Lessons: The case against writing manuals," he says, "One doesn't write out of some intellectual plan or strategy; one writes from a kind of beautiful necessity."

And no one can tell you how to transform that necessity into art.

Postscript: This post touched off a firestorm of responses online, most of them angry. Some bloggers attacked me for "gagging" choreographers; one tweeter said I should lose my job. I was surprised by the level of outrage. I hadn't realized the degree to which young people are attached to the Internet as a mode of communication (or, um, self-exposure). The hubbub gave me an insight into how outrage gets manufactured: People exaggerate what you say, and that gets passed on.

However, some bloggers appreciated the issue I brought up. A post from Dance Theater Workshop written by Isabella Hreljanovic speculated that this kind of continual blogging stems from a wish for early encouragement. She said, basically extending my argument, "The constant availability of material, however, diminishes the air of mystery about a piece."

In my follow-up post, fielding the various responses, I tried to address both sides of the argument. I also offered choreographers' websites of writings that are worth reading. These included those of Miguel Gutierrez, Deborah Hay, Liz Lerman, Tere O'Connor, David Parker, Jill Sigman, Charlotte Vincent, Kate Weare, and the Movement Research site. And then I offered the complete and correct Stravinsky passage, which I did not have at my fingertips when I wrote the initial blog. I repeat it here because it's one of my absolute favorite quotes:

> A composer improvises aimlessly the way an animal grubs about. Both of them go grubbing about because they yield to a compulsion to seek things out. What urge of the composer is satisfied by this investigation? . . . He is in quest of his pleasure. He seeks a satisfaction that he fully knows he will not find without first striving for it. . . . So we grub about in expectation of our pleasure, guided by our scent, and suddenly we stumble against an unknown obstacle. It gives us a jolt, a shock, and this shock fecundates our creative power. —Igor Stravinsky, *The Stravinsky Festival of the New York City Ballet*, edited by Nancy Goldner, 1973, p. 36, originally from Stravinsky's *Poetics of Music in the Form of Six Lessons*, 1942.

The Times They Are A-Changin'

Feature story, *Dance Magazine*, July 2010

In our second Race Issue (the first was in 2005), we set ourselves this simple question: How diverse is the up-and-coming generation? This soon splintered into other questions: What opportunities are available to young dancers of color? How are students engaging with cultures other than their own? What is diversity, anyway?

In talking to artistic directors, educators, and performers about this unwieldy topic, two things became clear. The first is that multiracial dancers are a growing part of the discussion. And second, it's impossible to separate race from culture.

Eduardo Vilaro, the new director of Ballet Hispanico, says, "Younger audiences are looking for a reflection of what they see in their environment, which is a technology-filled extravaganza that reaches beyond their hometown, their city, their school. It broadens their connection to the greater world. They already understand what it is to be a global village."

Cuban-born Vilaro feels that young dancers thrive on diversity. "I see them joke around, using racial stereotypes in very fun ways. But to me that's questioning, and that's investigating. They are taking chances and opening up the dialogue—talking about your nappy head, or your funny accent. At the same time they'll say, 'Hey, let me tell you a little more about this,' or 'No, you've got it wrong.'"

Vilaro enjoys the wealth of Latino dancers in New York, many trained at Juilliard, Ailey/Fordham, or ballet schools. "But then you have this mixture, these other students of color, often mixed race, that are coming from a university background that are well-trained also, but not so classical." Vilaro, who is of mixed heritage (Asian, African, and Spanish), says that many of the Ballet Hispanico dancers are also mixed. One dancer's parents are Dominican and Armenian; another is Mexican and African American. "It speaks to me as someone who is of mixed race and who grabs at many different cultural backgrounds in order to create my identity."

On the college and university scene, we spoke to Susan Lee, who directs the dance program at Northwestern University. Active in American College Dance Festivals for years, Lee says that the Midwest region has grown in diversity in the last ten years, especially African Americans and Asians. In a recent improvisation course, she says, "I had B-boys in the class and kids who studied bharata natyam. I was thrilled! In the discussions they are really sharing their unique perspectives." She says they quickly learn "that they need to find common languages. When they talk about nuances from their form, they have to recognize that not everybody knows what they are talking about at first. They love to rise to that challenge."

One way that diversity can be measured is in student-run companies. Lee says that when she started at Northwestern thirty years ago, there were only two on campus. Now there are at least twenty-two, and they have helped attract African American students to dance. "I think it's the fusion forms they are really excited about," she says. "They are doing African dance and whatever else they have brought in as part of the mix."

These student companies have lively names like Boomshaka (hip-hop, tap, drumming); Deeva Dance Troupe (all-female group blending Indian classical, folk, jazz, modern, and hip-hop); the NAYO Dance Ensemble (modern, hip-hop, tap, Latin, African, salsa, ballet—whew!); and Typhoon Dance Troupe (dances of East and Southeast Asia).

As more culturally specific forms become available in colleges, they are opening up to students of other cultures. D. Sabela Grimes, a hip-hop dancer formerly with Rennie Harris Puremovement, offers a course called Funkamentals at the Department of World Arts and Cultures at UCLA, which has a heavily Asian student population. He teaches not only technique but also the lineage of black social dance forms.

Grimes says getting into hip-hop is a matter of finding a way in. "Someone that's Asian coming into the class has to negotiate their access point. How do I enter the circle? A lot of people still believe that if you're black you have easier access, but I would say it's different." He continues: "It's like you're going through chambers. You reach one chamber of the community and you explore it, only to find out that you can go further down the rabbit hole, so to speak. There are other chambers that exist."

One Asian who has passed through some of those chambers is dancer/ choreographer/actor Harry Shum Jr., now appearing in the TV show *Glee*. As a kid learning street moves, he says, "hip-hop was mainly minority driven, so it was something I felt comfortable in. With my friends, it wasn't about a color. We weren't like, 'You can't do this because you are white or you are black.' We had this universal thing, which was dance, and we all just had fun with it."

However, when he got to Los Angeles, things changed. "When you start going into the business it's a little different. Some people do have a lot of struggle, but for me, my ethnicity worked to my advantage. In Hollywood they can say, 'We want this certain look.' The first iPod commercials were silhouetted, but when I did the ones where you could see me dance, it was, 'Oh, he looks good for it, and we love his dancing, so let's do it.'"

He feels the industry is discovering the appeal of diversity, especially with backup dancers. "For Beyoncé, they brought me in because they wanted an Asian guy," he says with a laugh. "It's a give and take. I don't feel that they hired me just because I was Asian. I was a good, capable dancer."

Shum is very clear that he hasn't gone through all the chambers. "There are people who are really hard-core that feel that once it hits the mainstream it's not real, it's not legit," he says. "I don't think that'll ever go away."

But that doesn't bother him. "I don't consider myself a popper. I don't consider myself a B-boy. I consider myself a dancer, a free-styler, and I don't feel that anybody can take that away from me. I put all these things together myself; I made my own salad."

Ananya Chatterjea leads a dance company based on contemporary interpretations of classical Indian dance forms for women of color in Minneapolis. She believes that the younger generation of women is more open, but less motivated. "When a huge, momentous event happens in their lifetime, like the election of President Obama, they have this idea that things are okay now. So yes, they are more open, but that doesn't mean that the difficulties around race have gone away." When she came to New York in 1989, she recalls, "it felt really urgent to have a space for conversation among different communities of women of color."

Currently involved in a multiyear community project on antiviolence, Chatterjea decided that the issue is broader than women of color. So she started what she calls the Allies program, to include white women as well. "If they have the training and the form, and they understand the ideas on which the work is based, then we can say, 'Yes, dance with us.'" And in fact, a white woman who was her student at the University of Minnesota has joined the group.

"The dancers in my company are women of color," says Chatterjea, "but most of my students are white. They talk to each other, and it is no longer a ghettoized situation. So they can say, 'Oh, okay, you go to this Pilates studio? You're doing hot yoga? Is that helping your back?'" But her first commitment is to artistic merit. "The mainstream can stop me from going anywhere, but I am committed to excellence in my dancing and in my craft."

Like Chatterjea, Benoit-Swan Pouffer, artistic director of Cedar Lake Contemporary Ballet, says his first priority is artistic excellence. "I have the option to hire different nationalities, but I am looking for good dancers first. Dance doesn't have a race, doesn't have a palette." With a Parisian mother and Caribbean father, he says, "I am mixed race, and I am drawn to diversity."

Pouffer came to New York after his training at the Conservatoire in Paris, where he was one of the very few students of color. Attending The Ailey School was a revelation (pardon the expression) for him, as in, "Wow, I'm seeing a lot of black dancers out there!" Recalling his time at Ailey, he says, "The first word that comes to mind is normalcy. I felt, 'Now it is not about my color.' It made me push harder. I had to stand out differently."

He feels that diversity within a company creates a certain synergy. "When I have someone who was born and raised in Paris and someone who was born and raised in Korea, two individuals dance together and without knowing it they tell a story. I think half of the company is from another country. So all this generates energy, and it brings out of my dancers the combustion of all those energies."

In the seventeen years Pouffer has been in New York, he has seen the opportunities grow. He cites reality TV shows like *So You Think You Can Dance*, as well as companies like Complexions and Cedar Lake and Broadway musicals like *In the Heights* that made dancers of color more visible.

Even the School of American Ballet, that stronghold of purity (and whiteness), is working to boost its diversity. Kay Mazzo, cochair of the faculty, has seen growth since the nineties, when the school started giving community auditions. At first they were just to find boys, but since 1998 the auditions, which are now given in Harlem, the Bronx, Queens, Brooklyn, and Chinatown, feed girls into the school also. As a result SAB has doubled its minority population from 12 percent to almost 24 percent. "We're getting a lot more diversity than we ever had before, which is what Balanchine and Lincoln Kirstein wanted, and what Peter Martins wants," Mazzo says.

However, the community auditions are mostly for the children's division, ages six through ten. For the advanced classes, auditions are held year-round at SAB and there is an annual audition tour, which attracts mostly white kids who are already steeped in ballet. SAB's executive director, Marjorie Van Dercook, admits, "Our advanced division is not as diverse as we'd like it to be—although we've made a lot of strides."

For companies and schools that have attained a measure of diversity, they are finding that it's not just politically or socially correct, but also artistically vital. Eduardo Vilaro has stretched the "Hispanico" of Ballet Hispanico in terms of both dancers and choreographers. "I find that in diversity there is a richness, a contrast, a yin and yang. It gives a beautiful mix onstage. I'm looking forward to broadening even more. Now that we are diverse, let's start the conversations."

Biennale de la Danse de Lyon

Lyon, France

September 9–October 3, 2010

Festival review, *Dance Magazine*, December 2010

Where else does a dance festival overtake an entire city? With forty compa-nies spread out over thirty-four venues (plus three outdoor sites), this year's Biennale de la Danse was the main event in France's second largest city. It attracted ninety-five thousand spectators, young and old (not counting the even larger number that showed up for the parade that opens the festival). Tickets were moderately priced, and most shows sold out—even a national transit strike didn't put a dent in attendance. Performances routinely ended with rhythmic clapping, especially for Lyon's favorites like Bill T. Jones, Deborah Colker, and Compagnie Käfig.

My week (as a guest of the festival) started off with a bang. Pina Bausch's *Nelken* (1982), gorgeous and giddy, planted the dancers of Tanztheater Wup-pertal in a field of carnations—as intoxicating as a field of poppies. They played a raucous street game led by the droll Lutz Förster in a dress. Their antics exposed the power plays of children—or, rather, children as played by adults—with mounting hilarity. In a later episode, Dominique Mercy yelled in French, "You want to see a manège? I'll show you a manège," and furi-ously tossed off leaps and turns in a circle. "You want to see entrechat six? I'll show you . . ." and he executed a few perfect sixes. After he exhausted himself, he was still willing to defy his own reluctance, which was some-how terribly entertaining. Mercy has the gift of being funny and sad at once.

Of the commissioned works, the greatest achievement was *Lieu d'Être*— utterly delightful from the first meanderings to the last airborne swoops. A site-specific work masterminded by Lyon's Annick Charlot, it combined her five luscious dancers (herself included) with fifty-five residents of an apart-ment complex in the commercial center of Lyon. One dancer's task was to lead the crowd to the right place; another's was to gently embrace a resident of the building; yet another's was to shepherd residents in tableaux on the terraces high up. Every danced conversation was infused with charm, wit, and humanity.

Some of the big guns misfired. Angelin Preljocaj's elaborate collabora-tion with Bolshoi dancers, *And Then, One Thousand Years of Peace*, was so hard-edged that it didn't seem to be about collaboration at all. (The year 2010 was designated the "French-Russian year" by the cultural ministries of both countries.) In one scene, all dancers (more than twenty) had their heads wrapped in the flags of different nations. Perhaps it was meant as a statement about the blindness of nationalism—though a slightly sinister way of expressing that.

The duets were more human than the group sections. For those of us who had been to the press conference and heard Preljocaj say that every duet united one French and one Russian dancer, it helped just to know that. Plus the duets had a touch of vulnerability, which was lacking in the group sections. In one of them, two men alternated violence and tenderness, and ended up in a locked kiss. (The Bolshoi authorities couldn't have been too happy about that.) In a sexy, slinky, hetero duet, each partner pinned the other against a wall.

But the loveliest section was for three women moving stealthily with what looked like samovars on their heads.

The musical high point of the week was the Debussy String Quartet, which played selections from its classical repertoire for Compagnie Käfig's *Boxe Boxe*. Dipping into his past as a boxer, Käfig artistic director Mourad Merzouki wove together an unlikely mix of hip-hop, boxing, and classical music (Schubert, Ravel, Mendelssohn, etc.). Although the skit-like bits with red boxing gloves and punching bags were too literal and too long, the whole amalgam, with some nice interaction between the dancers and musicians, was admirable. My favorite moment came during a Philip Glass section where three dancers (including, in the center, the sole woman), wearing silky white boxer robes, moved through ghostly versions of hip-hop or boxing warm-ups. But the extended peak moment was Teddy Verardo's intense solo to Schubert's *Death and the Maiden*, showing the agony and the ecstasy of a prizefighter. In a coda, the musicians fiddled fast while the dancers pulled out all their hip-hop tricks, making us wildly happy.

The hip-hop dancer who stole my heart, however, was Artem Orlov, who appeared in *Na Grani* ("no boundaries") by Mickaël Le Mer. Another effort to bring together performers from France (Le Mer's Compagnie S'poart) and Russia (guests from Ekaterinburg), this piece combined contemporary and hip-hop. Orlov's virtuosity broke through the dim lighting. His speed, precision, sensitivity, and soaring energy captivated. Even when standing dead still, his strong focus made him charismatic. *Na Grani* used a set of large movable blocks (by Guillaume Cousin) to suggest an urban environment. The performers climbed on top of the blocks as though they were city rooftops. We waited, because the choreography seemed on the verge of taking off, but it never really did.

At the Maison de la Danse, an eleven-hundred-seat house just for dance,

Bill T. Jones presented the European premiere of *Fondly Do We Hope . . . Fervently Do We Pray* [Note: this piece had been reviewed in an earlier issue of *Dance Magazine*.] Though his text was spoken in English (subtitles were projected high above), and the subject matter was very American (Lincoln and the Civil War), the French audience responded warmly.

The Lyon festival has had a long relationship with Brazilian artists, and this year Deborah Colker brought twelve young dancers from favelas where she's been teaching. They performed her snappy three-part *Partida* with precision, humor, and great exuberance. Popular tunes by Stevie Wonder, the Rolling Stones, and Lou Reed helped make the piece both exhilarating and touching.

I missed major performances, including the Lyon Opera Ballet's Forsythe evening, Hofesh Shechter, Ailey II, Maguy Marin, and a clutch of other French choreographers. The only part of the Trisha Brown tribute I caught was the exhibition at Musée d'Art Contemporain, which included her drawings as well as posters and films—more evidence of Lyon's commitment to the artists it loves.

Sadly, this was the last biennale directed by Guy Darmet, who built the festival into the glory that it is.

Ralph Lemon

Blog post, October 18, 2010, dancemagazine.com

Ralph Lemon's piece was so resistant to the expectations of performance—and yet so powerful—that I found myself writing in the form of Yvonne Rainer's famous No Manifesto (see "An Improbable Pair on a Quest into the Past," Section V).

No to turning crying into laughing; no to ending the piece with an amazing unforgettable flourish; no to starting with wonderful, appealing dancing; no to choosing a famous collaborator in music or visuals; no to dancers forming shapes and patterns that keep your eye involved.

Ralph Lemon's *How Can You Stay in the House All Day and Not Go Anywhere?* at Brooklyn Academy of Music reminded me of the stubbornness of Yvonne Rainer's No Manifesto of the sixties. I loved her defiance then (though she has long since downplayed her statement of that time), and I love his stubbornness—or rather patience, now. A few people walked out of the performance at BAM because it wasn't what they expected.

Just as Rainer's no's to some things opened the door to yes's to other things, so too with Ralph Lemon.

Yes, he did go fully into sorrow. (When Okwui Okpokwasili cried with her back to us, it was so real. And don't we all have a river to cry?) Yes, his dancers were totally chaotic and alarmingly desperate (yet with a silver lining of humor). While moving fast, David Thomson released so far off balance that he looked like he'd lose his head.

Yes to the animal comfort of pulling toward each other, flesh to flesh, while improvising. Yes to layering of sources (e.g., Andrei Tarkovsky's 1972 sci-fi romance film *Solaris*; videos of Walter Carter, Lemon's hundred-year-old muse shuffling around during his last days; and Ralph's own account of being with his dying girlfriend.)

No to making a "show." Yes to making a contemplation on love and loss visible.

Crystal Pite

Peak Performances, Alexander Kasser Theater, Montclair State University

October 21–24, 2010

Web review, dancemagazine.com

This piece blew me away. The only way I could think to describe the impact was to use three adjectives followed by periods. Looking over my past reviews, I discovered, with chagrin, that I had employed the same device four years earlier in my review of Susan Marshall's Cloudless *(in "From 2004 to 2007"). I hereby vow never to use it again.*

Overwhelmed. Speechless. Awestruck. That's how many of us in the audience reacted to this monumental work. Crystal Pite's *Dark Matters* plumbs the depths of the unconscious by giving shape to fears as dark shadowy figures. Sometimes these figures lurk in such dim light that you're not sure they're there; other times they manipulate a puppet assembled by the maniacal Peter Chu. Dressed in black, they recall Bunraku handlers but also (as Pite explained in the "Shop Talk" that I moderated before the performance) refer to the concept of "dark matter" in space that inspired her.

The wooden puppet, about waist high, buckles at the knees, inclines its head tenderly, and springs up with no preparation. A luscious creepiness ensues as affection turns to mischief, and mischief turns to menace—with murderous results.

Doubt is a theme in Pite's work. This was highlighted by clever moments, like someone holding up a sign that says, THIS IS FATE but after a light flashes the other side of the sign shows the words THIS IS FAKE. Or when the shadows dance together—a quirky, funny, taunting dance that turns them into clowns.

After intermission, the dark figures have morphed into humans, and now the ratio is reversed: instead of one human (Peter Chu) and five Bunraku shadows, we have one shadow (Sandra Marín Garcia) and five humans. But the humans uncannily echo the puppet's moves: collapsing knees, disjointed arms, and sudden soarings.

Like William Forsythe's *Three Atmospheric Studies* (Pite danced with Forsythe for five years), the group dashes around, helping or hindering each other so fast that you almost don't notice the repeated tableaux: Eric Beauchesne is held upside down with his legs sticking straight in the air; Peter Chu side-kicks another dancer away from him.

Toward the end, the shadow figure activates Jermaine Maurice Spivey into an astounding solo. He billows from within, slides on the sides of his ankles, and melts upward. The sheer kinetic excitement of it could make you holler the way people do when Angel Corella whips off umpteen pirouettes or leaps above everyone's heads. These weren't jumps and turns, but insanely virtuosic stops and starts.

As the bounty of creativity accumulated, one could subliminally begin to connect all that was happening. The soundtrack, an ancient voice repeating lines from Voltaire—"This temporary blend of blood and dust / Was put together only to dissolve"—helped place the dance in a cosmic setting.

The final scene was transcendent, with its message of forgiveness—or was it a love-your-worst-fear message, or was it some kind of resurrection? The one shadow disrobes to reveal herself as a dancer too. She moves like a colt with wobbly legs, or, if you can imagine, a newborn puppet. She performs some kind of rescue on Chu, miming sewing his heart back together. Was this to give him a second chance—for his creation to be a savior rather than a destroyer?

All the elements blended to transport you to another world. Jay Gower Taylor built a dingy carpentry shop; the original music by Owen Belton transformed sounds of cutting and scraping into something both musical and sinister. And the puppet, designed by Robert Lewis and Valerie Moffat, had so much personality that it not only turned creativity into destruction in the first half, but the memory of it loomed over the second, dance-y half as an animating spirit.

The dancers of Pite's company, Kidd Pivot Frankfurt RM, were the most amazing of all. They embodied the initial innocence of the puppet (shades of *Petrouchka*) as well as the destruction-from-within phase of the puppet. *Dark Matters* expanded our range of movement imagination—thrillingly.

Politeness: Is It Crucial to the Future of Ballet?

Blog post, October 24, 2010, dancemagazine.com

Jennifer Homans's Apollo's Angels *caused a stir when the last chapter, "The Masters Are Dead and Gone," was posted by the* New Republic *online. This was the conclusion to a 500-page book that claimed to detail the history of ballet. A former student at the School of American Ballet, Homans is an exemplary member of the Church of Balanchine. She is not alone in thinking that ballet died along with him. Although her writing is eloquent, with a refreshing edge, and her historical knowledge is formidable (though certain gaps—almost nothing on the Joffrey Ballet or Ballet Nacional de Cuba—make one wonder), my hunch is that Homans has attended very few ballet performances of living choreographers in the last two or three decades.*

I was still thinking about Crystal Pite (see the previous entry) when I decided to add my two cents to the controversy. It's choreographers like Pite, William Forsythe, and Wayne McGregor who make me excited about ballet. They go beyond the Balanchine courtliness—or, um, angelhood—that I found dated and annoying (see "Seeing Balanchine, Watching Whelan," Section V). So I cited Pite and all the recent ballet I could remember that gave evidence of its vibrancy—a vibrancy that has nothing to do with courtliness. Thus you will see some familiar names and descriptions.

The following year I developed these ideas into a talk entitled "Seven Reasons Why Ballet Is Thriving" that I gave at a luncheon sponsored by the Carreño Festival in Sarasota, Florida. It then circulated on Twitter quite a bit. But I selected this earlier posting because it's more immediate and less of a lecture.

While Jennifer Homans has been mourning the death of ballet in her book *Apollo's Angels*, Crystal Pite's *Dark Matters* has been streaking across the international landscape. A monumental work that uses the ballet vocabulary as a basis, it tells a harrowing story of fearful shadows, human creativity, and willful destructiveness. Her craft is brilliant; the dancers' virtuosity is astounding. Not Balanchine-type virtuosity with its crisp footwork and open, long-lined upper bodies, nor the Bolshoi kind with its multiple pirouettes and bounding grand jetés. But a virtuosity of initiating movements from a precise place in the body and sending currents of energy with startling complexity and daring, corresponding to the mercurial routes of human thought and emotion. The cumulative power of *Dark Matters* grabs you by the throat and won't let you go. (I saw it this weekend at Peak Performances in Montclair, New Jersey.)

This kind of work is the descendent of classical ballet. Crystal Pite emerged from William Forsythe's Ballett Frankfurt, where dancers learned to exaggerate the principles of classical épaulement while decentering alignment. This is ballet today. Yes, it's about fragmentation, as Homans suggests, but the most accomplished of these choreographers, like Forsythe and Pite, can corral such methods to serve the larger ideals of art: to create a strange beauty that stimulates minds and hearts.

Here is a quick sampling of other recent ballets that speak to today's audience:

A landmark in contemporary ballet, Forsythe's *In the Middle, Somewhat Elevated* (1987), plays with the line between casual walking and full out, crash-landing dancing. With brazenly stretched legs, off-kilter pelvises, and otherworldly music by Thom Willems, the ballet sends us into a new, ultra contemporary planet of dance.

Wheeldon's *After the Rain* duet (originally the second half of a 2005 sextet for New York City Ballet) challenges the ballerina to dance—and float—with pristine simplicity. Wendy Whelan is a sylph for the twenty-first century who draws us into a hushed, celestial reverie. At least four other ballet companies have taken *After the Rain* into their reps; it is now a classic of our times.

Jorma Elo's *Slice to Sharp* (2006), also for NYCB, delivers a shock of delight to audiences. The eight dancers tear through big, wheeling lifts and scissor-sharp leaps at top speed, with a sprinkle of odd little mimed gestures. It's exhilarating to watch.

Wayne McGregor's *Chroma* hit the public with the force of Balanchine's *Agon* (1957) when it premiered at the Royal Ballet in 2006. It takes the long lines of ballet and pushes them to extremes, particularly during partnering, leaving you gasping at what's possible. Talk about rigor and discipline!

Back to Wheeldon: His *Within the Golden Hour* (2008) for San Francisco Ballet is one of the most haunting ballets I've seen. It's both melancholic and mesmerizing—the kind of ballet you want to see over and over.

Ratmansky's *Seven Sonatas* (2009) for American Ballet Theatre infuses the dancing of three couples with whiffs of romance. Exquisitely matched to the Scarlatti music, it touches us with hints of regret mingled with tenderness. Inventive, elegiac, and satisfying, it could be Ratmansky's *Dances at a Gathering*.

Sure, ballet can be "civilization," as Homans quotes Arlene Croce as saying. But it can be a lot of other things too. It can have a savage beauty as well as an ennobling beauty; it can be intimate as well as grand; it can have menacing male swans (as in Matthew Bourne's *Swan Lake*) as well as fragile female swans.

In an excerpt from her book, *Apollo's Angels*, posted online by the *New Re-*

public, Homans writes that ballet "is an etiquette as much as an art, layered with centuries of courtly conventions and codes of civility and politeness."

Do those codes have to be taken into twenty-first-century ballet? Are the other arts forever saddled with such civility? Would we have the disorienting paintings of Picasso, the spiritual music of Philip Glass, or the gritty novels of Toni Morrison if they had all stuck by codes of etiquette from centuries ago?

This is an exciting time for ballet. But, while some choreographers are looking ahead, some critics are looking to the past. This is the natural order of things. Artists are always ahead of their watchers, always pushing the envelope. To the watchers, I say, If you're looking for gold in a silver mine, you won't see the silver.

National Ballet of Canada

Four Seasons Centre for the Performing Arts, Toronto, Canada

November 24–28, 2010

Review, *Dance Magazine*, February 2011

With this triple bill, the National Ballet of Canada plunged headlong into ultra-contemporary weirdness in ballet and came up triumphant. They are the first company outside of the Royal Ballet to dance Wayne McGregor's astonishing *Chroma*. In this landmark work, the glare of lights seems to push the dancers into extreme territory, crooking the wrists, splaying the legs, and swaying the spine. One part of the body can be small and cramped, while another part is yanked open. The women can be stretched wide and pressed to the ground—more reptilian than human. In the first duet, Bridgett Zehr is a drastic creature on the edge of control, at times even looking like a cripple. You can't take your eyes off her. Tanya Howard's fine articulation is noticeable, and Greta Hodgkinson powers through with serenity. The music by Joby Talbot and Jack White is sometimes pounding and sometimes lilting.

There is no affection per se, but there are tender moments, and they are almost shocking within the cold, clinical context. The sense of caring is expressed not in romantic looks or swoons, but in a shared respite from the take-no-prisoners pace.

Thank goodness *Serenade* softened the stage before Crystal Pite's *Emergence*, because otherwise there would have been too much prehuman turmoil at one stretch. With the help of NBC's orchestra playing the Tchaikovsky live, the dancers rendered the Balanchine masterpiece with strength and sweep. Sonia Rodriguez was solid, energetic, and crisp as the Russian Girl. Elena Lobsanova's beautifully open chest gave the Dark Angel's arabesque a swelling look. In the final surrender, Xiao Nan Yu, held on high, opened into such a deep arch back that it seemed she might throw herself off balance.

In *Emergence*, dancers emerge from a cave-like barrel upstage. As in the movie *Days of Heaven*, we see insects—only here they are dancers—crackle and snap and mate close-up, and then from a distance they coagulate into a menacing swarm. In the opening scene, Rodriguez seems glued to the floor, trying to free up her hands by jerking her shoulder—a fly caught in a spider's web. At times there seems to be a chase between predator and victim. At other times there's a lovely overlap, like when the guys hunker down with their strong contractions while a few women bourrée through them.

In a large group they whisper, making the sound of cicadas on a summer night; eventually we can discern that they are whispering the counts. Everything—the dancing, the hornets' nest–type set design by Jay Gower Taylor, and Owen Belton's ominous sound—adds to the feeling of a swarm. Black markings on the men's upper backs make them look ready to sting. At the end, all thirty-eight dancers are counting and scratching in unison—just before a light from inside the cave blasts at us. And then they are gone.

Choreographers like McGregor and Pite are redefining what it means to be organic. The movement may look deliberately odd, but it's all part of what the contemporary dancer can do, what the curious body wants to do. In both cases, the set and music were organic to the dance, and it all came together into a complete experience. As complete as *Serenade*, only instead of divine, these ballets are diabolical.

Is Appropriation the Same as Stealing and Why Is It Happening More Now?

Blog post, January 31, 2011, dancemagazine.com

I took offense to Sarah Michelson's obvious appropriation of In the Upper Room, *Twyla Tharp's 1986 masterwork, but it seemed that no one else did. Perhaps appropriation is just an accepted part of the culture now. And maybe that's not a bad thing. After I posted this blog I learned about choreographers who "borrow" in a more transparent way than Michelson in her piece* Devotion. *See also my postscript.*

Watching Sarah Michelson's piece *Devotion* at The Kitchen, I was getting more and more upset as her dancers donned a series of outfits that mimicked Norma Kamali's costumes for Twyla Tharp's *In the Upper Room*. That ballet was heavenly for me, whether danced by Tharp's own dancers or by American Ballet Theatre. I loved it for both its supreme challenge to, and faith in the dancers, and for the spiritual uplift, riding on the celestial waves of Philip Glass's music.

In *Devotion*, the costumes were not the *exact* design of Kamali's for *Upper Room*, but you couldn't miss the little black-and-white-striped dress, the red racer-back leotard, the red socks, and the rolled down leotard over baggy trousers. At least two of the moves were also borrowed from *Upper Room*, namely, a jolting run, and a run-and-leap by a woman caught mid-leap by a man. After the show I got even more upset when I searched the special thanks page (the longest I've ever seen) and did not find the names of either Norma Kamali or Twyla Tharp.

So how deliberate was this connection? Did Michelson want us to recognize Tharp's piece inside hers? Was she creating an ode to *Upper Room*? Or was she exploiting a twentieth-century masterpiece? Clearly the paintings by TM Davy, mounted high up on the walls, with their saintly glow, were odes to baroque religious paintings—and I didn't mind that. And I didn't mind the fact that Michelson was using some of the same Philip Glass music ("Dance IX") that is heard in *Upper Room*. A lot of choreographers use his music, and it was credited in the program. (I also want to say that, before the first Norma Kamali costume made its entrance, I was enjoying Rebecca Warner's long solo quite a bit.)

I called Jodi Melnick, who had danced in *Upper Room* as part of Twyla's company, and who *was* listed in Michelson's special thanks. She calmed me down, and together we recalled some of the times we've seen this kind of appropriation before. Jodi herself ran off with Giselle's mad scene in a piece of Vicky Shick's called *Repair* in 2005. I loved it. I thought it was hilarious and moving at the same time. Vicky had embedded an over-the-top melodrama within her cooler, more fractured phrases.

And in 2008, Juliette Mapp inserted Trisha Brown's short "Spanish Dance" in her piece *Anna, Ikea, and I*. ("Spanish Dance" is something I had been in long ago and was pleased to do it again, with Juliette.) She loved that iconic piece of Trisha's, just as Michelson, presumably, loved *Upper Room*. But in this case, Juliette got permission from Trisha to do it, and we were coached by (and joined by) Diane Madden, Trisha's rehearsal director. And Trisha was invited to attend.

However, in that same concert, Juliette also replicated the exact choreography of a section of Merce Cunningham's *Septet* (1953). For this she did *not* get permission, thus stirring up some indignation from the Cunningham foundation. She had seen the segment on YouTube while looking for traces of Viola Farber's dancing. (Viola was a ghostly but definite presence in *Anna, Ikea, and I*.) Juliette told me recently that she never meant to antagonize Merce or his people, and, looking back, she wished she had requested their permission.

YouTube: It's changed the dance landscape. So much of our dance past is posted on it that we are awash in our history. I think the reason visual artists started appropriating way before dancers did is that their past is out there, in galleries and museums, for anyone to snatch ideas from. Duchamp drew a mustache and goatee on a reproduction of the Mona Lisa in 1919 (titling it *L.H.O.O.Q.*). This was called an assisted readymade, and the readymades challenged the notion of originality in art—just as Andy Warhol's Campbell's Soup cans did decades later.

But the soup cans and *L.H.O.O.Q.*) were immediately recognizable. Warhol and Duchamp were not trying to pass those things off as their own original work. Their own work consisted of Doing Something with iconic materials. And I admit, Sarah Michelson Did Something with her *Upper Room* materials. She combined text (by Richard Maxwell), actors (from the New York City Players), dancers, and especially lighting (by herself and Zack Tinkelman) together in a striking way. The piece had a hypnotic quality.

Appropriation as an artistic device caught fire in the eighties. Visual artists like Barbara Kruger, Cindy Sherman, and Sherrie Levine made careers out of appropriation—taking something that exists and putting it in a new context.

In that environment, choreographer Susan Rethorst actually titled a piece *Stealing*. For a publicity shot, she posed as Laurie Anderson, with white jacket and white opaque sunglasses, to simulate Anderson's look for her album *Big Science*. Rethorst later wrote a brilliant essay on the topic, in which she says that when an artist borrows from someone else, that artist does *not* lose her own voice. "As if, in forcing a move that comes from outside oneself, the self imposes itself with more clarity." She concludes that there really is no such thing as stealing, and "that any part of any dance, aided by the power of suggestion . . . can be said to be [either] derivative or referential."

Derivative or referential—or reverential: Which one was Michelson being in *Devotion*? No one else I spoke to was upset about this. Puzzled, maybe, but not upset. So I had to ask myself, why did it bother me so much that Michelson's dancers wore rip-offs of the *Upper Room* costumes? And would I have been appeased if due credit had been given on her special thanks page? I do think it's fair to refer to, and even borrow from, older works, since we owe so much to our dance heritage. One of the many examples is about to come our way: Merce spoofed Martha Graham in his piece *Antic Meet* (1958), which is currently part of the company's Legacy Tour.

A couple years ago, Levi Gonzalez showed a solo at the Association of Performing Arts Presenters conference. He started with a sly confession that he couldn't think up anything new so he decided to do other people's dances. As he went through some moves, he said, "This is from Miguel Gutierrez" . . . and "this is from Juliette Mapp." Of course he *had* come up with an idea: a concept for how to frame his appropriations. I really appreciated that he credited his colleagues' ideas. . . . But I wonder if he got any nibbles from presenters that day.

How far can an artist go—responsibly—in appropriating another artist's materials? It seems to be happening more in dance these days. And isn't that what an artist does: take materials from life and rearrange them? So what's my problem? Am I stuck with an outdated expectation that everything has to be created from scratch?

I think it's possible that this problem could have been resolved with a simple fix of the program notes. In Michelson's program for *Devotion*, the costumes were credited to three people. I think that if the credit had read, "Costumes by James Kidd, Shaina Mote, and Sarah Michelson partly based on (or inspired by) Norma Kamali's costumes for Twyla Tharp's *In the Upper Room*," I would have considered this a responsible borrowing. And then I might have been able to focus on the more original aspects of *Devotion* that other people found amazing.

Postscript: Julia Rhoads, artistic director of Lucky Plush in Chicago, responded to my posting with a spirited statement of her own, saying she's been fascinated with appropriation for years. She combines live performance and Internet "to unpack ideas about authenticity, originality, and the ownership of dance." On her website, www.StealThisDance.com, people could "buy dance moves as a way to provoke discussion about the value of dance, dancers, choreography." It also includes a video section called "Lineages and Derivatives" where dancers cite several sources for certain steps in their choreography. In her tongue-in-cheek way, Rhoads is celebrating—rather than exploiting—threads back through the past.

And recently Amy O'Neal, who has pioneered her own dazzling mash-up form in Seattle, made a solo in which the words projected on a screen include this quote: "We live in a sampling society. We imitate to learn, associate to process, and categorize to keep sane. Our brains work this way. How we mix the samples of our experiences is what makes us original, or merely an imitator."

Is There a Blackout on *Black Swan*'s Dancing?

Blog post, March 3, 2011, dancemagazine.com

Aside from the horrific portrayal of a ballet dancer gone mad (Natalie Portman) in Darren Aronofsky's popular movie Black Swan, *I was again bothered by the lack of credit given. In this case, Sarah Lane, a beautiful soloist at American Ballet Theatre, served as a double for Portman: In the more technical dance scenes, Lane's pirouettes and pointe work were shot instead of Portman's.*

Do people really believe that it takes only one year to make a ballerina? We know that Natalie Portman studied ballet as a kid and also had a year of intensive training to prepare for the film, but that doesn't add up to being a ballerina.

I think there have been deliberate omissions in the media that have reinforced the idea that Portman did all her own dancing in the movie. Here are what I consider two glaring examples:

First, in the video of special effects used in *Black Swan* that's been circulating on the Internet, a certain crucial three seconds have been deleted. When the video was first released a couple weeks ago, it showed, among its many techno-alterations (mirror double takes, gore enhancement, adding skin rash, puppet legs, etc.) an even more rarely used device: face replacement. Toward the end of the video, the Black Swan starts a manège of piqué turns quite a distance from the camera. When she gets close enough for the viewer to discern her face, it is swiped over and replaced by a different face. If you paused the video, you could recognize the first face as Sarah Lane's and the second face as Portman's. Then, with Portman's face, the dancer finishes her piqués, goes into fouettés, and by this time has big black wings that she swoops down and up and back in her final, triumphant arch.

The day before the Oscars, I looked at this video on several sites so that I could show this moment to my son, who's a film guy. He'd known that face replacement was used in other films but didn't believe that it was used in *Black Swan*. And it wasn't there. I mean the special effects video was still on the website, but those three seconds had been deleted (along with other deletions). When I tweeted about this, someone tweeted back that the original video had only been posted for one day before it was replaced by the curtailed one.

Second, at the Oscars, Natalie Portman thanked about twenty people (including Mary Helen Bowers, the former NYCB dancer who trained her for that year). But Sarah Lane's name was not among them. I wonder, was this Portman's forgetfulness in the heat of the moment? Or was this omission, and the deletion from the video, masterminded by the studio's publicity machine?

Sarah Lane is not just a dancer who happened to be the right size. She's a beautiful, enticing soloist at ABT who was our cover story in June 2007. Last December, we interviewed her about her hard work for *Black Swan* and she told us about face replacement. But was she prepared for credit replacement? (In the credits of the film she is only listed as an extra.)

It seems to be far more accepted that your run-of-the-mill movie star needs help singing rather than dancing. When Natalie Wood starred in *West Side Story* in 1961, I think it was common knowledge that her singing was done by soprano Marni Nixon. But maybe I'm wrong. Did United Artists try to hide this fact? Does anyone know?

Putting the *Black Swan* Blackout in Context

Blog post, March 11, 2011, dancemagazine.com

After reading my previous blog, a mutual friend contacted me and put me in touch with Sarah Lane. This is what I posted after that talk. It generated a furor online, both for and against Sarah, and for and against Portman. Some entertainment websites picked it up and escalated the controversy, claiming that Portman would not have won the Oscar if the judges had known how little of the dancing she'd done. The general commotion led to both Sarah and me appearing on the TV news show 20/20 later that month.

Sarah Lane, whose heavenly dancing helped make Natalie Portman believable as the ballerina Nina Sayers—thanks to face replacement—was not acknowledged by Portman at the Oscars. Not only that, but Lane was suddenly deleted from a video showing *Black Swan*'s special effects that was circulating on the web. In my blog last week I called it a blackout.

Sarah Lane calls it a more polite word: a façade. I asked her if she was expecting to be thanked when she heard Portman reel off ten or twenty other names during her acceptance speech. Lane said no, because a Fox Searchlight producer had already called to ask her to stop giving interviews until after the Oscars. "They were trying to create this façade that she had become a ballerina in a year and a half," she said. "So I knew they didn't want to publicize anything about me."

As she said in *Dance Magazine*'s December interview, she felt good about her work—though it was exhausting and frustrating—on the set. "It was a great experience to see the whole process of making a movie," she told me. But she didn't realize until just before the Oscars just how exploited she was. All the pirouettes, the full-body shots, and just-the-legs shots were her. (She also said that fellow ABT soloist Maria Riccetto doubled for Mila Kunis in one long shot.) The publicity campaign from the studio, however, spread the word that Portman did 90 percent of her own dancing.

Is it unusual for real dancers to get shoved under the rug in Hollywood? From the responses I got to my previous blog, no. John Rockwell reminded me that Savion Glover, whose tap dancing and choreography were the heart of the animated movie *Happy Feet* in 2006, was barely acknowledged. In a very funny take on this ("Penguin, Shmenguin! Those Are Savion Glover's Happy Feet!" *New York Times*, December 28, 2006), Rockwell tells us that *Happy Feet* director/producer George Miller admitted the movie would have been impossible without Savion—and yet the tapper's name appears way down in the credits.

Likewise, on IMDb (Internet Movie Database), Sarah Lane's name appears way down the line, not as a double but as "Lady in the Lane," which she explained to me was a split-second scene where she appears as an incidental, nondancing figure. Obviously she was not as crucial to the film as Glover to *Happy Feet*; Darren Aronofsky could have hired a lesser ballerina. But the idea is the same. Get a real virtuoso to make your story believable, but pour all your publicity into the studio's star.

It seems that when a movie star needs a singer to double for her voice, that's common knowledge. No one is surprised to learn that Audrey Hepburn and Natalie Wood didn't do their own singing when a trained voice was required. But people seem to believe that Natalie Portman did her own dancing. Of course to nondancers, Portman was entirely believable. (I myself found her upper body fairly convincing.)

Sarah says she's talked to her colleagues about "how unfortunate it is that, as professional dancers, we work so hard, but people can actually believe that it's easy enough to do it in a year. That's the thing that bothered me the most."

Can a Floor Give You Spiritual Energy? Ask Jared Grimes

Blog post, April 22, 2011, dancemagazine.com

A surge of energy went through the crowd the moment Jared took the mike and vamped to the beat of his own voice. What a natural—as a dancer, as a host, and as a voice of encouragement to younger dancers.

Wednesday night Jared held a special edition of his monthly Broadway Underground variety show at BB King Blues Club. This time he ran a competition called Run the Night that included tap, hip-hop, modern, and more. A panel of six industry judges, of which I was one, voted after each piece.

Jared wasn't planning to dance himself, but he couldn't help it. His terrific dancing—part Fosse, part Astaire, part Greg Hines—flowed out of him every time he paced the floor. He talked about the floor, watched the floor, "warmed up" the floor for the next dancer. He made it seem like the floor itself was radiating energy.

The deserving winner, out of the eleven acts, was a pair of guys from Seattle in a number called *Tap This*. They were Josh Scribner, a very fluent tapper, and his appealingly eccentric student, Vikas Arun. But what boosted them up a notch above the rest was their rhythms. They started off soft, silky, and slide-y and worked up to sharper rhythms with unexpected holds that played with the music.

Another group also took my eye: the Beat Club, from Monmouth Junction, New Jersey. A rag-tag bunch of B-girls and B-boys, they made great formations in their first number. But in their second one, their true colors came out. They started kind of chaotic and built up to show true individuality. They strutted in their best Don't-mess-with-me style—especially the girls, one of whom was only sixteen.

All the participants were completely committed to their movement and quite skilled. But no one compared to either Grimes himself or his special guests. These included the AmountBoyz in their fantastic break dancing. I would go pretty far to see them again. It also included an impromptu appearance from Bill Irwin, the great dancer/clown/actor—and a fellow judge that night. Jared called him onto the stage, and if I hadn't heard their conversation beforehand, I would have thought their nifty interaction was carefully choreographed. Bill did a couple of scrumptious body doodles, grabbed Jared's hat, and then finally tossed it back—and Jared caught it with the crown of his head.

As a finale, Jared made a big improv circle and invited any game dancer to go solo in the center. Even the ones who hadn't shone during the competition danced up a brief little storm. (Blame it on the floor!) After all the solos, one of the barefoot girls crossed with a hip-hop guy, amazing the audience with their on-the-spot chemistry.

And so it went. Everybody walked out bopping and smiling. That floor at BB King's was generous to all of us!

Eiko & Koma: The Unnatural Side of Communing with Nature

Blog post, August 1, 2011, dancemazine.com

Eiko's face floats, partially submerged in the water, like a bright moon gliding across a dark sky. She is a doomed Ophelia who is rescued by Koma. The driftwood that mysteriously sails toward them is their survival raft, but it also ensnares them in some kind of trap.

These images are part of a timeless dreamscape in *Water*, the version of *River* that Eiko & Koma have made for Lincoln Center Out of Doors. There is no exact beginning or ending of this seventy-minute work. Kathy Kaufmann's light finds Eiko first, Koma later. In the darkness, you can gradually discern a direction to their drifting—toward each other. When they finally touch, he seems to lift her out of the water, perhaps to protect her. Native

Eiko & Koma in *Water* in the reflecting pool at Lincoln Center: timeless charisma enhanced by elusiveness. (© Kevin Yatarola)

American drummer Robert Mirabal, also immersed, is circling his arms on the surface of the water to send a cluster of branches out toward them.

I look away for a second and when I look back Koma has disappeared. Is he behind Eiko? Is he under the water? (The level in the Milstein Pool of Lincoln Center Plaza is only knee deep.) Later he is ferrying a container of lit candles toward her, and then he's trawling it to the far side of the pool. It's so dark that the candles look like they are traveling on their own, past the huge Henry Moore sculptures. Have we lost Koma again—or is it my eyes?

Eiko & Koma's performances are based on their affinity for nature—and yet there is nothing carefree or even natural about the preparation.

Last Thursday, a few hours before that evening's performance, I moderated a talk-and-film-showing with Eiko and Koma at the New York Public Library of Performing Arts at Lincoln Center, just behind the Milstein Pool. In describing their lives as artists, they tried to deflate any romantic notions of their affinity for nature. In visiting their retrospective exhibit, "Residue," now at the library, you can see evidence of the meticulous work that goes into each of these purely "natural" performances. For instance, that bunch of branches they cling to in *Water* looks haphazard but has actually been carefully constructed. When I asked about it during the talk, Eiko responded, "Yes, nothing is natural. What we do is not natural." The films they showed give a glimpse of how arduous the preparation is, whether hauling branches around, scorching a canvas for a piece called *Raven*, or sewing themselves into their costumes.

Likewise, in the film *The Retrospective Project*, Koma says, "I'm expecting some mysterious moment which I couldn't imagine, I couldn't anticipate. As a performer, if we don't look for that kind of moment, we have no reason to do this." At the talk, he explained that he is a professional who takes into account audience expectation.

To the naked eye, those moments of his performance look inevitable— as though some kind of fury or mischief wells up inside him and has to explode. Those actions make us feel something, but they do not give us anything to know. We ride with the uncertainty. (Are they moving or still? Where is the light coming from? Is he saving her or drowning her?)

I think their idea of Delicious Movement, the name they give their workshops, can be applied to the state of watching them: Delicious Uncertainty. You don't really know anything for sure, but your mind stays very active watching them. You can make up your own stories about who, when, and where.

Eiko said at the talk how much she admires the cave drawings of thirty-eight thousand years ago that are the subject of Werner Herzog's 3D movie,

Cave of Forgotten Dreams. They try, added Koma, to be denizens of a time long before us (humans) and long after. Maybe that's why they are so mesmerizing to watch: There's a timelessness that allows all circumstantial things to fall away.

Last Thursday I felt as immersed in the experience as Eiko & Koma were in the water. I felt grateful that their time on Earth coincides with mine. With their chalky faces and kimonos, they were ancient Japanese paintings come alive. (So many of those paintings have water in them—tsunamis even.) Their timeless charisma is enhanced by their elusiveness. But they are also two people dealing with ordinary problems. Eiko has actually been contaminated by the water—getting fever and shakes—in a previous outing.

Eiko & Koma are now celebrating forty years of their work together with a three-year retrospective, the brainstorm of Sam Miller (former director of Jacob's Pillow and current director of Lower Manhattan Cultural Council). If you go see their installation "Residue," you'll get a glimpse of how powerful and mysterious their work has been over four decades. You can have the Eiko & Koma experience pretty much in the privacy of your own thoughts. The exhibit is strange, informative, eerie, even a little bit creepy; it's perfect for people who don't have the patience to sit through one of their performances. But I found it a bit shocking to be so close to their work—there are videos, fabrics, a film, a teahouse, piles of salt and sand—without them being there. It's almost as if they are preparing for their own death—their own version of Merce's "legacy tour."

Koma mentioned his wish for a permanent museum of their work. I think that the website they've been developing is the next best thing. A virtual museum, it's got their films, their book (*Time Is Not Even, Space Is Not Empty*), photos, videos, articles, and more. You can visit it at www.eikoandkoma.org.

For sheer originality, there is no one like Eiko & Koma. They go their own way, a way that communes with ancient archetypes. They play with our perceptions. They slowly immerse us in richly ambiguous images and leave us to our own devices.

Merce's Other Legacy

Blog post, January 1, 2012, dancemagazine.com

Yesterday I witnessed the very last night of Merce on Earth. I mean the last Legacy Tour date at the Park Avenue Armory. But I'm not going to talk about the event because plenty of dance writers have and will. Sure it was nice to see the dancers and guess what piece they were excerpting. And it was awesome to see/hear how the live horn music (by Takehisa Kosugi or John King or both) colored the dancing so that you felt impending disaster or a stream of serenity or many shadings in between. It was neat to see how the movement choices are just a hair's breadth away from seeming "arbitrary" but instead seem natural. It was heart-warming to see the complete trust the dancers have in each other, diving backward into another's arms without looking. I could tell you about some of the beautiful or bracing moments in the choreography. Or the stadium-like roaring when it was all over, and the many times we called them back for a bow.

But I won't. Instead I'm going to talk about who was in the audience because that is the other legacy. Cunningham's effect goes beyond the Legacy Tour and beyond the Merce Cunningham Dance Company. There's a piece of Merce in all of us.

Here are some of the choreographers I saw in the audience: Donald Byrd, Jane Comfort, Lar Lubovitch, Annie-B Parson, Helen Pickett, Trisha Brown, Sarah Michelson, Vicky Shick, Wendy Rogers, and Meredith Monk. And of course, dance artists who have performed in his company: Carolyn Brown, Steve Paxton, Neil Greenberg, Douglas Dunn, Kimberly Bartosik, Gus Solomons jr, and Foofwa d'Immobilité. All felt the loss of the Cunningham company in some way.

All these choreographers are very different from each other. When I think of Donald Byrd's raucous, in-your-face *Harlem Nutcracker*, or Jane Comfort's delving into the unconscious in *Underground River*, or Helen Pickett's challenge to super technical ballet dancers to be mercurial, or Gus Solomons's sly humor in *A Thin Frost*, or Trisha Brown's velvet-soft dancers, or Annie-B Parson's elusive, multisourced *Supernatural Wife*, none are imitating the Cunningham style. And yet they are all post-Cunningham dance makers.

Post-Cunningham means postmodern. Merce didn't just influence many artists; he changed the way we think about performance. One of the ideas that he and John Cage introduced is about the multiplicity of ideas. The dance could be one thing, the music entirely another, while each viewer gathers his or her own "meaning" from the juxtaposition. Cunningham and Cage had the knowledge—the faith—that we would each make our own sense out of the parts we witness. It's one of the things they knew about the human mind, and it is something about contemporary life that we now know. Whether multitasking, surfing the web, or choreographing, we have embraced the habit of encountering several, sometimes conflicting ideas at the same time.

Cunningham and Cage opened up so many doors—not just for artists but for audiences too. As we watch performances, we are open to the multiplicity of modes, moods, and styles. And we each perceive the jumble in our own way.

And yet, with the Cunningham company, it's never a jumble. That's where post-Cunningham artists have to be careful. Whatever Merce's methods—whether throwing the dice or relying on computer software—he had a touch. A friend of mine, the late Harry Sheppard, said that he would get chills during a certain perfect decision of Cunningham's, whether it was exactly when a dancer would enter from upstage right or how three dancers would interact with each other. The ability to give chills, when it comes down to it, cannot be explained by any idea or method.

Postscript: A DVD of the last performance of the Legacy Tour is now available from www.artpix.org.

A Debate on Snark

Blog post, March 6, 2012, dancemagazine.com

This post—and the panel discussion it was based on—garnered support from many dancers. Not surprisingly, a couple dance critics voiced their displeasure. I guess I got what I deserved. On the other hand, Robert Johnson, whom I take issue with here, remains a buddy; we often enjoy disagreeing with each other.

When writing this, I wasn't thinking of my 1991 screed about critics ("Beware the Egos of Critics," Section IV), but I can now see they are related.

Okay, I'm rolling up my sleeves. Robert Johnson and I were polite with each other in a "Meet the Press" panel at the sold-out symposium sponsored by Dance/NYC on February 26. Since then, Robert has posted his "In Defense of Snarky Reviews" in writing.

So now I'm gonna say my side of it.

I have no problem with a critic getting sarcastic once in a while. But I think the snarky negativity has gotten out of hand. Sometimes it's an automatic response, and sometimes it's got just a bit more venom than is necessary—under the guise of "just being honest." When I talk to dance people, the conversation often turns to this troubling topic. People are upset by the uptick in snark in NYC's main daily paper, the *New York Times*. Jamie Bennett of the National Endowment for the Arts, who moderated our panel, picked up on this and plunged right in. He asked each of us (me, Robert Johnson, Brian Seibert, and Gus Solomons jr) where we stand on "snark." (Do I need to define it? I think it's somewhere in the neighborhood of snide, condescending, and dismissive.)

Robert's point is that if a performance is bad, the critic should say so. Our fellow panelist, Brian, who writes for the *Times*, said that sarcasm is useful when you are trying to write a coherent review of an ephemeral art in a short space.

I can basically agree with both those points. (Though, as I'm sure you've noticed, critics have gotten snarky about excellent performances as well as bad ones.) And I appreciate how eloquent both Robert and Brian were about the challenge of putting dance into words.

What I object to is *excessive* snark, either in frequency or intensity. I don't think either Robert or Brian is guilty of this. But I think some critics don't realize when they've slipped into a default setting of snark. It's easy to throw the darts once you get into the habit, and I don't deny that snarky reviews are fun to read. I get it that readers and editors want a certain snap.

Robert wants his reviews to protect the ticket-buying public. But I've seen audience members who enjoy a night out at the ballet and then are appalled two days later when they read a totally dismissive review. I've heard one person say, "Are the critics trying to destroy the dance world?"

The snark habit is destructive—not only to dancers' psyches but also to ticket sales, bookings, and reputations. I think critics should feel free to write in their individual voice, but they should also have a sense of the responsibility that comes with their power.

And the *New York Times* has more power than most papers in most big cities. The English choreographer Wayne McGregor told me recently that when he does a premiere in London, there might be fifteen different reviews. As Gus pointed out, NYC used to be a multi-newspaper town too. But it's more centralized now, which is unfortunate. And that's where the blogosphere comes in: it can add more voices.

In the website *NJ.com* Robert writes, "In my opinion, snark is an especially appropriate gift for the high-and-mighty. It's the pin-prick that makes over-inflated reputations shrivel and sputter."

I wish snark were used that judiciously. But let's face it, there aren't many high-and-mighty people in concert dance, and the critics who get nasty are pretty indiscriminate. If a critic punctures the reputation of a TV personality or a movie star, it doesn't ruin a career. In our economically challenged art of dance, that puncture wound can be devastating.

Deborah Jowitt wrote in her collection *The Dance in Mind*: "Long ago I decided that it was pointless to use heavy artillery on small targets." I like how she keeps the bigger picture in mind.

I've been both an artist and a critic, and I see misunderstandings on both sides. Dancers don't understand that the critics' first commitment is to their readers, not "the dance community." And critics don't understand that for dancers, it goes beyond being hurt by an individual insult. When the arrows get slung with venom—or condescension—it's disrespectful to the art of dance, and that's what hurts.

I am not asking for critics of big publications to forgo their honesty. But I want them to have some sense of balance, so that one annoying thing about a work doesn't eclipse whatever is good about it. And I want them to have an awareness of how precarious our art is economically.

Gus has breached the dancer/writer divide nicely. At the panel, he said he tries to write reviews that are both engaging to the readers and instructive to the creators, while respecting the integrity of their efforts—however effective or not they turn out to be. I don't think a critic has to also be a dancer in order to have that basic respect.

I used to have a fantasy of starting a Devastated Dancers' Hotline, similar to a suicide hotline. Whenever a nasty comment in print cuts you to the bone, you could call in and talk to a sympathetic, balanced person. That person would assure you that the seemingly indelible remark is only one writer's point of view. But they would also ask you to examine yourself and your work and see if there is any truth to the critic's perception.

But to bring it back to reality, I think we need more dialogues like the panel at Dance/NYC in order to forge a greater understanding.

The Joffrey Ballet

Auditorium Theatre, Chicago

February 15–26, 2012

Web review, dancemagazine.com

With this bold triple bill, the Joffrey reclaims its place as the edgy American ballet company. No, it's not Robert Joffrey's sexy, trippy *Astarte* of 1967. It's not Tharp's visionary hybrid *Deuce Coupe* of 1973. And it's not the company's brilliant 1987 reconstruction of Nijinsky's riot-inducing *Rite of Spring* of 1913.

Instead, this is a gathering of three of the best choreographic minds of the twenty-first century—nary a Balanchine or Ashton in sight. "Winter Fire" gave us a company premiere by William Forsythe, a U.S. premiere by Wayne McGregor, and a returning favorite by Christopher Wheeldon.

Forsythe's iconic *In the Middle, Somewhat Elevated* needs dancers who can declare their presence fearlessly. Originally made for Paris Opéra Ballet in 1987, the ballet infuses precision with defiance. The nine dancers skew ballet positions into pelvis-thrusting tendus and whacked-out grand battements, then saunter offstage with a thrilling toughness. Every duet is pulled—rather yanked—off balance. Victoria Jaiani, in the role made for Sylvie Guillem, ate up the space with a ferocity that's rare for this exquisitely delicate ballerina. The men who stood out were newcomer Ricardo Santos and Graham Maverick.

The commissioned score by Forsythe's longtime collaborator Thom Willems, with its whooshes and crashes, has the feel of a Cage-influenced sound piece. It's a sign of Forsythe's utterly contemporary outlook that he dips into the Cage/Cunningham aesthetic of randomness. Yet the music has a strong beat, adding punch to the already aggressive choreography.

McGregor takes Forsythe's concept of destabilization even further. His dancers seem to coil and uncoil every corner of their bodies. Jutting heads and snaking spines are part of his vocabulary. When the dancers go all out, their frenzied energy seems natural. For *Infra*, Derrick Agnoletti charged into his opening solo with a springy, sensual gusto. Others who made McGregor's strangeness sizzle were Christine Rocas, Jeraldine Mendoza, and John Mark Giragosian.

Infra, made for the Royal Ballet in 2008, shows that McGregor can be dramatic as well as kinetically exciting, that his performers can be human as well as creature-like. Julian Opie's LED-animated figures walk serenely back and forth far above the dancers' heads. These simple though surreal figures add a pleasant double consciousness. In a moment of convergence, they accumulate to form a whole crowd, just as the stage floor fills up with human pedestrians crossing the stage in street clothes.

McGregor turns his inspiration for this piece—the underground bombings in London of 2005—into a private emotional moment for one dancer. On Saturday night, that was Amber Neumann, a wonderful choice because, with her girl-next-door looks, you hardly notice her in the beginning. But her intensity builds so that her breakdown is believable (though to these eyes, it seemed more motivated by her partner leaving her than an act of terrorism). After she joins the group walking offstage, we get a luscious, unfurling duet danced gorgeously by Jaiani with Rory Hohenstein. By this time, Max Richter's music has settled into a beautiful, melancholy violin solo.

Sandwiched between these two radical choreographers was Wheeldon's quiet, sculptural *After the Rain* (2005). Rarely done in its entirety, the first half, for three couples, seems to be more about shape, whereas the celebrated second half, made for Wendy Whelan and Jock Soto, is more about touch. Here, Rocas shone, giving it a girlish innocence. With more arm flourishes and less spirituality than Whelan, she still made it her own. Her front-of-ship lifts really sailed into the blue. However, her partner, Temur Suluashvili, rarely looked at her. This is not a gooey duet, but the man should be fully responsive to the woman. Suluashvili's blankness muted the sense of reverie created by Arvo Pärt's elegiac music. Some of the hand details were lost, too, for example, when the woman inches her fingertips over his shoulders from behind, or when the man does the "falling leaves" with his hands as his arms drift down. But the pairing of Wheeldon's spareness with Pärt's celestial music remains divine.

Afterword

What follows was a spoken story for From the Horse's Mouth *in February 2010. I have been part of this roving framework several times since its inception in 1998. Masterminded by Tina Croll and Jamie Cunningham, the dance involves thirty or so performers. One at a time, they talk for a minute and a half while others dance in an improvised structure. This particular edition was held at the 92nd Street Y, and we were encouraged to include something about the Y in our stories.*

When I was five, my mother started a school for "creative dance" in our basement. One of the exercises was simply to sit on the floor and point and flex the feet. Point and flex, point and flex.

Eventually my mother danced much less and I danced much more. She sometimes came to my concerts. Whenever I was moving around onstage, she was moving around too—bobbing and bouncing in the audience. It was embarrassing, and I secretly hoped she would stop coming to my shows.

I got my wish, because she moved to Santa Fe for a few years. When she came back, what she really wanted to do was be a volunteer usher at the 92nd Street Y, because here is where she studied with Martha Graham on scholarship, many years ago. But by then, she had congestive heart failure.

The last year of her life, she had trouble sleeping and sometimes hadn't slept for days. Whenever I came to her place, though, I would stretch out on the floor and start my exercises, and she'd fall asleep right away.

Two days before she died, she couldn't talk, walk, see, or eat. She sat slumped in her wheelchair, hardly moving. I bent down and took hold of her left foot and moved it, saying "Point and flex, point and flex." When I went to the right foot, she was ahead of me. She had already started moving it. Point and flex, point and flex.

Credits

Index

Page numbers in **bold** indicate photos.

ABOUT THE AUTHOR

Wendy Perron, a former dancer,

choreographer, and teacher, is the

editor in chief of *Dance Magazine*.